REMOVING THE MARGINS

THE CHALLENGES AND POSSIBILITIES OF INCLUSIVE SCHOOLING

George J. Sefa Dei
Irma Marcia James
Sonia James-Wilson
Leeno Luke Karumanchery
Jasmin Zine

Canadian Scholars' Press Inc.   Toronto   2000

Removing the Margins: The Challenges and Possibilities of Inclusive Schooling
George J. Sefa Dei, Irma Marcia James, Sonia James-Wilson, Leeno Luke
Karumanchery, and Jasmine Zine

First published in 2000 by
Canadian Scholars' Press Inc.
180 Bloor Street West, Suite 1202
Toronto, Ontario
M5S 2V6

We acknowledge the financial support of the Government of Canada through the Book
Publishing Industry Development Programme for our publishing activities.

Canadian Cataloguing in Publication Data

Main entry under title:

Removing the margins : the challenges and possibilities of inclusive schooling

Includes bibliographical references.
ISBN 1-55130-153-9

1. Inclusive education. 2. Minorities – Education. I. Dei, George J. Sefa (George Jerry
Sefa), 1954- .

LC1200.R45 2000   371.9   C00-932003-2

Managing Editor: Ruth Bradley-St-Cyr
Marketing Manager: Susan Cuk
Interior design and layout: Brad Horning
Cover design: Jean Louie
Cover image: DigitalVision

00 01 02 03 04 05 06   6 5 4 3 2 1

Printed and bound in Canada by AGMV Marquis

We dedicate this book to those youth who are struggling
to find a sense of place in the school system.

CONTENTS

PREFACE

This book has been a collaborative venture, and we have each grown and learned along the path of collective engagement. With a critical eye towards our own strengths and weaknesses, and our individual and group experiences, we have come to fully realize that knowledge is never owned, either individually or collectively. Rather, knowledge is produced as part of a collaborative process, and one of the most dangerous delusions of any academic project is to claim to know everything. To know is to be humble, and humility is the triumph of knowledge. We do not claim to have knowledge of, or ownership over, "the truth" of educational improvement in North American contexts. It is not our intention to "soap-box" preach. Indeed, if an attitude of certainty is conveyed in this book, it is a consequence of our deep convictions, and dedication to the work. Therefore, if such thoughts/impressions are conveyed herein, we call on readers to reject and resist them. When we began the research for this book, we had several objectives, but foremost among them was a desire to address and bring to light the positive work being done in the field today.

Following in the Freirian tradition, we see education systems both as a source of oppression and as a site for social transformation. So we didn't want to write yet another book that would re-examine and merely articulate issues of racism and oppression in education. While we recognize the enormity of these issues, particularly as they relate to the politics of ensuring equity and access to minoritized youth, we wanted to work within a philosophy of hope. That philosophy demanded that we focus on the positive initiatives being undertaken in schools, off-school sites, communities and families: transformative programs that demonstrate the practical benefits of inclusivity. We wanted to bring a more nuanced understanding to the notion of inclusivity: a reading that would move beyond traditional definitions of inclusive schooling as dealing only with issues of "special education." As schooling is rooted in the public/private moral and cultural domains, we felt that it was important to look at questions of identity, representation, community, equity and access, and spirituality. For us, inclusivity is intrinsically tied to how educational sites respond to the needs and concerns of all students from diverse racial, ethnic, gender, sexual, class, religious, linguistic, and cultural backgrounds. It is a view of "schooling as community": a concept of education that engages the implications for knowledge production and use, while addressing the myriad identities and bodies that struggle in the system. In other words, by collapsing the artificial boundaries between schools, off-school sites and local communities, inclusive education would seek to engage the physical bodies and multiple knowledges that students bring with them to their schooling experience.

   This project arose from a mutual desire to see our research culminate in a resource that would encourage, advance and facilitate the work of other social-educational theorists and practitioners. To these ends, we have sought to address the philosophical and theoretical bases for inclusivity in this book, while laying out a practical approach to inclusive education in the accompanying Teacher's Guide. It is our hope that this marriage between theory and practice has produced a resource that will be useful across disciplinary borders: that educators, student teachers, sociologists, anthropologists, and all those other partners in "the project" will find this work to be helpful, encouraging and uplifting. In writing this book, we held on to the ideal that education should be about the production of knowledge for social action, and not the reproduction of knowledge to affirm the status quo. We accept and assert that we are complicit in the current state of affairs if we do nothing to challenge the order of things. Therefore, as we are all (individually and collectively) implicated in the struggle for educational change, we must own up to our obligations and responsibilities when it comes to the transformation of education as we know it. As authors coming from different social locations and backgrounds we bring different but shared dreams to the project. It is our hope that these dreams will become a reality in and through this enterprise.

ACKNOWLEDGEMENTS

This book could not have been written without the aid and support of a great many people, their organizations and communities. We would first like to acknowledge those community-based educational programs that welcomed us so openly: The African Heritage Educators' Network (AHEN) Project 90; The Canadian Association of Black Educators (CABE) — Vaughan Road Project; The Jamaican Canadian Association; The Jane and Finch Concerned Citizens Organisation (JFCCO); The Muslim Education Network, Training and OutReach Service (MENTORS); The Milliken Mills African Caribbean Canadian Upliftment Program (MACCUP); and Saturday Schools/ Community Educational Outlets. The willingness of the community workers and organizers in these programs to allow us into their schools and homes was a testimony to their enormous dedication to this project and our collective struggle for positive educational change.

We would like to extend special thanks to: Alimamy Bangura, Kofi Barimah, Ana Costa, Carmen Hernandez, Tessa Benn-Ireland, Ekua Blair, Paul deLyon, Emmanual Dick, Jonas Ma, Pam Plumber, Joseph Rouse, John Viera, and Janet Wong for facilitating our research in their respective organizations. Also we would be remiss if we didn't thank all those parents, teachers and students who gave of themselves, their experiences and their knowledge.

There were several OISE/UT Graduate Students who worked on various stages of this research with George Dei. We would like to thank specifically

Paul Broomfield, Loreli Buenaventura, Maria Castagna, Awad Ibrahim, Erica Lawson, Josephine Mazzuca, Elizabeth McIsaac, Notisha Massaquoi, and Bizunesh Wubie. Their input, hard work and dedication to the completion of this project was invaluable and is greatly appreciated. Christine Connelley has assisted in a number of academic projects of George Dei and a great deal of scholarly debt is owed to her. We are all thankful to Elizabeth Price for spending numerous hours reading and making extensive comments on the draft of the manuscript. Her suggestions and insights were indeed helpful to us all. To Ann Nicholson we are impressed with your superb editing skills and suggestions you offered that greatly enriched this book. As is always the case, Olga Williams, an administrative assistant in the Department of Sociology and Equity Studies, OISE/UT has been there to assist George's academic and intellectual pursuits.

Finally, George Dei, as principal investigator, would personally like to thank the Social Sciences and Humanities Research Council of Canada (SSHRC) and the Ontario Ministry of Education and Training, for providing the funds that made this study possible.

ABOUT THE AUTHORS

George J. Sefa Dei

I am an African-Canadian male teaching in a premier Canadian institution of higher learning. I have come to realize that the position of tenured Professor (and also, serving as Associate Chair of the Department of Sociology and Equity Studies, OISE/UT) can open doors. The status is part of the trappings of privilege that come unequally to bodies working in the academy. But the position of an academic can also cover up many challenges. Thus, I maintain that the test of a true scholar does not lie so much in how we know but in how we come to know and what we do with the knowledge so acquired. I come to this project well informed by a personal and collective history of struggle, therefore, I endeavour to affirm social identities and personal/collective experiences as important sources of knowledge.

My educational journey has been shaped by interactions with colleagues, peers and students as we struggle to make sense of the world we inhabit. I believe that I have learned as much in these interactions as I have "impacted knowledge." My students have been my greatest teachers. I was recently asked whether I truly felt that the struggle was worthwhile, that is to say, that our individual and collective endeavours in "the project" might result in social transformation. While the work we do is difficult in the best of circumstances and can be disheartening at times, I firmly believe in its capacity to disrupt the status quo. I have a twelve-year-old son in the school system, so in some way at least, as a parent, I must believe in the capacity of the system to change and/or affect change.

As a pedagogue, if I didn't believe in the possibility of social transformation, I would have no right to speak with students and peers about working towards change. Bearing that in mind, I enter the debate on inclusion to recognize and acknowledge schools, families, and communities are doing well, and to ask that we go further for the sake of ourselves and the future generations yet unborn. Sometimes we may not know where we are coming from, but it is inexcusable not to know where we are going. It is often said that the future itself is being hotly contested. If this is so, then we must challenge the oppressive arrogance and the complacency of those who would design our futures.

Irma Marcia James

I am an OISE/UT Graduate in the M.A. program of the department of Sociology and Equity Studies in Education. I was born in Antigua, W.I., and emigrated to Canada as a young child. Since tutoring and teaching minority students during my B.Ed. at McGill University, I have been interested in studying how students' educational success may be achieved through co-operation among stakeholders with the student's school, home and community. During my work at OISE/UT, I have had the opportunity to observe students in a variety of learning environments, and working with parents, teachers and administrators from many different cultural, religious and racial backgrounds. Much has been made of the opportunities of the new millennium however, all students will be disadvantaged if educators fail to incorporate the multiplicity of their students' voices into the curriculum, policies and teaching methods in today's schools. I am now pursuing a career in law, also at the University of Toronto. I hope to incorporate my interests in education and social justice to challenge systemic discrimination in our legal system.

Sonia James-Wilson

Over the past few years, I have had the privilege of working with my co-authors on what for me has been a transformative project. As a newcomer to Canada, I have been embraced and nurtured by my colleagues in an exploration of possibility. As an African-American woman of Caribbean descent, I embody a variety of experiences, perspectives and sensibilities. Participation in this project has reiterated for me the unquestionable need to not only "make a space," for those who do not fit the description of the dominant, but to encourage them to "take the space" which is rightfully theirs.

As a teacher educator, I have struggled to help future educators understand their responsibilities to, and their potential influence on, the children that they will one day teach. More importantly, I want teacher candidates to realize that their students will come from homes and communities that exert their own formidable influences on the lives of these children, and that their work as teachers involves the ability to respect, recognize and reconcile those realities with life in schools.

As a mother of two young children, I have great faith in these individuals to re-build, re-form and re-think the types of schools we create for our children and youth; to implicate themselves in the process of knowledge construction; and, to push the boundaries of involvement towards inclusion.

Leeno Luke Karumanchery

In the writing of this work, I locate myself as a Malayalee-Canadian, male academic, and as such, I am speaking from an intersecting vantage point. While I benefit from my privileged position as male and an academic (I am a doctoral candidate in the Department of Sociology and Equity in Education of OISE/UT), I also occupy a marginalized position as a person of colour in what is a Eurocentric society. These and other such intersections place me at a crossroads of culture and identity ... I walk in the borderlands. It is a journey that often leaves me feeling isolated even though I know it is a path shared by a great many others. That being said, issues of appropriation, co-optation and competition plague the work that we did, and in many ways, we often find ourselves struggling not only against power and privilege, but against those "others" who should in fact be our partners in "the project." For me, working collaboratively in this type of endeavour carries an important message about community, co-operation and resistance. It is a message that I saw reflected in the organizations researched in this study. Their's is a vision of hope, it is a vision that I share; an idea that we work towards ... together in solidarity.

Jasmin Zine

As a doctoral candidate in the field of anti-racism education, my work has been informed by my own experience growing up in the Canadian public school system with the multiple identities of being female, Pakistani, Muslim, and hence, "other." Understanding the struggles many minoritized youth continue to face in our schools is something that has driven me to focus my academic and political work towards examining the transformative possibilities of education and schooling. As a parent, I also realize that our children must not inherit the legacy of oppression and disenfranchisement within our schools that occurs as the result of social differences. As such, my work is guided by the social and political need to critically re-vision education through new lenses which must look beyond the politics of difference toward a pedagogy of inclusion.

CHAPTER 1

RETHINKING INCLUSIVE SCHOOLING: THEORETICAL AND PHILOSOPHICAL FOUNDATIONS

INTRODUCTION

In exploring strategies for alternative schooling, Ernst and Statzner (1994) have stressed the imperative need to redirect social science research away from the often hopeless and stereotypical study of educational failure, to the heartening exploration of new and creative ways of meeting the needs of minority teachers, students, and their families (p. 205). This book addresses the pedagogical, curricular and instructional implications of a multi-year study to examine exemplary practices of inclusive schooling in Ontario schools. In addition, we discuss specific home and community educational strategies that parents, families, guardians, caregivers and community workers have successfully employed to promote effective learning and to enhance youth educational outcomes.

We begin this document with an unconventional declaration. It is a statement of the desires and subject politics that shape our venture into critical educational research. As argued elsewhere (Dei, Mazzuca, McIsaac and Zine, 1997), an important task of critical educational research is to delineate the causes and/or factors contributing to educational inequality, failure and success and to proceed to offer alternative solutions. Although it is not usually acknowledged, academic research is governed by specific political intentions and ideological perspectives that precede the research process. Educational research is as much contextualized by the political biases of researchers and participants as by their lived realities. The nature of academic inquiry, then, can never be characterized as neutral in its claim to represent the "authenticity" of experience. Educational researchers and their subjects are socially and politically located, situated and positioned. Positionality and situatedness influence interpretations and the making of meaning. We cannot claim political innocence in this study. What we write and speak about as "text" does not always (if ever) provide a mirror of real-life experiences (see also McRobbie, 1981; Walcott, 1995). Therefore, we have an expressed desire to ensure that our school systems strive to provide education to all groups so that all can equitably access the valued goods and services of society. To us, therefore, the educational challenge is to ensure that educational excellence is not simply accessible, but that it is equitable to all groups. Given the realities of social and institutional inequity, for a large number of people, participation in today's mainstream schooling is not only problematic, it is impossible. An acceptance of this truism, while basic to anti-racist theory and practice, is not the norm in society. Bearing that in mind, it becomes apparent that we not only struggle against structural inequity but against philosophical barriers as well.

Arguably, the new millennium will witness mounting tensions in schools, and these pressures will be fueled by the conflicting interests of multiple stakeholders. Whether these stresses are brought by parents, governmental agencies, communities, businesses and/or students, the result will be fractured and stretched educational system where only a few may thrive, while those unfortunate others are lost in the shuffle. At the moment, conventional schools are being developed to meet the challenges of the global market place. However, at the same time, we need to remember that the development and refinement of the human mind for critical and analytical thinking is fundamental to the concept of education. We fear that at this moment, concerns for money management, and the bottom line are taking precedence over the basic needs, desires and opportunities of *all* students.

As sound research is key to developing new ways of delivering education, we entered into this project with hopes of unraveling new concepts and understandings that would help to re-think schooling in North American contexts. Our politics moved us to do educational research that would result in more than a simple production/re-production of knowledge. Historically, as a direct result of its refusal to accept the status quo, critical educational research has shaped and informed much of the public debate about the course and direction of schooling. It has asked tough questions of educators, school administrators, policy workers and officials. Today, critical research continues to force a re-questioning of the role and purpose of education.

In recent years, schools have been effective in communicating ideas about change, particularly when parents and students challenge them to address problems of the contemporary world. Perhaps, it is not so much that education has failed society. The majority of educators have been encouraging. Most students have fulfilled their part of the bargain and engaged schools. Unfortunately, it is the inability of governments to work in collaboration with minoritized students, parents/guardians, educators and community participants with the requisite tools, guidance and leadership needed to respond to the competing (and sometimes contradictory) needs of a diverse student population that is at issue.

In presenting a new approach to schooling, we contend that contemporary problems require a reconceptualizing of educational aims and objectives. Critical educators (see Apple, 1986; Fine, 1991; McCarthy, 1990; McLaren, 1993; Lather, 1991; Scheurich and Young, 1997; Ghosh, 1996; Dei, 1996; Jervis, 1996; Razack, 1998; Taylor, 1995; Gaskell and Novogrodsky, 1989) argue that questions of difference (class, gender, sexuality, race, ethnicity, age, dis/ability, faith, et cetera) are consequential for schooling in North American contexts. They point to differential educational outcomes for students and learners given the unequal distribution of resources. These resources are unevenly distributed relative to race/ethnicity, gender, and socio-economic class such that social inequities are continually reproduced in the prevailing competitive market economy.

Important questions must be asked. For example, what is the goal and purpose of transformative education? What is the availability of educational resources in society? Who has control over the available educational resources? How are these resources defined, distributed and assigned? Searching for answers to these questions could lead us to rethink schooling and education in the new century. It is healthy when parents, students, and community workers continually challenge educators and governments to provide youth with the appropriate tools, skills and capabilities which they need to live in a plural, global society. In recent years, the educational system has come under intense scrutiny. Particularly in Ontario minoritized students, parents and communities have been calling upon public schools and boards of education to respond to the challenges of diversity and difference by ensuring that educational practices offer equality of opportunity and equitable outcomes for *all* students. Compounding this challenge is the fact that we live in a post-modern era that is remarkably different in its celebration of difference and diversity. As the report of the Ontario Royal Commission on Learning aptly highlighted, Ontario schools need to evolve because "… society has changed so dramatically … [and] … schools can't possibly be expected to keep up without substantial changes" (see Royal Commission on Learning [RCOL], 1994, p. 3 [short version]).

Therefore, we need to know what exemplary and best practices are actually being carried out in schools. Furthermore, we need to address the expectations and interpretations that students, teachers, and school administrators have for these programs and practices. How do these eductional practices promote academic retention, graduation and social success among students from racial/ethnic minority and working-class backgrounds? What does the notion of inclusive schooling imply for future educational practice in the specific context of Ontario? Educational research in Ontario continues to indicate that historically, education has not worked for all students (see Brown, 1993; Cheng, 1995; Dei, Holmes, Mazzuca, McIsaac, and Campbell, 1995; Brathwaite and James, 1996). We need to identify and address the problems that prevent schools from meeting the needs of a diverse student body.

In many ways, this document responds to some of these questions by spelling out actual school practices that promote educational inclusion and, consequently, enhance academic success, particularly among Black[1] youth and other students from racial minority and working class backgrounds. In addition to informing us of how exemplary practices of inclusion may be taken up in mainstream public schools, our research studies have also suggested ways in which knowledge about exemplary practices of schooling can inform the establishment of inclusive schooling for the academic and social success of all students.

REVIEW OF RELATED LITERATURE

General Context

Schools do not exist in isolation from local communities. Aside from dealing with questions about difference and identity, there is also an extensive body of works that has emphasized school-community relations as a crucial aspect of any approach to inclusive, multicentric education. A review of the specific literature on community/parent-school relations similarly suggests theoretical and discursive demarcations. As Gill (1997) points out in her review of the general literature on "parental involvement," at one level, the discourse of "involvement" is articulated with the "protection framework" (see Swap, 1993).

The educational literature employing this theoretical perspective views schools, and specifically teachers, as having primary responsibility for education. Teachers are professionals whose work must be "protected" against unwarranted intrusions from parents, community workers and social activists. The school-focused model (Irvine, 1992) identifies the primary role of parents and local communities as supportive to the school. For example, parents, families and the community provide remedial education to assist teachers in dealing with the educational "deficits" of students. The partnership model (Comer, 1989) stresses partnerships among local communities, parents and guardians in the redefinition of respective educational roles and responsibilities.

Besides these theoretical demarcations, much of the literature tends to focus on the *targets* of educational benefits that come with parental and local community involvement. The works of Ziegler (1987), Epstein (1990), Henderson (1981) and Cohen (1990) review the benefits of enhanced academic performance of youth. Bauch (1989), Comer (1988), Stallings and Stipek (1986), and Dei, Mazzuca, McIsaac and Zine (1997) show how parental and local community involvement is significant in dealing with the problem of youth disengagement and dropping out of school. Other studies deal with the benefits of school-community partnerships for parents, and particularly their understanding of schooling issues and the general educational system (see Epstein, 1986, 1990; Cohen, 1990; Comer, 1986; Bauch, 1989; and Gordon, 1977). While some studies (Epstein, 1990), highlight the benefits of school-community partnerships for teachers, others (Fullan and Stiegelbauer, 1991; Swap, 1990; Epstein, 1988; and Henderson, Marburger, and Ooms, 1986) look at the benefits for the entire school system. A host of studies touch on the practical implications and strategies for improving school-community relations. Most of these studies focus on the issue of parental involvement (see Hester, 1989; Fullan and Steigelbauer, 1991). To varying degrees, these studies examine the myriad ways for parents, guardians, families and community workers to fulfil educational obligations to schools (e.g., local community involvement in school activities, the promotion of students' prior learning activities in the homes/families, and the performing of educational advocacy and school governance).

In her synthesis of the literature, Gill (1997) argues that studies on parental involvement in schools can be delineated in terms of works that highlight parents and local communities as partners (Ramon, 1985), as collaborators and problem-solvers (Henderson, Marburger and Ooms, 1986), as audience (Dornbusch, 1988), as school supporters (Fullan, 1982; and Henderson, Marburger and Ooms, 1986), as advisors and co-decision-makers (Armour, et al., 1976; and Rich, 1987), and as educational advocates (Perry and Tannenbaum, 1992).

Within the school-community relations literature, critical studies (Fine, 1993; Dehli, 1987, 1994; David, 1992; Ball, 1993) have problematized conventional definitions and designations of "parents" and "families." Importantly, these studies have also addressed issues of parental exclusion and the marginalization of parents, guardians and minoritized communities in debates about public schooling that privilege the discourse of "choice," "free market," "voice" and "democratic participation." Critical educational research has recognized the barriers to effective community education and the need to encourage co-operative efforts between the family, the community and the school.

It has been argued that unless schools can build trust at a grassroots level within communities, significant educational change cannot occur. Dehli (1996a) argues that the "parent," featured in contemporary educational discourses and practices, is produced as an ideological "effect" of power and knowledge. Parent-school relations are socially constructed, idealizing the white, middle-class experience. The notion of "parent," however, cannot be separated from considerations of race, class, gender, sexuality. Schools, therefore, cannot disregard power relations, community cultures and differing locations of parents when it comes to parental involvement. Tools, resources and considerations of time and place are significant in evaluating how individuals are able to fulfil their roles and responsibilities as parents, guardians, caregivers, family members and community workers.

Besides a critical interrogation of what such notions as "family," "community," and "parental involvement" mean for rethinking schooling and education in Euro-Canadian/American contexts, this report addresses what families, parents, guardians, caregivers, and local communities are doing to promote youth education. The study works with a broader definition of "community school/schooling" to include educational outlets/sites in which families, parents and local communities promote education for all. "Community" refers to a collectivity of individuals engaged in common educational activities, and sharing some common interests regarding education. Education is for the entire community: parents, children, guardians, caregivers, young and old. Such community schools avoid a false delineation of the "educational" outside of local politics, economics, social ecology, and spiritual activity.

"Education" in community-based schooling is taken more broadly. It includes the options, strategies, processes and structures through which individuals and communities/groups come to know and understand the world and act within it. This form of "education" happens at/in multiple sites and contexts — schools, universities, workplaces, homes, churches and union halls — with a diverse body of participants involved. This perspective of community schooling and education assists a citizenry to provide a nurturing environment that fosters meaningful learning.

Community education aims at the intellectual, emotional and spiritual development of the learner. It draws on mutual solidarity and partnerships with educators, learners, community workers, parents, guardians, and caregivers. It combines the individual rights of all learners with the related/ relevant social responsibilities. In fact, community education serves to promote cultural, personal and political agency. These positive outcomes emerge from the reciprocal relationship that that is constructed between learners, teachers, schools and the community. However, communities are constituted by more than shared common interests in education. Their shared culture and heritage become politicized through the complex of formal education. In other words, "communities of learning" act as political bodies when they begin to challenge dominant concepts and structures of schooling. This politicized community works within a framework of solidarity that engenders both a shared ownership of knowledge and a joint commitment to succeed.

The task of education in North America has always been a collective responsibility, and historically, parents, families and local communities have been at the forefront of struggles for school reform (see Dehli, 1994; Castagna, 1997). There have also been situational and contextual variations at the intersections of class/gender/dis-ability/race in how parents, families and local communities relate to, and engage schools. Different stakeholders have defined and acted on their roles and responsibilities with differing outcomes. In Euro-Canadian/American contexts, minority parents have defined parental and community responsibility in education in ways that reveal deep anger over the long history of exclusion and marginality. The

exclusion and/or handling of parental concerns have understandably lead
to deep seeded frustrations in the community. The concerns voiced by
parents have all too often fallen upon deaf ears, and continued community
protests would indicate that these tensions are not going away. Parents in
today's diasporic societies are demanding more than mere equality of access
for their children. They want to see that the structures and cultural life of
schools are adequately geared towards the long-term success and well being
of their children. Mainstream schools have been successful in engaging
some students (e.g., students from the dominant society), while disengaging
others (e.g., poor, working-class and racial minority students, and student
bodies marked as "different" by gender, sexuality, faith, dis/ability ...). To
deal with the problem, minority parents and communities have continually
strategized on youth education. As Dehli (1996b) rightly points out, in
"... unequally structured material and social conditions parents draw and
construct different cultural scripts to constitute their identities and
community membership to make claims to schools" (p. 86).

There are two significant theoretical implications of such developments.
First, the question of who/what is defined as a "parent" or "family" in parental
involvement has required some rethinking. Within certain minority
communities, the family is the larger community and any adult is considered
a parent with responsibility for youth education. Second, the lessons of
myriad community involvement in schooling has meant that a working
definition of "parental involvement" is able to rupture white, middle-class
assumptions and challenge the idea of simply inserting parents and
communities into hegemonic structures of schooling. It is therefore important
for critical educational research on home/family learning strategies and
community-based educational outlets to articulate the different histories
and contexts of conventional discourses that highlight a perceived lack of
minority family/community involvement in schooling. Such discourses evoke
"blame," "pathology" and "individual responsibility" for systemic problems.

The redefinitions of the role, responsibility and meaning of education
has led racial and ethnic minority families, parents and local communities to
utilize local creativity and resourcefulness to respond to the challenge of
school-community relations. Such relations are mapped in the terrain of
resistance, advocacy, and the provision of both material and non-material
support to learners. Although parental input has not always been well
received and/or accepted in mainstream schools, parents have found ways

to establish their physical presence in the process of education. Parent activists have struggled to re-position schools within local contexts, and they have worked to move beyond rigid definitions of parent, community and family responsibility. Working from various locations, parents, guardians, caregivers and community members have endeavored proactively to advocate for and with their children. In advising learners of their rights and responsibilities to/in education, it is a struggle towards far more than simplistic notions of good grades and academic success. In today's age of diaspora and increasing social inequity, it is a necessary struggle for human rights, educational responsibility and general success in life.

Reading the Ontario Context

In the specific context of Ontario, much of the existing research data and scholarly writing promoting the idea of inclusive schooling focuses on the "problems" of minority education in general. A few studies have highlighted the question of minority youth disengagement from school (Radwanski, 1987; Dei, 1993, 1994; Daenzer and Dei, 1994; Dei, Holmes, Mazzuca, McIsaac and Campbell, 1995). These critical studies stress the need to examine how various factors of schooling, such as curricular and assessment practices, school/community relations, staffing profiles and the organizational life of schools, have a disempowering impact on minority and poor youth (Dei and Razack, 1995; Brand and Sri Bhaggiyadatta, 1986; Januario, 1994; Ogbu, 1987; Samuda and Crawford, 1980; and Gonzalez and Yawkey, 1993). These factors, along with others such as low teacher expectations, affect learning outcomes for students (see McLaren, 1993; Brown, Cheng, Yau and Ziegler, 1992; Nunes, 1994; Januario, 1994; and Becker, 1990). Among Asian students, often viewed as the "model minorities," those who face educational problems are often reluctant to seek help. This is directly related to the high expectations that are extended to Asian youth who are commonly channelled into the sciences (Found, 1991; Suzuki, 1977; Ryerson Polytechnical Institute, 1991; Maclear, 1994; and Razack, 1995a).

As noted by Dei, Mazzuca, McIsaac and Zine (1997), educational sites not only marginalize students, they actively push children out of schools. However, while many minoritized groups are commonly disengaged from their schooling experience as a direct result of this "push-out" factor (a complex combination of the school's culture, environment, organization, structure and curriculum), Black and Aboriginal students appear to be most affected. The assembly of First Nations Education (1988) and Brown (1993) are among the studies that show dropout rates in high school to be the highest among Aboriginal and African-Canadian students. This high dropout rate is usually related to the alienation and exclusion that racial minority students feel through their schooling experience. In focusing on the problematics facing Black youth in North American contexts, Dei (1996), Brathwaite and James (1996), Toronto Board of Education (1988) and the Black Educators Working group (1993), among many others, assert that schools have failed to make meaningful connections with Black students. This lack of connection can be influenced by the negative portrayal of Africans in history such as the depiction of slavery in the Americas. Blacks are not only shown as victims, but as one-dimensional objects. This type of negativity reflects society's views of Blacks, which has been referred to by Steele (1992) as double vulnerability. Specifically, a lack of Black success in the school system reinforces society's views of Black students as lacking the mental capacity to succeed.

At the more general level, much of the research documenting Black students' alienation in Ontario schools corresponds with literature on minority education in other Euro-American contexts (see Carby, 1982; Erickson, 1987; Asante, 1991, 1992; Shujaa, 1994; Hilliard, 1992; and Lomotey, 1990). In fact, U.S. research is focusing strongly on alternative visions of schooling informed by success stories in minority settings, rather than simply a critique of conventional schools (Ernst, Statzner and Trueba, 1994). As a result, case studies of schools that encourage inclusive schooling have appeared in the literature (see for example, Purkey and Novak, 1984; Purkey and Smith, 1985; Epstein, 1995; Raison, 1995).

In Ontario, the role of parents and local communities in the search for inclusive schooling is generally recognized. The Royal Commission on Learning (COL, 1994) detailed plans for increased encouragement of parent and community involvement in the form of school-community councils. Building on the COL, the Ontario Parent Council (OPC) outlined a plan for new school councils which called for community support that would question traditional school power structures and the reproduction of social inequities. The formulation of the school council still entrusted vast amounts of power to school principals, and this continues to challenge the success of school councils. Nevertheless, the Ontario Parent Council also found that parent involvement improves youth academic achievement (see also Ziegler, 1987, 1989).

Currently, some schools in Ontario are working toward genuine inclusion of youth, parents, and community members. Parents, guardians, caregivers, families, community workers and activists have worked together to promote and enhance youth education by establishing community educational outlets/sites, which exist outside the conventional school setting and often operate with the full support of school authorities. Such collaborative efforts have enhanced educational outcomes for youth. Parent, family and community advocacy for educational change has strengthened the efforts of schools to educate, while at the same time, teachers and administrators have offered material and intellectual support for family and community-based educational programs and outlets. As local communities devote time, energy and resources to supporting community-based educational outlets, the cause of education, particularly in the conventional school system, has been facilitated.

However, despite signs of collaboration, some parents often feel under-informed about school practices and find that their contributions to decision-making and knowledge creation in schools are peripheral to already formulated policies and formal school knowledge. In addition, very little is known about the home-based strategies used by minority parents to increase learning opportunities for their children. Yet, the expertise of parents regarding their children's learning styles and best learning environments is crucial in order for schools to assist youth. When minority parents, youth and community members maintain an integral role in decision-making and knowledge creation about school practices, they become genuinely empowered to contribute fully to the functioning of schools. With the accumulated knowledge of "what works" at the home and community levels, this book will assist in advancing the notion of developing schools into "working communities," where parents, youth, and community members, together with educators, are empowered to strive towards an equitable education system.

Not surprisingly, community organizations have been in the forefront, pressuring schools to initiate studies, policies and practices on inclusive schooling. Groups such as the Organization of Parents of Black Children (OPBC) (see Board of Education, 1988), the Black Educators Working Group (BEWG) (1993), the Working Group (1992) and the Canadian Alliance of Black Educators (CABE) (1992) have indicated how the absence of inclusive and anti-racist practices contribute to the sense of alienation and lack of connection that youth feel in relation to their schools. Studies such as those conducted by the aforementioned groups, illustrate the willingness and desire on the part of minoritized parents and communities to be genuinely involved in their children's schooling. Other studies also point to the importance of implementing and maintaining links between communities and educational institutions. For example, the partnership between the Ontario Federation of Indian Friendship Centres (OFIFC) and the Ontario Ministry of Education and Training (1994) led to the establishment of alternative school pilot projects for Aboriginal students. It is important that schools show a willingness to work in collaboration with diverse/minoritized communities, and that those communities have a role in determining school programs and practices (Barman and McCaskill, 1987; Yukon Native Brotherhood, 1972; R. & S. Consultants, 1993; Ontario Ministry of Education and Training, 1993b).

Within some community-based educational sites, Indigenous cultural values and local resource knowledges are utilized to empower youth. Through cultural-historical narratives of resistance learners deal with social and political realities. Central to parental and community involvement are political discourses of family encouragement, vigilance and support for the learner. Community-based education of minority youth deals with gaps in conventional schools as families, guardians and community leaders work with notions of pride, history and social justice.

The establishment of community-based educational outlets provides new opportunities to deal with questions of curriculum, pedagogy, staffing and instruction that are raised in mainstream schooling. Community workers, leaders and families ensure that the complex dynamics of the culture, environment and organizational lives of community schools work to enhance educational and learning outcomes for a diverse body politic. Through the insurgence of community involvement in schooling, we have begun to move beyond the traditional confines of mainstream education. Community educational efforts are beginning to pick up where the mainstream is leaving off, and as a result, parents, families and community members are finding/ developing a niche from which to inform the processes of formal education. For the educational practitioner in the conventional school system, there is a challenge to ensure that schools become an extension of community in the sense of youth identification with staff, as well as curricular, instructional, pedagogic and communicative change.

A DISCURSIVE [THEORETICAL] FRAMEWORK: TOWARDS AN INTEGRATIVE INCLUSIVITY

In writing about the urgency of educational change we have to confront an inherent danger. There is always the risk that theory will be vilified while practice is privileged. Yet, educators cannot unproblematically disassociate theory from practice. We must understand the philosophical basis for the specific practices that we seek to promote in schools to enhance learning outcomes for all youth. Hence the legitimacy of the questions: how can it be ensured that what is pragmatic does not stand in opposition to what is theoretical? How can critical social theory inform educational practice?

THEORIZING "INCLUSIVE SCHOOLING"

Our general theoretical approach to the idea of "inclusive schooling" is informed by the view that a school is inclusive if every student is able to identify and connect with the school's social environment, culture and organizational life. We acknowledge "inclusive schooling" as problematic insofar as inclusion is presented as an insertion of minoritized "cultures" as auxiliary or peripheral to a core dominant curriculum which remains intact as the legitimate site of knowledge/power. Similarly, we also recognize that "inclusivity" has been problematized in terms of its inadequacy to support substantive transformations in the social construction of power, privilege and difference beyond an assumption of universal entitlement to "hold one's own" place, opinions, or views. Rather, we intend our consideration of "inclusivity" to mean that viewing difference is political and not neutral. We also believe that for inclusive schooling and education to create substantive structural and social transformation, participants must avoid reproducing a dominant hierarchical ordering and classifying of bodies by race, class, gender and other hegemonic categories. Rather, the negotiation of multiple knowledges must take place on the terms of all participants and not just through conditions imposed by the ruling class.

In rethinking schooling and education, our academic project is to promote inclusive schooling. A study of the existing literature on inclusive schooling provides theoretical and practical insights into how Euro-American/Canadian schools can take up the notion/practice of inclusion.

Following the work of Banks and Banks (1993), Goodstein (1994) and Bracy (1995), we have conceptualized the literature on school inclusivity into two broad categories: "diversity as a variety perspective" and "diversity as a critical perspective." The first approach to inclusion is exemplified as viewing diversity in terms of teaching and sharing knowledge about the contributions of diverse cultures to enrich plural communities. This falls within the purview of multicultural perspectives of schooling. Educators' approaches to inclusive schooling may involve a shift from a colour-blind approach to schooling to the recognition of specific contributions of diverse groups to scholarship, as well as the recognition of "... exotic difference between cultures ... [but dealing] ... with surface aspects of celebrations and entertainment" (Bracy, 1995, p. 13). In other expressions of diversity, "difference" and "voice," when acknowledged or taken up in schooling, address various relations to the norms and values of the dominant society.

Generally, inclusive schooling practices embedded in this approach have the educational agenda to develop better intergroup communications, enhance co-operation and tolerance for people of diverse backgrounds, and foster respect for social difference (Bracy, 1995, pp. 3-5). In valuing and appreciating "difference," students, for example, are introduced to academic works that highlight the specific experiences, histories and contributions of the exotic "other." These works are decontextualized, and merely romanticize the "other" without necessarily centring marginalized groups in the dominant cultures of schooling. Marginalized groups and their histories and experiences remain peripheral to dominant educational discourses and practice. This approach to inclusion does not lead to equity, nor does it challenge power, identity or representational issues in education. In fact, the approach fails to rupture difference as the context for power and domination in schools and society.

The second approach to inclusivity adopts "diversity as a critical perspective" where schooling is seen as a racially, culturally and politically mediated experience. This approach deals directly with marginalization and exclusion in school contexts by centring all human experiences in the process of learning. In the analysis, the focus is placed on the twin notions of power and domination in order to understand and interpret social relations and structures (see Lee, 1985, 1994; Goodstein, 1994; Bracy, 1995: 3, Anderson and Collins, 1995). In our view, it is a critical integrative perspective on schooling and education (Dei, 1996) that is able to cultivate new knowledge and oppositional scholarship. The second approach avoids vacuous notions of bland pluralism and the "add and stir" approach to incorporating diversity (Tice, 1990). It focuses on a critical examination of the different histories and experiences of domination and subordination in plural communities. The more critical literature stresses identity, equity and representation as fundamental in schooling and education. The dynamics and relational aspects of difference (race, class, gender, sexuality, language and ability) are critically explored to illustrate how difference and power converge and intersect to shape the schooling experiences of minority youth. The emphasis is on transformative educational practices, which would ensure that students are equipped to challenge and resist dominance and oppression in the multivariant forms of racism, sexism, heterosexism, classism and abilism. Critical educational practices deal specifically with an understanding of, and resistance to "... hierarchies and systems of domination that permeate society and systematically exploit and control people" (Bracy, 1995, p. 6; see also Anderson and Collins, 1995).

The critical approach to inclusive schooling has a transformative educational and social agenda. It focuses on the asymmetrical power relations between and among social groups within the school system and seeks a redistribution of power to ensure fair representation, not only of the actors themselves, but also of the subjects of knowledge production. It seeks to equip individual students with the knowledge and skills necessary to confront their own biases and prejudices, and work for social change. In the process, it legitimizes oppositional and subjugated voices while engendering an educational atmosphere in which all youth can challenge and resist the structural forces that continually reproduce social oppression and inequality.

The relations of power that inform the schooling process are based in identity and difference. Schools are "contested public spheres" (Fine, 1993, p. 682), and as political sites for the production and reproduction of power and social inequality, the process of teaching, learning and sharing knowledge enters participants into power relations (see also Apple and Weis, 1983; Giroux, 1983; Apple, 1986; McCarthy, 1990). These relations are part and parcel of the lived experience of minoritized students today, and many critical educators argue that inclusivity cannot be effectively addressed without specific work to ameliorate their effects. To these ends, critical studies on "inclusive schooling" offer useful and often penetrating insights into the challenges of education in plural communities, as well as ways in which genuine inclusive practices can be implemented in schools.

In discussing the importance of inclusivity in school settings, the critical literature problematizes social oppressions that are developed and transmitted through the hidden curriculum of schools. Oppressions such as structural poverty, racism, and sexism, are consequential to schooling outcomes across the board, but the nature of intersecting and interlocking oppressions gives rise to multiple problematics for minoritized youth specifically. Bearing this in mind, when dealing with the lived experience of students and their families, there are no hard and fast rules that state how people will react to oppression. Eisenhart and Graue (1993), Gay (1994), Ogbu (1982) and Solomon (1992) discuss how minority students form groups to resist the dominant school culture. Siu (1994) suggests that minority students will often assimilate in order to succeed; a process that all too often results in a loss of cultural/ ethnic/personal identity (see chapter 5), and a deep sense of exclusion.

The structural processes of schooling foster unequal opportunities, and create differential outcomes, particularly for racially minoritized students and those from low socio-economic family backgrounds (see also Willis, 1977; 1983). This is a significant departure from conventional views that focus on family-school relations, conceptualizing homes and families as sites and sources of student educational problems. We would assert that such simplistic explanations of student failure only serve to blame the victims of systemic oppression by pathologizing the "trinity" of student-parent-community. We must look beyond conventional views that place learners and their families as the axis for educational failure. We must be look at the systemic problems as a starting point for change. Society as a whole must accept responsibility for educational failures, and acknowledge that if learners are not empowered through their schooling experience, then the system itself cannot be genuinely inclusive, and is in need of reform. Similarly, the notion of "centre" should be seen as a point of entry, a location for subjects and actors involved in knowledge production and use. The location of centre/margin is a power relation. To be included in the processes of schooling, all learners will have to be centred. This means that the experiences, histories, cultures and identities of all learners are considered as central to all levels of educational practices (e.g., teaching, instruction, curriculum and textual production).

One of the current oppositional stances to inclusive schooling in North America (see Bloom, 1987; Hirsch, 1987; D'Souza, 1991) takes the view that public schooling and education is unduly burdened with special interests and politically motivated demands. This view asserts that inclusive schooling is a concern of special interest groups, and that any such move towards a "minority curriculum" will place academic standards and excellence at risk. It is unproblematically argued that Canadians want a return to the "basics" and that "quality" education is better than equity education. This argument denies any linkage between academic "excellence" and educational "equity." However, are there truly "special interests" concerns when it comes to the education of a diverse student body? Is education not for a common good? Responding to the challenge of difference and diversity in Euro-American education requires a change in the educational status quo. Dealing with educational inequities and social justice issues requires differential and positive (i.e., solution-oriented) treatment of social groups given the lessons of history and the social reality of the racialized, classed and gendered society in which we live.

While the argument that teachers must treat all students the same may be sound in reference to teacher attitudes and expectations of students, this reasoning can be problematic at another level. This is the case when the debate addresses how best to deal with the marginality and alienation of minority youth in the mainstream school system. Put bluntly, our argument is that Canadian education cannot address concerns of minority youth's marginality and alienation in the schools without ensuring that school practices effectively succeed in centring these youth, their histories and subjectivities, in schooling. By history, we refer to the complexity of a people's past and lived experiences, as well as a politically situated, dynamic collective gestalt of time/place, rather than a decontextualized set of abstracted "facts" such as dates, heroes and place names. By subjectivities, we refer to students' sense of their individual identities and how these self-definitions intersect or converge with students' collective and historical existence as members of racial minority and majority groups.

Inclusivity must be defined broadly. It must mean including all human experiences in the education of every learner. Educational researchers and practitioners have frequently suggested strategies that can address the marginalization of racially minoritized students, women, and students from diverse sexual and socio-economic class backgrounds. In particular, heterosexism and homophobia work to disempower students within schools (see Friend, 1993). Lesbian and gay issues have historically been excluded from the curriculum and from the literature on inclusive schooling. Advocates for the inclusion of these issues argue that the use of resource materials and lesbian/gay literature should be infused into the curriculum to dispel homophobia within the school setting (see Anderson 1994; Firestone, et al., 1994; Lipkin, 1994; Pharr, 1993; and Russell and McCaskell 1995/96).

Studies have highlighted the fact that the combined framing(s) of radical multicultural, anti-racist, multi-centric and critical feminist teachings have the greatest potential to create ruptures within the school system (see Henry, 1992; Ladson-Billings, 1994; Dei, 1994; Bright, 1995; Brown et al., 1992; Gillborn, 1995; Lee, 1994; Malloy, 1994; Banks, 1989; Hilliard, 1992; Vann and Kunjufu, 1993; and Dei, 1996). Addressing marginalization openly is crucial if we are to provide a balance to the Eurocentric worldview presently found in the school system. Anti-racist feminism, for instance, distinctly challenges traditional feminist education practices (Bourne, 1983; Davis, 1981; and hooks, 1989). Mainstream feminism tends to speak to middle-class white women who favour class reforms in society without implicating themselves in the reproduction and benefit of a racist patriarchy (see also Razack, 1994, 1995b; Stasiulis, 1990; and Aziz, 1995). In other words, so-called "second-wave feminism" generally is unable to challenge critically the power that white, heterosexual women have in this society. An anti-racist feminism takes into account the interlocking levels of oppression in society. Men and women who recognize their relative positions of privilege and oppression are potential and valued allies in trying to rupture power differentials embedded in the Eurocentric and patriarchal system. The project of anti-racist feminism expands beyond changing the "face" of power in the system — it seeks to make serious changes in the way people are treated and portrayed.

Research indicates that in addition to race and ethnicity, achievement outcomes are also influenced by other social factors. For example, class combines with ethnicity and language to limit the opportunities of students (see Curtis, Livingstone and Smaller, 1992). The organizational structures of schools often work to reproduce and reinforce existing patterns of class and ethnic dominance. Students of low socio-economic status are often streamed into inferior programs and schools, thus restricting their educational options and reproducing a working class (see McLaren, 1993; Nunes, 1994; Januario, 1994).

These studies clearly indicate that minority students face problems in our educational system that must be addressed. While some studies provide useful background information, they generally fail to focus on the expressed concerns of the students with regard to their educational histories and how real and perceived institutional structures may have served to alienate them from the school system. In the literature, the lack of student perspectives, especially from subordinated groups, also reflects society's tendency to ignore their voices. In general, teachers, administrators and other educational professionals are reporting their findings from their subject position. This position, no matter the intentions of the participants, does little to challenge the traditional power relations between teachers and students.

Fortunately, recent studies have started to present voices from students who have traditionally been silenced (see Brathwaite and James, 1996; James, 1990, 1995a; Dei, Mazzuca, McIsaac and Zine, [forthcoming]; Solomon, 1992; and Greer, 1992). These studies inform the discussion on inclusive schooling by highlighting the need to hear and learn from the narratives of racial minority and working-class students. However, centring the lived experiences and personal accounts of students within the curriculum and pedagogical practices of schools cannot be effective without addressing notions of power, privilege and domination (Bracy, 1995, p. 3; Anderson and Collins, 1995; Apple, 1993; and Holdberg, 1990). Critical educational practitioners have noted that white teachers often resist acknowledging their privilege and *a priori* assumptions regarding minority cultures (Sleeter, 1993; Solomon, 1995; James, 1995b; Blair, 1994). This resistance prevents teachers from recognizing, for example, the extent of racism faced by Black and other minority students.

The issue of inclusion in education extends also to factors of ethnicity, class, gender, sexual orientation, faith, dis/ability, health, body size, age, language/culture, et cetera. Certain ethnic groups face similar prospects in terms of success in the school system. For example, Becker (1990), Brown, Cheng, Yau and Zeigler (1992), McLaren (1993), and Nunes (1994) reveal how racial/ethnic minority students underachieve in school. The notion of merit, or "achievement" can serve a political function. In evaluating student success based on the arbitrary conventions of a presumed authority, the notion of merit serves to regulate the ways in which bodies, voices, knowledges and power are registered, approved and written as legitimate. In this way, the structures of meritocracy attain the power to eclipse/mute "othered" ways of knowing. For example, patriarchal structures dominate our school system to the extent that the contributions of women are hidden, not seen, ignored, or devalued. Many women learn through phallocentric, sexist school practices not only that the pursuit of learning is generally reserved for males, while child-rearing is the domain of women (see also,

Gaskell and McLaren, 1991; Gaskell, McLaren and Novogrodsky, 1989; and Staton and Larkin, 1993). For Lewis, (1988, p. 15), phallocentrism is sustained as a system of entitlement extending patriarchal power into the realm of sexualizing and objectifying women's bodies as reproductive sites of male-centred and male-directed economic and political control. Moreover, when phallocentrism dominates conventional paradigms of schooling, women's knowledges/ways of knowing, including feminist informings, are not visible or else are dismissed as incommensurate with the rationality of education. In the academy, race and gender intersect such that "rights and wrongs, values and counter-values, are defined from the perspective of those (often white) men, who have the authority for making definitions and imposing them on others, and that difference and non-conformism are not tolerated when they threaten the status quo" (Moghissi, 1994, p. 230). Similarly, students who are gay or lesbian face uphill battles in seeing themselves depicted positively in school (see Friend, 1993).

The "hidden curriculum" in schools also affects the extent to which schools are actually inclusive. The colour of the teaching staff, for example, speaks to the commitment individual schools have towards inclusion. This lack of diversity among school staff may signal a school's reluctance to embrace meaningful diversity in a non-curricular way. Racial minority students may question why they are not being represented even though the student population is diverse. Identification with teachers of similar ethno-cultural backgrounds could highly influence the motivational level of diverse students not only to stay in school, but also to achieve. The level of support the school gives to school clubs is also important. The type of support and leadership offered by staff and administration can greatly affect the students' feelings of connection to the school setting. Practices of inclusion at any school also take into account the viewpoints of subordinated groups. All students must feel comfortable in the school setting. If students feel that the school is ignoring or marginalizing them, they will have a tendency not to "buy into" the program.

The role that schools play in the community reflects the level of commitment they show towards inclusion. A school that links up with the communities of subordinated groups will show that they are at least attempting to meet communities' needs (e.g., providing school spaces for African-centred learning and Indigenous forms of education). Conversely, the inability of schools to meet regularly with community groups or parents signifies a disrespect that is duly noted within that community. In addition, not implementing the occasional community proposal suggests that the school cares little for the concerns of that particular community.

It is also important to start inclusive schooling from early childhood and at the primary school level. Disengagement from schooling is a process that often begins in and through a child's early educational experiences. As is the case in all human interactions, there are no hard and fast set of rules as to when, where, and in what shape this disengagement may occur. For many minoritzed students, and particularly for Black and Aboriginal children, the lack of visible and "other" minority teachers can serve as a precursor to disengagement. Students may be going through the motions throughout there entire student career. That is to say that a child can be disengaged while attending school. For example, students who feel severe alienation and marginalization may stay in school simply because their friends are there, because it is the norm, or even in response to parental pressures. In contexts where the classroom climate accentuates a capitalist-oriented individualism while negating the students' affective and spiritual subjectivities, students may seek spaces elsewhere outside of the content and context of the classroom.

Inclusive schooling would recognize that schools are obligated to make real connections with new students, particularly those from non-Western cultures. So-called "immigrant students" have to feel that they have the same access to equal and quality education as those who are already here. Assimilationist or "melting-pot" approaches to schooling must be scrutinized as they automatically reject the new student's background and also reduce her or him to a singular identity. At the same time, they have the effect of silencing or negating students' voices.

Recent critical educational studies assert that genuine power-sharing among parents, community members, and school personnel from diverse racial and ethnocultural backgrounds can empower youth to become more effectively involved in their own learning (Dei, Holmes, Mazzuca, McIsaac and Campbell, 1995; Cummins, 1996; Dehli, 1996a). Parent and local community knowledges of "what works" are a valuable, yet untapped resource for improving schools. Traditionally, parents (and particularly African-Canadian parents) have been blamed for their children's difficulties at school. Educators who view minority family life as culturally deprived express feelings of powerlessness to overcome their students' "deficiencies" (see Dei, Holmes, Mazzuca, McIsaac, and Campbell, 1995; Brathwaite and James, 1996; Lee, 1985, 1994; and Dei, 1996). As a result, a culture of mutual misunderstanding may develop, inhibiting learning in the classroom and widening the gap between home and school cultures.

Working Toward a Critical Integrative Framework

Our study utilized a critical integrative approach to understanding social difference as related to issues of inclusive schooling. We view inclusive schooling as an approach to education which stresses that the socially constructed concepts of race, ethnicity, gender, class, language and sexuality are fundamental to education and the schooling process. Through a critical integrative analysis of social difference we are able to learn how the diverse knowledges and concerns of youth, parents and communities are embraced in schooling and educational sites in plural contexts. To understand the role of students, teachers, parents and local communities in the process of developing inclusive schools, a critical integrative approach to research would connect educational issues with questions of social difference.

An integrative framework maintains that educational practitioners need to be aware of the historical contexts and institutional structures that sustain educational inequities in Euro-Canadian/American contexts. It follows that parents, community members, and youth from diverse racial, ethnocultural, and class backgrounds must be jointly involved in both the decision-making and the delivery of education. An integrative perspective examines ways in which the rich knowledge of parents, families, guardians, caregivers, and community workers can aid in "empowering" minority youth to achieve both academically and socially. This approach encourages a critical reading of how race and social difference might mediate the power of communal social practice into actions that address educational inequity. The framework argues that power and resistance are not intrinsic to the dominant group, and that discursive agency and resistance also reside in/among local, minoritized and marginalized communities. In plural societies, subordinated groups develop both theoretical and practical conceptions of how they might engage in social and political reform. For these marginalized groups, collectively produced knowledges that are embedded in local culture, history and daily social interactions inform communal agency, and act as the basis for collective political action.

These knowledges are basic not only for the well being of the community, but for the health of schools as well. That being said, educational practices have limited value if they recognize the importance of community knowledge and difference among students without changing the physical/cultural environment of schools. As an educational approach, inclusive schooling moves beyond a mere recognition of inequity and enables educators to encourage/employ the differences, knowledges and identities that students bring with them to school.

Following the pioneering works of Brandt (1986), Mullard (1980, 1985), Carby (1982), Jeffcoate (1984), Nixon (1984), Gilroy (1982), Cohen (1988/9), Bains and Cohen (1988), Abella (1984), Thomas (1984), Lee (1985), Troyna and Williams (1986) [see also Reed, 1994], Dei (1996) developed an integrative anti-racism discursive framework for understanding the issues of educational inclusivity and social change. Dei's framework interrogates how local communities (e.g. students, parents, families, community groups), interact with the institutional structures of education. At the centre of this interrogation is an insurgent perspective on oppression and the pragmatic potential for educational change. The integrative anti-racist framework recognizes that race and social difference constitute the context for power and domination in society in general, and schools in particular. To expand on this notion, identities in general are multi-accentual, and are informed though the myriad experiences of life. In this same way, marginalized identities are formed in relation to the exclusions and inequities of life. Anti-racism asserts that identity must be linked with the process of schooling, and therefore the intersecting and interlocking nature of oppression must be taken up in educational sites. So discussions of racism in schooling must necessarily entail discussions of class, gender and sexuality, and we can no longer assume that a policy of tolerance is enough to create an equal playing field.

As Dei (1996) argues, integrative anti-racism moves beyond a simple acknowledgment of the material conditions that structure social inequality. The anti-racist framework employs a critical interrogation of white power/ privilege as well as its accompanying rationale for dominance. As a point of clarity, this interrogation does not only seek to determine and clarify sites of white power. Rather, with respect to the dichotomies inherent in any discussions of oppression, we seek also to illuminate and examine the sites of negation and repression that stand relative to all that is good and beneficial about whiteness. Bearing this in mind, anti-racism questions the marginalization of minority voices, experiences and histories. The anti-racism discursive framework questions the roles that social institutions (schools, home/family, museums, workplaces, arts, justice, and media) play in reproducing racial, gender, sexual and class-based inequalities. It acknowledges the pedagogic need to confront the challenge of diversity in schools, and the need to develop educational models that are more inclusive and capable of responding to racial minority concerns and aspirations. However, as social structures have historically served the material, political and ideological interests of white privilege and capitalist social formations, affecting change must, almost by definition, be an insurgent project. To these ends, anti-racism praxis stands openly in opposition to established hegemonic social, economic and political interests.

Put succinctly, anti-racism deals foremost with *equity*: the qualitative value of justice. It also deals with the question of *representation*: that is, the need to have a multiplicity of physical bodies, as well as diverse voices/ perspectives entrenched as part of mainstream social knowledge. Anti-racism also examines institutional practices to see how educational institutions respond to the challenge of *diversity and difference*: that is, the socially constructed intersections of race, gender, class, sexuality, language, culture and religion (see Dei, 1996).

TOWARDS NEW RESEARCH FRAMINGS FOR THE CONSIDERATION OF INCLUSIVE SCHOOLING

In this book, we attend to some fundamental questions of contemporary Canadian education. What do educators know and understand about diversity in their schools? How can schools create a learning environment in which the needs, concerns and aspirations of a diverse school body can all be met? How do educators and learners understand within a context of power and privilege? How do schools deal with racial, sexual, gender, class and ethnocultural diversity? What are the challenges of being a minority in a Euro-American/Canadian school setting? What does it mean to be "different"? What is the relationship between race, difference and schooling? How can teachers and educators teach about race and difference in schools? What are the personal and collective responsibilities in fighting racism and social oppressions? What are the intersections of race, class, gender and sexuality? These questions generally centre around the educational challenge of dealing with difference and diversity. The search for an understanding of a common humanness and the need to learn about our social difference should not be seen in conflict. In fact, they are not incompatible. We cannot abandon the search for understanding and appreciating human differences in a desire simply to accentuate our commonalities. Understanding social differences and their educational implications is basic to the development of inclusive schooling. We believe difference should be a source of strength for communities. And, we also believe, the practice of inclusive schooling is fundamental to achieving equity and justice in Canada.

In this introductory chapter, we frame some of the fundamental issues and problematics that inform our politics. We wanted to clarify that anti-racism and inclusivity are not "special interest" projects, but rather, human projects that work directly against the forces of oppression that affect and damage society as a whole. Further, this theoretical backdrop serves to frame the best practices considered in this work. Chapter Two discusses aims, current research context, methodologies and data analysis with respect to a three-year study conducted in Toronto schools to assess "best practices" in inclusive education and schooling. Chapter Three extends one of the themes identified through the best practices research to consider the implications of Indigenous knowledges for inclusive schooling. Chapter Four further expands on the theme of spiritual and intuitive learning to present holistic approach to learning and indigeneity. Chapter Five addresses issues in multilingualism, language integration and retention. Chapter Six examines broader conceptions of educational success. Similarly, Chapter Seven looks at questions of representation in education. In Chapter Eight, the authors revisit community-based education as a strategy for social transformation. Finally, Chapter Nine summarizes the tensions and possibilities inherent to inclusive, integrative approaches to education.

NOTES

1   In this study, the term "Black" refers to those students of African descent who identify themselves as such. Although Black students do not constitute a homogenous group, we believe there exist significant commonalities in the educational experiences of students born in Africa, the Diaspora or those of mixed parenthood (Black and non-Black) to allow discussion of issues experienced by these students in the collective. For this reason, the term Black is used throughout this report to include all students of African heritage.

CHAPTER 2

RESEARCH AND METHOD: EXEMPLARY PRACTICES OF INCLUSIVE SCHOOLING

INTRODUCTION

We ask that readers do not interpret this work solely as a theoretical treatise on anti-racism and school reform. We wanted to peel away the veil of equity that hides oppression in education today while proposing pragmatic alternatives to the existing systems and structures of mainstream schooling. That being said, we would clarify that many of the theoretical and practical concepts discussed in this book were informed by critical educational research that has spanned the last decade. Since the early 1990s, George Dei, one of the authors of this book, directed numerous collaborative investigations into the State of education in North American contexts.[1] Dr. Dei, as the principle investigator (PI) for this project, worked alongside the four co-authors of this book, and numerous other OISE/UT graduate students, in an effort to examine innovative new approaches to school reform from an anti-racist/inclusive perspective. It is with a critical eye towards the findings of this research project, that we undertook the task of writing this book. We wanted to obtain in-depth, site-specific ethnographic information on the practices that most effectively promote educational equity and academic excellence for *all* students. Further, we wanted to interrogate these issues from the viewpoints of students, teachers, school administrators and parents. The primary research objective for this work was to examine in detail innovative practices that target the needs of identifiable school bodies (e.g., Black/African-Canadian students). It was proposed that the study would highlight exemplary practices that particularly enhance learning outcomes for Black youth (e.g., studies of culture-specific programming, including programmes that tap the cultural resource base of Black communities, as well as educational practices that seek community and parental involvement in, and shared control of, schooling and educational processes). We felt that a project of this nature, while ambitious in scope, would best illuminate the inspiring concepts and initiatives being undertaken to ameliorate the problematics of oppression in North American schools today.

AIMS AND OBJECTIVES OF THE STUDY

Between June 1992 and November 1995, we conducted a study to examine the dilemma of Black and minority youth disengagement from school. The primary learning objective was to understand the processes of students' disengagement from school from the vantage points of the subjects and actors themselves (see Dei, Mazzuca, McIsaac, and Zine, 1997). In the study, we argued that, while conventional schools are capable of engaging many students (particularly but not exclusively students from the dominant groups), a good many students are correspondingly disengaged in and by schools. It was our contention that a combination of factors, ranging from the culture and the environment to the organizational lives of schools coupled with off-schools (home, family and community), contributed immensely to the problem of minority youth dropping out of schools. There is a growing realization that in spite of the general concerns of some youths failing and "underachieving" in schools, there are also "success" stories. These success cases emerge out of exemplary practices of inclusive schooling at the level of schools, families, homes and local communities. We believe these cases can provide useful lessons for rethinking schooling and education in North American contexts. There are numerous examples of dedicated teachers, educators, parents and community workers actively engaged in promoting enhanced educational outcomes for all youth, and they should not be overlooked.

To this end, between June 1995 and May 1999, we conducted another study on the challenges of making excellence accessible and equitable to all students through an inclusive approach to education. The first phase of this major research study looked at exemplary practices of inclusive schooling in a select number of schools in Ontario. Our research touched on issues of curriculum, pedagogy, instruction and materials, with a focus on practices that created inclusion for all students. In the second phase, the study goal was to learn how the diverse knowledges and concerns of youth, parents and communities could be incorporated in schooling and education in Ontario. To better understand the role of parents and local communities in the process of inclusive schooling, a critical integrative approach to research was employed to connect educational issues with questions of social difference. The research methodology sought to obtain in-depth, site-specific ethnographic information on home-based learning strategies and autonomous community-based educational initiatives. Also, we sought to ascertain the extent to which community liaison officers' were bringing family, home and cultural knowledge into schools.

Independent learning strategies employed by parents and youth, including the prior learning styles that youth bring to the school environment, were to be examined through interviews with youth, parents and community members. In addition, research would focus on how community liaison work facilitates effective school-community linkages to ensure that home educational strategies are made relevant in schools. Examination of community- and home-based learning strategies, as well as the work of liaison officers were to take place concurrently.

An important research focus was the detailed examination of the ways in which community-initiated programs are working to empower (Dei, 1996, p. 22) African-Canadian and other racial minority youth through teaching about rights, responsibilities and advocacy. We wanted to examine how elements of non-hegemonic cultural capital are produced in the home, and how those elements might be integrated into mainstream schools. We would mention that home/community-based knowledges should be seen as more than simply assimilationist. In fact, particularly around issues of agency and access to educational resources (via community liaison counsellors and school councils), community-based knowledges whether employed in the mainstream or in the community should be read as subversive. Gaining access to dominant institutional languages and discourses, for example, allows communities to engage within a politics of subversion, because they appropriate this knowledge to articulate positions of dissent. Through discussions with minority parents, youth and community members, information on the incorporation of local communities' knowledge, concerns and issues in the operation of the newly established school councils would also be generated. The inclusion of minority voices would assist in reforming the organizational and curricular practices of schools, making the educational system more responsive to the needs and aspirations of a diverse student body.

The third phase of our research had three main goals. First, to develop innovative practices that would promote participatory research, and facilitate inter-faculty collaborations at OISE/UT. Second, to develop curricular and instructional resource guidelines and innovative pedagogical approaches for practising teachers and student teachers in the elementary and secondary school panels in Ontario. Third, to assist teachers and student teachers to implement integrative anti-racism and anti-discrimination curriculum guidelines, instructional materials and innovative pedagogical approaches in their classrooms.

QUALITATIVE METHODOLOGY

"Space" is conceptualized here with respect to the process that invites participants into the research, but also in terms of ethical/epistemological issues of power and voice/difference. This methodology was informed by the assumption that research is not neutral but rather is a political activity with consequences for the social construction of privilege, power, authority and knowledge (see Cherryholmes, 1993, p. 2; Kirby and McKenna, 1989, p. 169; Eisner and Peshkin, 1990, p. 15). Through a critical content analysis of the narratives developed herein, we sought to identify salient themes as they arose. Further, in using in-depth interviews and participant observations as the principle methods of data collection, we felt that we would be able to both negotiate and create spaces. Respective of these issues, our research highlights the contingencies and contiguities between qualitative research as a politicized methodology of knowledge production and anti-racist/ inclusive educational research praxis creating spaces. Respective of the "richness" of "lived experience," we feel this methodology opens research to possibilities that could not be found in traditional qualitative methods. While there are competing paradigms which have attempted to discredit such work, we assert that this methodology has a great deal to offer. Qualitative approaches to critical race and anti-racist research create a platform for voices that have been otherwise silenced and muted.

The approach used in this research considers that the data cannot speak for itself, but that it must be sufficiently contextualized. This is a delicate proposition in that the work must take care not to eclipse the voices of the participants, while attending to the shifting locations of the researchers. To the extent that we read our data collection and analysis through the lenses of our informed experiences, our observations and analyses were not external to us, nor were our phenomena/interpretations static (Kirby and McKenna, 1989, p. 155). Rather, as participant observers embodying the accounts of our research (Haraway, 1988, p. 578), our involvement in a historically situated symbolic construction or data collection/construction process was both integral to and constituted by our dynamic subjectivities and positionalities (Popkewitz, 1997, p.132; Houle, 1995, p. 97). Such participation involves the ongoing negotiation of meanings beyond problematized essentialisms or univocal theories of experience at the intersections of race/class/gender/disability/age/sexuality/language/ culture/ethnicity (see also Harris, 1997).

CRITERIA FOR MEASURING "BEST/EXEMPLARY" PRACTICES OF INCLUSIVE SCHOOLING

Following Dei and Razack (1995), our study conceptualized "best practices" as exemplary educational strategies that promote both equity and academic excellence. The best, most inclusive initiatives seek to address questions of equity and power-sharing in education by centring students and their lived experiences in schooling. Thus, our approach to research has been to measure successful practices by criteria that take into account significant facets of inclusion. We believe that genuine educational inclusion is indicated by high retention rates for all groups; the relatively even distribution of all groups across academic programs and levels of the school system including the post-secondary level; and effective parent/school/ community relationships. Of equal importance is the principle of "inclusivity" which seeks to transform schools into "working communities" by bringing the notions of co-operation and social responsibility into the centre of mainstream schooling. Schools that demonstrated these indicators and principles were chosen in order to examine the practices that contribute to inclusion. We should also reiterate that more work can be done on these "exemplary practices," our discussions are not conclusive or definitive, and we are not claiming that these practices represent the ultimate practices of inclusion. Rather, we assert that they must be read as starting points for a process of educational transformation. Often, these processes are part of the existing hegemonic structures but do not represent the kinds of transformation that need to take place to allow for broader systemic change. Our theoretical framework allows for a pragmatic perspective that moves beyond existing practices, and into a more fully integrative approach that combines all the domains covered in this book.

We did not want to focus on educational practices that simply acknowledge the need for inclusive education. Rather, we wanted to examine school, home and local community initiatives that actually adopted inclusive practices in order to enhance the schooling experiences of their students. We have identified some of these initiatives as 'exemplary', and noted them to be the 'best practices of inclusive schooling'. This notes insurgent initiatives that work towards youth success and empowerment in/through the process of education. The best practices work to restructure the conventional processes of schooling such that Eurocentric educational models give way to integrative, multicentric ways of knowing and learning. This distinction is important because it specifically questions "multicultural" efforts that seek to mainstream marginal discourses within the current educational and cultural framework. Contemporary multicultural programs amount to little more than sugar-coated reforms that compartmentalize and/ or particularize alternative forms of knowledge. In contrast, the disruptive and revolutionary nature of inclusivity gives birth to new readings of educational reform, and fresh interpretations of how education might be delivered.

Unlike models of education that endorse and sustain dominant/ privileged understandings of the world, an inclusive perspective views marginalized knowledge and experience as valuable resources to be centred in processes of schools. Bearing this in mind, we must reiterate that inclusive practice is not geared towards the interests of any one sector of society. We cannot abide rhetorical arguments that seek to pigeonhole inclusivity under the auspices of an "interest group" agenda. All students need to be aware of the diversity of ideas, events and histories that have informed, and continue to shape human growth and development. The promotion of an inclusive "global education" is basic to these ends.

To effectively promote inclusive education, it is crucial that schools distinguish between inter and intra-cultural initiatives. We must draw a very clear boundary between practices that tolerate minoritized students, and those critical anti-racist initiatives that actually address the relations of domination and power in educational sites. We make this point of clarification because school policies may tolerate cultural difference and social diversity without necessarily dismantling the barriers that plague minoritized students. The notion of "tolerance" itself is fraught with problematics of power, privilege and opportunity. Who gets to tolerate whom? Who is in the position to tolerate, and what are the power relations relative to that position? If we adopt a policy and practice of tolerance without dealing with the questions of power and privilege, then we cannot realistically address concerns about race, identity and representation in education.

The best practices of inclusive education challenges the fundamental relations of power that run through mainstream educational sites. By dealing directly with the dynamics of oppression and its implications for educational success, these inclusive practices promote positive learning outcomes for all students and stakeholders alike.

RESEARCH ACTIVITIES AND METHODOLOGICAL FOUNDATIONS

As already noted, one of this book's authors, George Dei, has been the principal investigator (PI) for the entire research project. Since 1995 he has been working with a number of graduate students from the Ontario Institute for Studies in Education of the University of Toronto to conduct document studies, field/ethnographic research (observations and interviews), data analysis and dissemination of research information.

Field Activities: 1995-99

The entire research project had three phases extending from October 1995 to May 1999. The initial research phase was devoted to a study of innovative/exemplary practices at three levels of the Ontario public school system: elementary (K-6), intermediate (7-8) and secondary. Research focused on ethnographic studies of specific curricular practices designed to seek the inclusion of all students, as well as those practices that specifically targeted the needs of African-Canadian and other minority students. Four major research questions guided the examination of best practices:

1. How do school practices seek out and integrate inclusive resources into school curricula?
2. How does the school take into account students' home and off-school cultures in the teaching, learning and administration of education?
3. How does the school deal with difference and diversity among the student population?
4. How do particular school practices seek out and recruit, particularly, Black and other minority teachers and staff?

The exploration of these questions involved ethnographic observations of actual practices in classrooms and schools, a review of written materials, and the examination of innovative programs and policies designed and implemented with an eye to inclusion. Of particular concern was how schools might integrate diverse histories, experiences and viewpoints into teaching and learning practices; how schools promote courses and non-academic programs, taking into account students' concerns and interests around race, ethnicity, class, sexuality, dis/ability, language, culture and difference; and the extent of school support for special programs, student clubs, organizations and events aimed at full inclusion. Our study also focused on the organizational life of the school (e.g., power structures of schooling, as well as the particular practices that account for student context in counselling programmes). Finally, attention was given to the nature and extent to which schools make use of the cultural resource knowledge of the local community (e.g., approaches to communicating and interacting with minority parents and community groups).

An appropriate evaluation of inclusive schooling must take the voices of students and teachers into account. Students are the immediate (but not exclusive) beneficiaries of such reform and a central resource in assessing the effectiveness of identified exemplary practices. We therefore conducted in-depth interviews with a select number of students, teachers and administrative staff to explore the ways in which the school is a "working community." For example, important guiding research questions included: How do students, teachers and administrative staff work together to read and understand themselves and their worlds? How do students and teachers imagine and act in creative and innovative ways to enhance schooling and learning outcomes for everyone? Interviews focused on an understanding of how teachers and students manipulate the school system and transform the social world they inhabit by speaking, teaching and learning collectively about race, social difference, power, oppression and social justice. We also sought an understanding of how students empower themselves to succeed in the school, as well as how, through dialogue and social awareness, students and teachers work together to overcome domination within the culture of schooling (see Ernst and Statzner, 1994, pp. 203-4).

While we have attended in detail to the voices of the secondary school participants involved in this project, there is an absence of their elementary student counterparts' voices in the text. The student narratives chosen for this book reflect a sample selected for their relevance to the specific themes we have been discussing here. From listening to the tapes of elementary student interviews, many elementary students tended to talk about inclusion in terms of whether available programming was related to their interests (e.g., sports, et cetera) While this knowledge is valuable in its own right, we do not find it to be directly relevant to the discussion of the domains selected for emphasis in this study.

In phase two of the project, research documented the pedagogical, curricular and instructional implications of specific home and community educational strategies that parents, families, guardians, caregivers and community workers have successfully employed to promote effective learning and to enhance youth educational outcomes. The learning objective was to see how the diverse knowledges and concerns of youth, parents and communities are embraced in schooling and education in Ontario contexts. In the third phase of the project, we analysed the field data and identified certain domains around which to organize professional workshops with students and practising teachers and community educators. Workshop sessions were organized around particular domains. Researchers were assigned responsibilities of brainstorming and dialoguing with educators, teachers and community elders on respective domains, and engaging in action research in classroom settings to understand the practical constraints, realities and challenges of integrating theoretical ideas and philosophies of educational change in Ontario contexts.

Specific Areas of Data Collection

Phase I
In the 1995-97 school years, the study focused on six schools selected from two former boards of education in Metropolitan Toronto. We studied two schools in each of the elementary (Grades 4-6), intermediate (Grades 6-8)

and secondary (Grades 10-OAC) levels. We interviewed 30 teachers, including eight school administrators (six principals and two vice principals), as well as 94 students (30 students at the secondary level, 29 at the intermediate level, and 35 at the elementary level). At one high school, Black students, who constituted a high proportion of the student body, were the main targets of study. The remaining schools from each board were racially and ethnically diverse.

Beginning in mid-October 1995 to March 1996, we observed school and classroom interactions while interviewing students and teachers. Students were selected to reflect race/ethnicity, gender, sexuality, faith, and family backgrounds. In March 1996, focus group interviews were held with high school students. Interviews with teachers and school administrators began in November 1996. A maximum of five staff from each of the six schools, representing educators in history, arts, mathematics and science, and those engaged in innovative programs, were selected for interviews. The month of April 1996, was spent on a preliminary data analysis and write-up of initial findings on schools' "best/exemplary practices" for conference presentations and community speaking engagements.

Over a twelve-month period (May 1996 to July 1997) the principal investigator (PI) and six OISE/UT graduate research assistants conducted ethnographic observations, in-depth interviews and focus group discussions with youths, parents, community liaison workers and members of community-based, grassroots organizations. In the examination of community-based learning initiatives, seven community-based, grassroots organizations working to promote youth education were identified. Between the months of May and August 1996, we interviewed parents for their reflections on school practices as well as their views on how schools can be made more inclusive for all youth. Sixteen adult community members from different organizations were interviewed about their educational strategies. From September 1996 until March 1997, we focused on a number of Community Saturday School projects/programs to examine how their practices related to inclusive schooling. We examined the content of these projects/programs and also conducted in-depth interviews with the individuals who led them, as well as with parents and students who were involved in the programs. In the examination of community-based learning initiatives, we identified seven community-based, grassroots organizations working to promote youth education. Sixteen adult community members from different organizations were interviewed about their educational strategies, as well as a total of 30 youth participating in each of the community-based schools. Since these programs were established to empower youth, it was necessary to understand how young people themselves viewed these programs as meeting their needs and enhancing their educational outcomes. The study sample included students in OAC programs and those enrolled in community-initiated educational programs. With the assistance of community groups, we were able to identify parents whose children were achieving academic and/or social success within the conventional educational system. The families provided a sufficient sample to obtain study participants. Community-based youth programs participating in this study included:

- African Heritage Educators Network (AHEN) Project 90;
- Canadian Association of Black Educators (CABE) — Vaughan Road Project;
- Jamaica Canada Association;
- The Jane Finch Concerned Citizens Organization (JFCCO);
- Muslim Education Network, Training and OutReach Service (MENTORS);
- Miliken African Caribbean Canadian Upliftment Program (MACCUP);
- Saturday Schools/Community educational outlets.

Regarding home-based learning strategies for youth, 23 families (parents/youth) were interviewed. We identified learning strategies employed in the homes and ways in which parents help their children to succeed. To examine the role of community liaison counsellors, we interviewed nine liaison officers from Ontario school boards to learn their strategies for facilitating community-school partnerships, and how local community concerns and knowledges are incorporated into schools. Data regarding the inclusion and participation of minority parents in the formation and implementation of school councils has been generated through interviews with study participants. The month of April 1997 was spent conducting three separate focus group interviews with families, students and community members.

Phase II
In each year of the project, two months were devoted to a preliminary data analysis and dissemination of findings. However, the 1997-98 phase can appropriately be designated as the year of comprehensive data analysis.

Research activities in May and June of 1997 focused on data analysis and compiling the findings on school, home- and community-based learning programs and on the work of liaison officers. We have, as much as possible, cross-referenced interpretations of parent, youth and community worker narratives with the study participants. Research data was analyzed for general trends about school, community, and home-based educational programs, the work of community liaison counsellors, and ways in which these programs can inform curricular and organizational practices and the operation of school councils. We compared individual narratives between and among youth, parents and community workers. We also organized workshops and held professional development seminars for educational practitioners, administrators, students, parents and community groups/associations. Information gained from these sources was used to develop curriculum units that summarize, explain, and suggest the implications of our research, and make the information available to curriculum departments of the Ontario Ministry of Education and Training (MET) and boards of education in Ontario. These curriculum units will be useful for pre-service and in-service training.

The dissemination of research findings is continuing with the intention of reaching a wider audience, including those engaged in academic teaching and practice, as well as others involved in educational planning and policy and curriculum design in the boards of education and MET. Researchers have written some papers for publication. There have also been presentations of preliminary study findings at scholarly international conferences. We have developed a resource guide of best/exemplary practices for teachers and administrators. To serve differing audiences and purposes, our research findings will be disseminated to community-based groups, such as the Organization of Parents of Black Children in Toronto (OPBC), Black Educators Working Group of Toronto (BEWG), the Anti-Racist Multicultural Educators' Network of Ontario (AMENO), Toronto Portuguese Parents' Association, and Paise Filhos (Parents and Children), as well as participants in several community-based education programs for youth in the greater Metropolitan Toronto area, including African Heritage Educators Network (AHEN) Project 90, Canadian Association of Black Educators (CABE) — Vaughan Road Project, Jamaica Canada Association, The Jane Finch Concerned Citizens Organization (JFCCO), Muslim Education Network, Training and OutReach Service (MENTORS), Miliken African Caribbean Canadian Upliftment Program (MACCUP), and Saturday Schools/Community educational outlets.

In the second phase, we also continued with the investigation of research areas and educational sites identified in the first year. We accomplished four objectives. First, starting in October, 1997, we studied the Toronto Board of Education's alternative educational program, the Nighana Project. In an effort to ensure that they complete their education, the program is intended for Black students who have dropped out of school. The Nighana Project school opened up in 1995 in response to the community's concerns about the lack of inclusion of Black studies and experiences in the mainstream school curriculum. We interviewed program co-ordinators and program officials (e.g., teachers, child and youth workers, guidance counsellors and students, individually and as part of a focus group). Our research team also joined the Nighana Coalition, a watchgroup for the Nighana program. Second, we compared best/exemplary practices identified in local community educational outlets with those best/exemplary practices of inclusion found in our previous study of Ontario public schools (Dei, et. al, 1996). Through a comparative analysis we were able to gain a deeper understanding of how inclusion operates within various settings. Third, we also initiated our investigations into the Faculty of Education and its practices of inclusive schooling. Fourth, during the year, we held two well-attended teaching workshops at OISE/UT with educators, student teachers from the Faculty of Education and community workers on the implication of the preliminary research for Ontario schools.

Phase III

In this third phase of the project, during 1998-99, we continued with our examination of the Nighana Project. We also conducted a literature review. For example, we completed a document review of the best/exemplary practices of inclusive education identified by one faculty of education in Ontario. Adopting criteria similar to those used for defining best/exemplary practices in elementary and secondary schools (see Dei, et al., 1997), we also reviewed inclusive practices in the faculty of education in terms of how teacher training faculties prepared students for subsequent teaching positions. Faculty course outlines, curriculum materials and teaching practices representing an inclusive schooling and reflecting anti-racist teachings were analyzed in order to understand how these were precursors to the best/exemplary practice examples we saw in the elementary and secondary school classrooms.

Other research activities included interviewing instructors in the faculty of education, and collaborating with educators to incorporate our research findings into the design and assignments of pre-service courses and to examine the pedagogical implications of our research for pre-service teaching and research. We developed a workshop summary of "best/exemplary practices" and made presentations on our research findings to a number of pre-service classes. Working with a member of our research team who teaches a pre-service class, we prepared a checklist for teacher candidates in her pre-service class to use as a reference during their teaching practicum to apply our research findings (domains). As part of our action research, student teachers were given assignments based on our research findings as "domains." The teacher candidates developed urban microethnographies in the schools and communities where they completed their practice teaching. We also encouraged other teacher candidates to add to our list of "best/ exemplary practices" and to share their teaching experiences with the research project.

During the third phase, we also revisited our school-based knowledge and community/parent-based best/exemplary practices. We examined and "unpacked" what had been considered "best/exemplary" practices over the previous two years of the research project. The learning objective of this exercise was to identify and address gaps in our work to strengthen our final research document.

A primary outcome of the longitudinal studies was to develop educational resources (curricular and instructional guidelines and alternative pedagogic approaches) from previous ethnographic research findings/ information on exemplary school practices, family/home-based prior learning styles, independent learning strategies, and autonomous community-based educational initiatives. The key research questions and interests have been: How can the expertise and knowledge base of parents and local communities be taken up in the schools? What specific practices undertaken through community initiatives can be adopted in the school curriculum? In which ways can practices reflecting diverse ways of knowing be integrated in classroom teaching to deliver education effectively in the elementary and secondary schools of Ontario?

Perhaps more importantly still, we spent the final part of phase three developing a set of domains around "best/exemplary" practices that we believe are key for rethinking schooling and education in Euro-Canadian/ American contexts. Specifically, we studied best/exemplary practices of inclusive schooling identified in mainstream schools as well as in community-initiated contexts in terms of the implications for pre-service and in-service teacher training in faculties of education in Ontario. We have been developing a preliminary set of learning outcomes for inclusive schooling.

Three main research goals were achieved. First, we identified and described concrete strategies and directions to be addressed in pre-service training, the organizational and cultural life of schools, and in the search for alternative models of community schooling and education. Second, we held two additional teaching workshops at OISE/UT with educators, student teachers from the faculty of education and a few parents and community members to discuss the application of the research material/findings from the first three years of study in a variety of new school settings. We worked with over 40 educators, students teachers in elementary and secondary school panels in action research, applying the findings to real-life situations. Third, we spent much of the year developing a curriculum unit that summarized, explained, and suggested the implications of all three phases of our research. We also completed the first draft of this book.

DATA ANALYSIS

We devoted the third phase of the project to in-depth data analysis, validation of research interpretations, and writing-up and disseminating our research findings. Focus group meetings with students and teachers provided a cross-check/reference to our interpretations of individual student and teacher narratives on best practices. Research data has been analyzed qualitatively for general trends and principles of successful inclusive practices. Through triangulation, it has been possible to compare individual narratives between and among students and teachers, and locate general patterns. We developed a code system to identify themes in student and teacher narratives. Seven operational domains of best practices emerged from the themes highlighted through our coding procedures. Generally, home/family prior learning strategies, independent learning styles and community educational practices offered valuable lessons for rethinking schooling and education in Ontario and Canadian contexts. To help us reconceptualize schooling and education in North American contexts, we have identified certain themes running through our longitudinal research. Among the relevant findings and important lessons from research studies that will form the basis of curricular, instructional and pedagogical development for/with practising and student teachers are the following seven domains:

1. *A recognition of the important role of Indigenous, traditional and culturally-based knowledges in schooling* as valuable educational resources for the learner.

2. *The promotion of spiritual and intuitive learning*: The philosophy of family/home-based prior learning and community education is anchored in a broader definition of education that encompasses emotional and spiritual dimensions, parental and community advocacy and youth empowerment. A personalized, subjective identification with the learning processes makes it possible for the learner to be invested spiritually and emotionally in the cause of educational and social change.

3. *Language integration*: In family/home-based prior learning and community educational practices, home language (often a vernacular) is used in instruction in conjunction with English. Language becomes a fundamental component to cultural identity. Family/home, community and innovative school educational strategies validate learners' first languages [local vernacular], and facilitate English skills development.

4. *An emphasis on co-operative education and a broader concept of "educational success"*: While school, home/family, and community education cultivates high academic expectations, in effective schooling the learner's *"successes"* are defined to recognize the extent of community work and involvement, as well as non-academic proficiencies in areas such as psycho-social development and cultural knowledge. Thus, the learner is helped to improve and sustain her/his self-esteem, and sense of identity.

5. *The adoption of an inclusive, integrative approach to learning and education*: The ideas of "equity pedagogy" and "culturally-relevant pedagogy" are central to effective school, family/home and community educational praxis, dealing directly with issues of power and equity. Educational stakeholders allow learners to participate fully in their education while developing and practising home cultures and personal and collective identities.

6. *Representation in Education:* Effective school and local community educational practices address issues of representation in three areas: *visual representation* or the inclusion of racial/ethnic and religious minorities and their cultures within the visual/physical landscape of the educational setting; *knowledge representation* or the centring of non-European cultural knowledges, cultures, histories and experiences; *staff equity*, or the integration of teachers and educators from different racial, ethnic and gender backgrounds.

7. *Emphasis on community schooling and the important roles of parents and community workers in youth education*: In community schools, parents become knowledge producers. Parents, guardians, caregivers, and adult community workers are seen as initiating, creating and resisting subjects. They are not simply inserted into the existing structures, allowing adults to claim an important degree of collective ownership of community schooling.

In the following chapters, we will discuss the above seven domains with a particular focus on their implications for school pedagogy, curriculum, and classroom instructional change. The theoretical and practical applications associated with "inclusive education" tease out compelling new implications for school reform, and teacher educational development in North American contexts. It is important to note that we pointedly speak to North American contexts because these are not site specific reforms. The themes addressed in this book speak to the possibilities of educational improvement for all youth across a broad range of educational settings. At the heart of these possibilities is a framework that encourages students, educators, and other stakeholders to work towards social justice through an ongoing reconsideration of personal biases, and critical examinations of systemic oppression.

NOTES

1   George Dei, as the principle investigator (PI), the other co-authors of this book and numerous other Graduate Students at the Ontario Institute for Studies in Education of the University of Toronto (OISE/UT) worked on numerous research projects over the last decade. Some of the studies included: *Making Excellence Accessible and Equitable; Unpacking What Works: A Critical Examination of "Best Practices" of Inclusive Schooling in Ontario*; and *Untapped Resources: Home, Family and Community-Based Learning*. These projects were all funded through the Social Sciences and Humanities Research Council of Canada. The initial proposal for this research was submitted to the Ontario Ministry of Education and Training, for both the OISE Transfer Grant funding, and the Social Science Research Council.

CHAPTER 3

SCHOOLING AND EDUCATION
IN NORTH AMERICA:
RECENTRING INDIGENOUS KNOWLEDGES

INTRODUCTION

We begin by posing a question: What are the implications of Indigenous knowledges for school curriculum, classroom pedagogy and instructional change?

The heightened pace of global change and the associated developments of intensive information flow, massive population movements and the "traffic in cultures" call for rethinking conventional processes of schooling and education. There is some urgency in searching for multiple knowledge forms in different social settings to provide meaning and understanding to individual and collective thought, experience, action and activity. The study of Indigenous knowledges offers insights in changing the course and direction of educational process, as well as social practice.

Despite their specificities, Indigenous knowledges are generally applicable across cultural boarders and in all school settings. Their situational, contextual, and localized nature position them as fundamental resources for educational reform, and central to the promotion of critical pedagogy and practice in schools. The incorporation of Indigenous knowledges into the mainstream is basic to the future of school reform because conventional Western policy and practice do not make "space" for the changing face of society. Mainstream schools are deeply enmeshed in the relations of power and difference that position knowledge as emerging from one site, the site of power and privilege. In contrast, Indigenous knowledges are understood as being open for general ownership and public consumption; they cannot be privately owned.

Knowledges are produced within multiple contexts, but some originate within the self and the body. Through the generation of such self-interested knowledge, ideas emerge to offer readings of larger social and political contexts. Intuition works with the body and the spiritual. There is a primordial consciousness that understands intuition to be an important source of knowing. From self-generated knowledge, the learner, teacher and educator can produce broader social understandings for the larger social contexts. This knowledge translates into a shared, collective consciousness.

The promotion of Indigenous knowledges works towards agency and the empowerment of oppressed groups. Educators can employ these ways of knowing to assist students to engage in social action that is both emancipatory and revolutionary. The undeniable possibilities of Indigenous knowledge arise in that they are articulated on the basis of language and the cognitive power of subjects. That is to say, that such knowledges are not part of a privileged paradigm that speaks from only one specific location of power. Rather, Indigenous ways of knowing are shared by marginalized groups. They speak to community, the open exchange of ideas and perspectives, and most importantly, their political/insurgent nature makes them invaluable in the process of education. The power of cognition, language and symbolic thought allows the learner to articulate immediate and practical concerns that emerge from experiencing the social world, and in the articulation of these concerns, new theoretical frameworks emerge. Informed by daily practice, local peoples are able to provide their own accounts of what is happening to them and what they plan to do about social change. Further, local peoples are able to make theoretical and practical sense of their worlds and take up the challenge of acting within contested and contradictory terrains. For the educator, this knowledge is an important source of information to be imparted to all learners.

However, to appropriately teach Indigenous knowledge, educators must deal with questions of credibility, accountability, practice, relevance, sustainability, appropriation, validation and legitimation. Credibility is a question of the educator providing knowledges that students can trust to reflect their social reality. Accountability calls on students, educators, parents, and community workers to be accountable to each other in the search for, and sharing of knowledge. Practice means that knowledge is not only experiential and can be tested, but that it can also be used to address pressing social problems. It is in this latter understanding that the relevance of Indigenous knowledge is articulated. To put it succinctly, Indigenous knowledges are dynamic, and in their ability to adapt to new challenges and new environments, they have stood the test of time. One central reason for its sustainability is that local people view and employ them collectively to work towards personal and communally beneficial ends. In this communal perspective, there is an open directive against the appropriation of knowledge for narrow individualistic interests.

As we seek to integrate these knowledges into the conventional school systems, we must guard against appropriation and misappropriation. This is a contemporary challenge for educators. The process of validating Indigenous knowledges must not lead to Indigenous peoples losing control and ownership of knowledge. In other words, it must be recognized that these knowledges are valid in their own right and that the process of bringing them into the academy should not itself constitute the measure of validation. Closely tied to the question of validation is the issue of legitimation. The legitimacy of Indigenous knowledges is based on the right of peoples to define and articulate their own accounts of what is happening to them and how they intend to deal with pressing problems. In other words, an acknowledgement of the varied ways, options and strategies through which people continually make sense of their world and act within it.

An exploration of the instructional, pedagogical and communicative implications of Indigenous knowledge for schools, and for teacher development in particular, will help all learners to develop a sound critique of the conventional ways in which knowledge is produced and used. As an approach to rethinking educational change, the teaching of Indigenous knowledges will help students and learners to understand the importance of combining home and school pedagogies in order to accentuate students' identities, cultures and histories. By appreciating the importance and relevance of subjugated/marginalized knowledge forms for developing a pedagogy of subversion, students, educators, parents and community workers can work together to challenge stable knowledges and the status quo. All educational stakeholders will come to know the partiality of every way of knowing, that is, the limits and the uncertainty of all knowledges. Partiality is understood here as both an inclusive/multicentric *gestalt* and a statement of *gestalt* as political, or informed by political contextualizations/ groundings. Also, we present the appreciation that dominant paradigms construct partialities as part of a normalization of othering/difference to the extent that othered knowledges eclipsed to the margins by the dominant framing. Learners will also develop a holistic sense of self, culture and society, and understand the intuitional, emotional, spiritual and psychological dimensions of knowledge forms.

In meeting the contemporary challenge of transnational and global knowledge production, formal school systems, in particular, could learn from the informal and non-formal learning practices, networks, structures and systems found in off-school environments. Such knowledge is useful in promoting education in a post-modern world that genuinely acknowledges and celebrates difference and diversity. In our world today, new knowledges play a crucial role in reforming actual/formal classroom practices, pedagogy and curriculum instruction for youth and adult learners. However, if such new knowledge forms are to be socially relevant, they must be constructed relative to the present moment, and the real lived experience of real people. That being said, incorporating marginalized knowledges into mainstream educational sites would not only contribute to general educational improvement, it would foster collective reliance, mutual interdependence and strengthening of individual/group identity. These issues may not reflect conventional calls for a return to the basics and a continued reliance on the three Rs. But they do take up the pressing educational concerns that have developed and continue to develop in our increasingly globalized contexts. They work to develop the essential analytical and critical thinking skills needed to address today's complex social issues and problems.

The task of educational transformation is not simply to reform existing curricular and pedagogical practices. Transformative educational change must address the challenge of integrating social and cultural values that promote alternative and multiple readings of the world into classroom pedagogies, instruction and school curricula. Among the critical questions that may be posed are: What is the role of Indigenous culture, language and social politics in knowledge production? What contribution do local cultural resource base knowledges make to the search for genuine educational options? What are the nature and content of eco-cultural knowledges of local peoples? What are the ways and strategies of popular knowledge creation for problem identification and solution in communities? What cultural norms, and social values/ideas are privileged in home, family and communal settings for use in school and classroom instruction? Finding answers to these questions and applying the knowledge in classroom setting could assist in enhancing learning and educational outcomes for all youth.

Educational change means problematizing the marginalization of voices and ideas in school systems, as well as the legitimation of the knowledges and experiences of subordinate groups in the pedagogic and communicative practices of schools. The use of Indigenous knowledges can contribute to educational change in the Euro-American context. Education today can be said to be in a state of contention. Quite often, well-meaning educational policies and practices (curriculum, texts, pedagogies) fail to speak adequately to the variety of human experiences or to the diverse history of events and ideas that have shaped and continue to shape human growth and social development. Genuine and effective educational options must be appropriately contextualized in the local human condition and social realities. Fortunately, in some circles, Canadian, African and American educators have been pioneering new analytical systems based on Indigenous concepts and their interrelationships for promoting education for youth (see Almeida, 1998; Barnhardt and Kawagley, 1998; Castellano, 2000; Dore, 1976; Dove, 1995; 1998a; 1998b; Howard, 1995; Karenga, 1988; Shujaa, 1996; 1994; Tedla, 1992). There are signs of cultural renewal and a revitalization of an Indigenous cultural resource base that might be used to address current social problems. Our approach to educational change in Canada will explore how locally-initiated curricula, pedagogical and policy options inform alternative and viable educational options.

INDIGENOUS KNOWLEDGES: CONCEPTUALIZATIONS AND OPERATIONALIZATIONS

The significance of the Foucauldian concept of knowledge as power cannot be overemphasized (Foucault, 1980). Arguably, one of the primary/urgent goals of critical education is to assist the learner in interpreting and changing her/his social worlds. Knowledge acquisition is for self and group enhancement, as well as collective actualization and well-being. The possession of knowledge can help empower the student/learner/teacher not only to solve daily problems, but also articulate a vision for a collective future. In examining Indigenous knowledge as part of the multiple knowledge systems for use in schools there must be an initial understanding of what Indigenous means.

By Indigenous knowledges, we refer to the common-sense ideas and cultural knowledges of local peoples concerning the everyday realities of living. These knowledges are part of the cultural heritage and histories of peoples (see Fals Borda, 1980; Fals Borda and Rahman, 1991; Warren, Slikkerveer and Brokensha, 1995). We refer, specifically, to the epistemic salience of cultural traditions, values, belief systems, and worldviews that are imparted to the younger generation by community elders. Such knowledge constitutes an "Indigenous informed epistemology." It is a worldview that shapes the community's relationships with its environments. It is the product of the direct experience of nature and its relationship with the social world. It is knowledge that is crucial for the survival of society. It is knowledge that is based on cognitive understandings and interpretations of the social and physical/spiritual worlds. It includes concepts, beliefs and perceptions and experiences of local peoples and their natural and human-built environments.

More specifically, the term/notion Indigenous means knowledge resulting from long-term residence in a place (Fals Borda, 1980). Indigenous signals the power relations and dynamics embedded in the production, interrogation, validation and dissemination of global knowledge. It also recognizes the multiple and collective origins as well as collaborative dimensions of knowledge and affirms that the interpretation or analysis of social reality is subject to different and sometimes oppositional perspectives (Dei, Hall and Goldin Rosenberg, 2000).

In an excellent paper Castellano (2000) identifies three broad aspects of Aboriginal knowledge that are of relevance to the general discussion of Indigenous and alternate knowledge forms. These are: *traditional knowledge* which is intergenerational knowledge passed on by community elders; *empirical knowledge* which is based on careful observations of the surrounding environments (nature, culture and society); and *revealed knowledge* as provided through dreams, visions and intuition. The main characteristics of Indigenous knowledges are that they are personal/ personalized, i.e., there are no claims to universality but the trust of knowledge is tied to integrity and the perceptiveness of the speaker. Such knowledges are also orally and visually transmitted. The sharing of Indigenous knowledges is tied to considerations of responsibility in the use of the received knowledge. Indigenous knowledges are experientially-based and depend on subjectivity and the inner workings of the self in generating social interpretations, meanings and explanations. Indigenous knowledges are also holistic and relational. Indigenous epistemologies are grounded in a deep appreciation of the cosmos and how the self, the spiritual, the known and the unknown worlds are interconnected. They draw direct connections from economic, cultural, political, spiritual, and ecological facets of life to the material forces and conditions of society. In this respect, they relate the physical to the metaphysical realms of life. An appreciation of the outer self and space is tied to an understanding of the inner sense of self (see also Ermine, 1995). The dimension of spirituality in Indigenous knowledges provides the strength and power in physical communication. Indigenous knowledge forms are expressional and narrative. They are metaphorical in the use of proverbs, fables and tales. Indigenous knowledges view communalism as a mode of thought.

In the body of this text, we usually refer to Indigenous knowledges in the plural form because we understand these ways of knowing to be dynamic and continuous. To refer to Indigenous knowledges in the singular would be to imply a distinct perspective that does not take the diverse and complex nature of history, culture and the lived realities into consideration. They offer important insights into the development of a multiplicity of centres through shifts in knowledge production. Historically Indigenous knowledges have been used by marginalized peoples to make sense of and live in the contemporary world in ways that are continuous and consistent with traditional worldviews, principles and social practice (Dei, Hall and Goldin Rosenberg, 2000).

A critical approach to understanding human society must deal with the dilemmas and contradictions relative to the continued devaluation and fragmentation of traditional values and beliefs, the erosion of spirituality, and the distortions in local, regional and national economies. These developments emerge from the unprecedented pace of globalization. Rethinking schooling and education in contemporary times requires that educational change is well-rooted in complementing Indigenous and Western worldviews. Strategies for educational change must reclaim and tap local peoples' worldviews if they are to identify, generate and articulate new and alternative visions of social transformation. An understanding of local experiences provides the requisite building blocks for the development of strategies that will be both relevant and insurgent.

Teaching and learning in Euro-American contexts must speak to the social, cultural, economic, political, spiritual and cosmological aspects of local peoples' lives, as well as their specific needs and aspirations. Current and on-going debates about "educational change" must be situated in appropriate social contexts that provide practical and social meaning to learners as "subjects" and "creators," rather than as "objects" of the educational discourse. This is a part of critical perspective on educational change that argues that local communities should own and control the search for solutions to their own problems.

Elsewhere, Dei (1998) pointed out that the works of Charles Taylor and Jurgen Habermas are very informative in discussions of Indigenous knowledges and their usefulness in Euro-American schools. For example, Habermas (1994) argues that "[a] correctly understood theory of rights requires a politics of recognition that protects the integrity of the individual in the life contexts in which his or her identity is formed" (p. 113). He further points out that individuals can only "acquire autonomy ... to the extent that they can understand themselves to be author of the laws to which they are subject as private legal persons." (p. 112). While Habermas is dealing with political rights in particular, his conceptualization clearly has to do with membership in a diverse community and how the system itself must deal with this diversity. To have inclusion, each group must provide and define its own needs, its own political substance and, we would argue, its own educational content. The challenge then is for educators to learn to incorporate these ideas and create a synthesis.

Taylor (1994) notes in his essay, "The Politics of Recognition," that there are a number of reasons why alternative "knowledges" should be part and parcel of the public school curriculum. He argues that previously silenced groups are currently fighting for recognition, and that the need for this recognition emerges not only because of the omission of other voices, but largely because this view, by the existing structure, is negative and demeaning. However, what is most profound about Taylor's discussion is that he links this need to the Fanonian conceptualization of the process of liberation. Taylor suggests that, like liberation from colonial occupation, there must be a transformation of the status quo so as to find a basis for incorporating alternative viewpoints. This stand is not only profoundly political, but rooted in a deep moral belief that the status quo must be reformed before the oppressed can ever find a space and place in society (Blanford, 1998). We do not mean to suggest that such change would/could/will occur through sites of privilege and without the input of the oppressed. In fact, alternative voices will necessarily play an intrinsic part of any such movements toward change because the process of intellectual liberation does not simply appear out of a vacuum. In other words, minoritized peoples will respond to the history of negation that silenced/silences their voices and devalues their accomplishments and contributions to human history and social development. Their response will be the catalyst for change.

THE CHALLENGE OF SYNTHESIZING KNOWLEDGES

As argued in another context, (Dei, 2000), the discourse of Indigenous knowledge brings a complex array of theoretical and methodological issues to the debate on inclusive education. Before Indigenous knowledges could be incorporated within the orbit of the mainstream, some fundamental barriers would have to be addressed. Disturbingly, Eurocentrism continues to masquerade as universalism, and old school sentinels fiercely discredit any political academic projects that seek to break the silence that surrounds marginalized knowledges. For Indigenous knowledges to find a space and place within the mainstream there would need to be an informed dialogue about the complimentary nature of knowledge systems and the benefits that accompany the practice of synergetic co-operation.

Indigenous knowledges challenge Eurocentrism's commodification of values in the "consumer cultural paradigm," as well as the associated notion of "unlimited material progress" through science, technology and competition (see also, Dei, Hall, Goldin and Rosenberg, 2000). Eurocentric knowledge infuses a hierarchical ordering of things that overglorifies "quantification" and engenders scepticism towards anything that cannot be quantified. Historically, positivism and traditions of "rationality," "objectification," "reason," "progress" and the "certainty of knowledge" were seen as the hallmarks of Western scientific knowledge. Social phenomena would often be presented in structural forms, downplaying the human element and dimensions of emotionality and intuition. These are the concerns that Indigenous knowledges bring to the debate about creating a truly inclusive body of knowledge.

To promote and institute Indigenous knowledges in conventional schools, certain theoretical questions must be addressed: For example, what is the place of Indigenous knowledge in schools? What is involved in teaching Indigenous knowledge? What are the pedagogical styles/ instructional strategies of producing, interrogating and disseminating Indigenous knowledge within/out schools? What will be the curriculum content of teaching Indigenous knowledge? How does the content reflect the idea of multiple, collective and collaborative dimensions of knowledge. How is identity linked with/to schooling? What is the linkage between "identity" and "knowledge production" drawn in the school setting? How can educators use "practice" and "experience" as the contextual basis of knowledge? What does it mean for the educator to take into account the spiritual, emotional, intuitive and analytical dimensions of knowledge/

knowing and learning? How can educators present teaching and learning as emotionally-felt experiences?

Dei (2000) asserts the importance of getting schools, colleges and universities to recognize Indigenous knowledges as central to the academy of knowledge production. This calls for validating the legitimacy of Indigenous knowledges as a pedagogic, instructional and communicative tool in the processes of delivering education. The challenge starts with hiring Indigenous, racially minoritized scholars to join teaching faculties and to integrate Indigenous knowledges into the curriculum, and the instructional and pedagogic practices of educators and learners. Bringing diverse physical bodies and addressing the question of knowledge representation involves systemic change.

To synthesize multiple ways of knowing genuinely into the orbit of the mainstream, schools must accept and work with the varied, collective and collaborative dimensions of knowledge. Synthesizing different knowledges means shifting to a restructured and reconstituted space, where issues of content and physical representation are dealt with to recognize the multiplicity of human ideas. Synthesizing different knowledges will be an educational practice that leads to systemic change rather than the remedial patchwork of unsustained efforts. Synthesis is not simply opening up the club to new members, but rather examining the whole idea/structure of the club.

In order to initiate the process, the distinction between traditional thought and modern scientific thought must be rendered as only useful in the theoretical sense but false in terms of the application of knowledge. We must be able to deconstruct the false dichotomy that separates the two ontologies. In synthesizing multiple knowledge systems, we work with an understanding that Indigenous moral and cognitive conceptions are compatible with those of Western science. Furthermore, it means that we can develop meaningful discursive frameworks that consider both philosophical traditions. Yet, the question of whether we can use another's language to attain a deeper conceptual and philosophical understanding of the other's knowledge system(s) still remains. This is why culture and language instruction and retention are crucial to the promotion of Indigenous knowledges in schools. [We address this issue in Chapter Five.]

Integrating Indigenous knowledges into Euro-American school systems is itself a recognition that different knowledges can co-exist; that different knowledges can complement each other; and also that knowledges can be in conflict at the same time. A false dichotomous thinking between

Indigenous and non-Indigenous knowledges can be avoided by understanding the "past/traditional" and the "modern" as not frozen in time and space. The past continues to influence the present and vice versa. We live in the past today and the future in terms of its (past) lessons. There is a continuity of cultural values from past experiences that helps shape the present. Similarly, the present also influences the narration of the past. Bearing these concepts in mind, there are important reasons for working towards a synthesis of different knowledge systems. Aside from issues of the partiality and uncertainty of knowledges, there is the inadequacy of science knowledge (both Indigenous and Western) to account for the totality of the human experience and social practice. In fact, the worlds of the metaphysical and the physical, the worlds of mystery/invisible agents and of science and modernization are not oppositional realities (Prah, 1997). Different knowledges represent different points of a continuum; they involve ways peoples perceive and act in the world.

We see schools as a most important starting place for promoting Indigenous knowledge forms in the academy. In everyday classroom pedagogic, communicative and instructional practices, teachers and educators must grapple with the following issues (see also McLeod and Krugly-Smolska, 1997, pp.16-17, in another context):

1. First, developing an awareness and a deeper knowledge base on Indigenous knowledges (e.g., discussing the topic with students, use of Indigenous guest speakers, resource materials, posters, displays, films). Teachers can also target Indigenous concerns and issues in classroom discourses and undertake research trips to Indigenous communities. They can also plan cultural celebrations of Indigenous histories and experiences. Such acknowledgements and celebrations need to be placed in appropriate contexts and histories in order to serve as a form of decolonized education, and also to speak to the unfortunate and unpleasant consequences and outcomes of the colonial encounters between the subject and the colonizer.

2. Second, promoting critical teaching through the use of Indigenous knowledges. Indigenous knowledges address the relationship that people have with nature, culture and society. It is about a peaceful co-existence in a just planet. It recognizes the self and collective worth of all peoples. Thus, Indigenous knowledges offers a critique of social/ global inequality, and provides an opportunity for the educator to teach

students to ask critical questions about the nature of things in the current social order. To achieve this end, conventional curricular, pedagogic and instructional approaches to schooling and education must be rethought to promote communitarian learning and schooling, holistic and intuitive thought, and other alternative ways of decoding information. Also, engaging Indigenous knowledges allows educators, learners and students to ask about the absences of Indigenous writings/texts on syllabus, teaching and learning of Indigenous spirituality, languages, myths, legends and philosophies.

3.   Third, developing advocacy and support networks to promote the hiring of Indigenous faculty and to pursue holistic, communitarian and co-operative learning and teaching strategies in schools. Educators can assist in initiating political actions (e.g., student and teacher protests and submissions to university administrations) to recruit and sustain a diverse teaching faculty. Such actions can also ensure that the curricular content of academic courses reflects the works and contributions of Indigenous scholars, as well as women and other racially and sexually minoritized scholars.

4.   Fourth, developing a sustainable community support (e.g., memberships and linkages with Indigenous communities groups; promoting meaningful educational partnerships with Indigenous communities, and seeking guidance and informed advice from Indigenous communities). Sustainable community support is crucial if initiatives are to have long lasting impact on the processes of delivering education.

PRACTISING INDIGENOUS KNOWLEDGES IN SCHOOLS

Incorporating Indigenous knowledges into mainstream school settings will require a most pragmatic strategy. Educators and administrators will need to establish a clear plan of action for addressing each of the above pedagogic, instructional and communicative stances. This design should clearly define the principles, objectives, resources and probable outcomes for the project. Also, we must be able to identify those crucial agents of change who will be responsible for executing the necessary action plans (see McLeod and Krugly-Smolska, 1997, p. 18). Pedagogically, teachers can use diverse, different and multiple modes of communication. These include the use of oral traditions, stories, legends, myths, traditions, fables, visual and textual aids. Teachers can also use elders and community leaders in their classrooms to teach about cultures, traditions and ancestral histories. Parents may be invited to teach about parenting and socialization skills to youths.

In connection with the structural and social organizational issues that relate to an educator's pedagogy and her/his classroom teaching, schools could create spaces for parents, elders, students to share in a collective learning exercise. In specified areas, students can learn together with parents, adults and community workers. It is through teachings about cultures and local histories that schools and educators can most positively work with Indigenous knowledges. Parents and community leaders can come into schools to teach about traditional discipline, authority, and social responsibility. Also, students could teach about their off-school cultures and experiences; a powerful innovation in that the language of the street could be used as an important pedagogical tool. By validating such approaches to education and schooling, students, parents and community workers see themselves not only as significant partners and stakeholders, but as critical agents of educational change.

In order to reform education genuinely it is crucial to deal with the problem of local curricular relevance. That is, providing curriculum that meets local needs, concerns and aspirations while framing those issues within global contexts. By appropriately and respectfully using Indigenous knowledges grounded in local/specific contexts, the general curriculum is shifted toward a non-hegemonic multicentricity.

As a more direct approach, educators can use a working knowledge of diversity and difference as significant entry points. By recognizing the existence of multiple knowledges about self, history and identity, educators can create spaces within schools to learn about diverse epistemologies or knowledge systems. In the teaching of Aboriginal epistemologies, the educator can lay emphasis on general trends of thoughts while Indigenous peoples themselves can speak and teach about the specificities of practice, experience and knowledge systems. At the very least, teacher education faculties could ensure that pre-service teachers interact with Indigenous educators in local communities in order to understand alternative learning styles and pedagogical practices. Teachers could be supported and encouraged to do community work in local communities. Alongside these approaches, the more fundamental question of structural representation could be vigorously pursued by actively recruiting aboriginal/Indigenous/minority students into teacher education faculties.

Classroom practice could shift beyond event-oriented teaching, to a model that is context-based. This means placing ideas and events in broader structural and political contexts. Activity driven teaching and instruction may also be pursued in a way that places the understanding of specific activities within a broader global politics. Teachers can use storytelling in many ways to show the power of oratory and the significance of myths, fables and folktales to understanding local histories and cultures. However, while the spoken word is a primary mode of communication in Indigenous communities, there are visual representations as pictographs (e.g., paintings on rocks) and Indigenous writing/communicative forms such as petroglyphs (e.g., carvings or inscriptions on rocks) that are widely used as well.

An emerging challenge in bringing Indigenous knowledges into the school system is how best to convey spoken words (as narrated in stories, fables, myths, and oral accounts of life histories) from another culture. There are issues of language and cognition with significant pitfalls and implications for understanding Indigenous knowledges. One such pitfall arises in that stories, fables, proverbs, myths, folklore and folksongs have long been treated as objects to be collected, coded, stored and/or disseminated. Cruikshank (1992, p. 2) asks, can cultural knowledge as "… linguistic expression and material manifestation of ideas" be collected, represented and/or stored without losing meaning? Fluency in the local language is critical to textual representation of the oral.

Material artifacts, museum exhibitions, stories and oral accounts are all part of the Indigenous knowledges of local/colonized peoples. Rosaldo (1980, p. 91) is very deliberate when she argues that we must see oral traditions as texts to be heard, not as documents to be stored. What happens to the spoken words when they appear on paper, or are "recorded in magnetic or digital codes on tapes, disks or in film or videotape" (Cruikshank, 1992, p. 1)? What are the uses of material artifacts, museums exhibitions, stories and oral accounts as written texts in Euro-American centres of learning? Oral traditions, stories, fables and proverbs collected from Indigenous communities and written as texts in Western academies can become a material manifestation of colonial encounters (Trigger, 1988 cited in Cruiskshank, 1992, p. 1). Once located in Euro-American centres of learning, they become "symbols of cultural oppression" since these institutions are places that have historically participated in colonizing the other (e.g., the processes of academic imperialism through the establishment of knowledge hierarchies) [see also Cruikshank, 1992, p. 4].

In discussing alternative approaches to schooling, we cannot minimize the powerful influence that myths and symbols can have on communication, pedagogy and instruction. Historically rooted stories and legends that speak to an idealistic or glorious past can have a profound influence on individual and group learning. In this respect, the role of myth in defining the Indigenous sense of place cannot be underestimated. As argued elsewhere (Dei, 2000), conventional resistance to the use of Indigenous myths and symbols in mainstream education serves to negate the sense of connection that marginalized peoples can have towards history and tradition. In other words, presenting Indigenous histories as little more than romanticized storytelling serves to disengage minoritized peoples from a sense of their own history. Further, these negations actively discourage and censure the spaces in which oppositional and insurgent discourses might be developed. Lattas (1993) correctly observed that there is "… an intolerance of [Indigenous] people's romantic fictions of the past, especially when these idealize and essentialize the core truths of their being" (p. 248). No epistemic saliency is offered for "… the idea of an essence passed automatically from generation to generation by either a biological or social mechanism" (Thiele, 1991a, p. 157, cited in Lattas, 1993, p. 248). The past, however imagined or fictive, cannot be edited out of the human condition. The mythic past is a constitutive part of the imaginary structure of all human existence. It is connected to the production of individual and collective memories, as well as a sense of self and group identities. It is through memory and our sense of self that we produce the real.

Teacher education is key to the promotion of Indigenous knowledges in schools. Educators must have a clear understanding of what Indigenous knowledges are if they are to help implement them within mainstream contexts. Furthermore, we should note that understanding is only the first step. Teachers must have a firm grasp of the inherent potential of these knowledges for social transformation and educational improvement. It is a communal project that engages learners, educators and other stakeholders alike. But, unless the educators are invested and dedicated to the proposal of multicentric and inclusive classrooms, the project cannot sustain itself. To these ends, with respect to teacher training, education about Indigenous knowledges must begin with the interrogation of Eurocentrism as a hegemonic knowledge system. This is an important beginning, because the recognition of Indigenous knowledges as a valuable and important resource located in multiple communities, works to rupture that hegemony. By upholding Indigenous knowledges in everyday classroom practices, educators not only create space for minoritized youth to exercise the power of imagining themselves, but also to create and control what is imagined about them. In order for the educator to recognize the existence of Indigenous knowledges, and be able to acquire and apply such knowledges, she or he must know these local communities. This calls for the educator to interact continuously with parents, community workers, caregivers, youth, parents and elders. Such interactions are important because they allow educators to make "real" interpersonal connections with the people in the community. This does more than foster positive home-school communications, it established a clearer sense of the complexities that are specific to the community and further, it allows teachers to ground those complexities in a concrete reality. This speaks to the old adage that you cannot really know a person until you walk a mile in their shoes. The educator could develop some familiarity with the norms, values and beliefs systems of a people and how these systems of knowledge provide context and meaning to daily social practice and action.

Teacher education also needs to focus on [social] identity and representation as relevant to educational change. Addressing the issues and challenges associated with the concepts of culture, identity and representation allows educators to rethink the processes of delivering education in plural contexts. Multicentric approaches to schooling posit different vantage points for learners and stakeholders in the school system. The existence of different vantage points implies that differential consequences and means of educational access and outcomes can be acknowledged and dealt with. Similarly, history and contexts, as well as race, gender, class and sexual identities are crucial to how students access educational resources and privilege. As a factor contributing to academic success, we cannot overlook the importance of identity. Identity is the lens through which one views themselves in relation to history, culture and society. A non-essentialized approach to identity allows us to understand and acknowledge the power of agency and self-actualization. That is to say, through identity development we can reflexively engage in political action that resists dominance and works towards insurgent social change.

The concepts of self/person-hood that are inherent within understandings of identity are particularly relevant to how students construct and make sense of their schooling experience. By either defining or imagining the self, students, parents and educators are able to place themselves in specific spaces within the politics of schooling. Students, for example, engage in a politics of collective educational resistance and change to the extent that they see themselves connected to particular identities. A racialized identity politics is embedded in understandings of self and group existence within a social order. Within Aboriginal epistemology, scholars speak of different levels of self. These are: self-worth, self-esteem, self-confidence, and self-image (Corbiere, 1998). These levels of identity are also expressed in myriad forms in other Indigenous communities. Self-worth allows students to articulate their place and power in society. By developing self-esteem students not only resist dominance, but also, challenge the educational system to respond to their needs and aspirations. Students gain self-confidence by seeing themselves in the school curriculum, and will use the received knowledge to further the cause of social justice. Students are also able to project a positive image of the self onto others as they come to assume roles, duties and responsibilities.

Schooling is an enduring agent of socialization. As a formalized, institutional structure, schools can be made to function appropriately to provide all learners with the requisite skills for accessing society. The success of this endeavour requires that schools be seen not simply as providing knowledge, but also as providing broad-based education. Education is a life-long journey, and throughout our lives, we are engaged in a constant process of learning and unlearning. This is a powerful realization. It allows us to bend around the paradigms that currently frame our perceptions of reality. When it comes to educational pedagogy and practice, we must always be in tune with the fact that as life changes, so too must we. With this in mind, educational practices need to change with the diversifying face of school communities. In today's Diasporic society, that change necessitates moves toward collaborative educational ventures that genuinely promote power-sharing and inclusivity. For example, educational researchers, experts and consultants in curriculum guidelines, policy planners, school teachers and administrators, community leaders, elders, parents, students and youth should all have some input in developing the appropriate structures and procedures for delivering education. While the target audience for imparting Indigenous knowledges will be the students, educators and teachers also have something to learn. We can begin by recognizing the utility and relevance of multiple knowledge systems.

SPIRITUALITY AND CLASSROOM TEACHING

How are intuition, emotionality and spirituality to be recognized as ways of knowing? What do spirituality and emotionality mean? We offer a fuller discussion in Chapter Four. Words mean different things to different audiences. The challenge is not to dismiss these words, but for us to interrogate how educators recognize themselves as spiritual/emotional beings while working within this understanding.

The initial approach for an educator is to establish entry points. For example, using experience and subject identity as a basis for talking about Indigenous knowledges and its forms and content. Teaching spirituality in the classroom will mean engaging "the self" in knowledge production. It is important for the educator to help students engage what they know about spirituality from a personal perspective. This strategy allows for the development of a self-referential knowledge base that can implicate and account for the dynamics of power and identity as well as spiritual definitions of self. This pedagogical approach recognizes that students are embodied beings who bring their experiences to bear on knowledge. That is to say, that their bodies are classed, raced and gendered, and so these specificities are part and parcel of their experience. For example, do people feel similar issues differently? Can educators deconstruct gender roles in terms of spirituality? Are there different ways of thinking and relating to groups and each other that educators need to be aware of? If this is the case then the educator can develop a knowledge base on how males/boys and females/ girls feel emotions, and express empathy. This could lead to a recognition of spirituality and emotionality in the everyday practice.

Yet what would teaching spirituality look like in the classroom? It will mean the emotional investment of the learners in the act and process of meaning-making. Spirituality as part of coming to understand, know and act in the world will mean learning to engage in social and political change.

Religion, unlike spirituality, is taught in schools. Yet, spiritualities are interconnected. For many people, religion is part of their understanding of spirituality in that religion and religious values help mold personal character. Given that religion has a place in schools, how can religion be integrated into the understanding of spirituality? Should religion be divorced from spirituality? Why are we looking at spirituality at this time? What is the connection between cultural beliefs and spirituality? Which religions do schools privilege and why? Why do mainstream schools separate religion and spirituality? Which religion or spiritual belief is the educator to value? To answer these questions, we must begin to interrogate how some knowledges become classified as cult, myth, belief, value or religion. We must question how discourses are policed, and in turn, how discursive regimes of truth are established.

Historically, the separate school system was founded on Catholicism while the public system was founded on Protestantism. The question is, at what point did it become convenient to separate religion from spirituality? The move towards an emphasis on the secular served the needs of capital and material interests of the state. There has emerged a powerful relationship between the secular, capital and market forces. In rethinking schooling, it should be possible to develop an educational system that would integrate all forms of religion. Spirituality and religion are inseparable although not coterminous. Spirituality cannot be equated with religion, but religion is part of spirituality. What is needed therefore is a broader definition of spirituality that includes religion, values, beliefs, and myths.

The teaching of spirituality has a place in schools. This will include tapping into religious norms and values and appreciating the sacred and spiritual dimensions of human existence. Religion is part of every culture. However, we cannot equate spirituality with religion. Educators must distinguish between doctrine and enforcement of religious norms and values, on the one hand, and the enunciations of values, norms and beliefs that guide a people's sense of self, personhood, individual and collective actualization, as well as relations with each other and their environments. Spirituality and spiritual values have to do with the development of the inner sense of self, feelings and personal character.

THE NEW PEDAGOGY OF INDIGENOUS KNOWLEDGES

Multiple pedagogical and instructional strategies might be used to integrate Indigenous knowledges within the mainstream. While some of these reforms might require the partial or wholesale rebuilding of curricula and a redistribution of power, others will be far less difficult for those accustomed to the privileges afforded by Eurocentrism. Other knowledges may be integrated by welcoming local community members, parents and volunteers into schools so that they might teach and contextualize Indigenous educational materials and concepts. To use community workers/elders, schools would have to build trust with local communities. Within these communities there are a core group of elders who can be seen as custodians of Indigenous knowledge. Nevertheless, since such knowledge is shared, it is important not to focus solely on the custodians.

Teaching will involve educating about values, cultural norms, alternative ways of knowing, complexities of life, and the relevance of Indigenous languages. The teaching of Indigenous knowledges could also start with those committed to the promotion of effective learning. These will be educators who value the knowledges of all peoples, and appreciate students' knowledges as much as teachers' knowledges. Through a dialectic of mutual interdependence and interactions, knowledges are produced.

Teacher education programs must equip new educators to deal with different and multiple knowledges. They must be able to interrogate power and its role in knowledge production. For example, it is important to question who teaches what and why; who can teach Indigenous knowledges and how; and who makes decisions about curriculum. Curricula must move beyond an "old school" reliance on the three Rs and adapt new educational forms that are relevant and appropriate to the needs of the new millennium. Such courses would be able to utilize Indigenous knowledges to address issues of social difference, diversity and oppression.

We cannot overstate the need for educators to be appropriately schooled in how to deliver Indigenous knowledges. This is an important point because change is always met with opposition. Therefore, teachers must be able to engage the new framework in ways that diffuse the rhetoric generated by false dichotomies. Teachers should be able to point to the commonalties as well as the philosophical differences that exist between the old and new frameworks. However, these discussions of difference should always be framed relative to their mutual interdependence. Those alternative knowledges should never be positioned in competition with one another. Among the shared commonalities of Indigenous knowledges are respect for land, and the power of human-nature interactions. The idea of relation not only emphasizes relational knowledge, but also highlights the fact of the intricate connections between humans, society, culture and nature. Classroom teaching can be approached within a context and a history, relating information to other issues and concerns.

To incorporate Indigenous knowledges in the school, the educator must also tap the sophistication and depth of the knowledge of local communities. This includes knowledge about folktales, legends, beliefs and spiritual norms. Particular strategies to access Indigenous and cultural resource knowledges will involve making home visits and forming alliances, building relationships with local communities, parents, and youths. The information obtained will be a valuable resource in teaching about social values and cultural norms. Teaching can proceed from sharing sessions in which students, parents, educators, and community workers talk, understand and critically evaluate each other's views and opinions.

The integration of Indigenous knowledges into mainstream education could be used as a basis to develop a more critical approach to learning and teaching. Alternative ways of knowing could help to develop strategies that would work to challenge and overcome Eurocentrism. Moreover, Indigenous knowledges carry a great deal of potential to expand the existing Western knowledge base, but that potential remains unrealized so long as Eurocentrism retains its grip on the mass psyche. For example, the herbal medicinal knowledges of Indigenous peoples will only secure legitimacy when they appear in the supermarkets of Western societies. Through listening to and learning from spiritually-grounded Indigenous knowledges, education will accrue tremendous socio-cultural and political benefits.

C H A P T E R   4

SPIRITUALITY IN EDUCATION:
A CRITICAL PERSPECTIVE

INTRODUCTION

Over the past few years, interest in spirituality has grown considerably. As a result of the increased public attention, a great deal of work has been done to interrogate whether there should be a place for spiritual perspectives within mainstream schooling. Much of the contemporary research suggests that the inclusion of spiritual frameworks within the mainstream could only improve the existing system. One perspective speaks of the specific potential to enrich the quality of life, for those who adhere to non-mainstream religious principles, and for those who are actively involved in spiritual development. However, in a more general context, research asserts that an active engagement in religious and/or spiritual practices can be an effective means of maintaining psychological well being across the board. This perspective becomes all the more significant when placed relative to the education of children and adolescents in the formative years where identity and social understandings begin to develop.

A religious and spiritual orientation has been said to act as a control against "deviant" behavior in adolescents and to increase one's ability to resist negative social influences. It has also been correlated with recovery from alcohol and drug addiction and child sexual abuse (Langehough, et al., 1997). In Steward and Jo's 1998 study of 121 African-American adolescents, spiritual support was significantly related to their ability to cope and adjust to the developmental changes and environmental circumstances in their lives. Those who reported themselves to be the most spiritual were the most well adjusted, had the highest academic performance, and were most likely to use family and social support networks.

Miranti and Burke (1998) explain the resurgent interest in spirituality as a response to the "values vacuum" created as a result of movements and events in the 1960s and 1970s that led to the questioning of the values used to govern institutions like the family, church and education system. Others see interest in spirituality as an effort to "return to our roots" — or our "inner selves"; a response to "the Age of Materialism," where people are engaged in a pursuit of material pleasures (Dickman, 1980, p. 8). This widespread acceptance of spiritual perspectives in the mainstream has certainly had repercussions for educational pedagogy and practice. Case in point, the movement towards wellness models and the general acceptance of spiritual issues by self-help groups has stimulated efforts to incorporate spiritual issues into school counselling frameworks (Miranti and Burke, 1998, p. 164). Likewise, in efforts to teach and guide "the whole child," teachers are being encouraged to include spiritual development in their curriculum. However, while research would suggest that spirituality might improve the schooling experience for youth, educators, and other stakeholders alike, considerable opposition to such reforms continues to forestall systemic change. There is a reluctance to engage with spirituality as a viable pedagogical tool. This hesitance is directly related to both the pervasiveness of "individualism" in Western belief systems and the mainstream's refusal to interrogate educational paradigms that glorify logical thought. These philosophical paradigms sustain false dichotomies that demarcate spiritual knowledges as irrational in relation to sensible science-based knowledges. Further, much of what is written about the "spiritual dimension" is ambiguous and the ways in which teachers can work to include spiritual concerns into their teaching are largely unarticulated. Many popular descriptions of spirituality are centred around world peace and global harmony — commitments that are not always shared, appreciated or understood by the mainstream. For example, Kolander and Chandler (1990) suggest that:

> The spiritual dimension serves as a guide for drawing us together, for recognizing our oneness and alikeness rather than our separateness and differences. As we tap into our creative personal powers, our focus becomes a commitment to helping others. World balance is achieved as all people move toward international harmony

and peace. Our internal interrelationship and interdependence with others becomes balanced regardless of our perceived external differences in color, sex and status. We recognize that we are ONE (p. 9).

This chapter is an attempt to investigate and interrogate some of the popular thought surrounding spirituality in education and to rethink this notion in support of inclusive schooling practices. This chapter will "unpack" notions of religion and spirituality, and offer an alternative way of coming to terms with the implications of each for teaching in a diverse and ever changing world.

In this chapter, we argue that to work towards an inclusive environment in mainstream schooling we must first recognize "other'" experiences and knowledges as valuable and indispensable. Recognition is only the first step, however. For inclusive pedagogy and practice to be infused within the mainstream, reform must resonate with a commitment to redefine social reality respective of the multiple knowledges, experiences and histories that have heretofore been silenced. To these ends, we will examine spirituality's appropriateness and/or potential in educational contexts. We focus on spirituality at this point because people must have a commitment to helping others before they begin working towards reformation and social justice. That is not to suggest that a spiritual education will necessarily instill an overriding concern for social welfare and justice. However, studies have shown, that spirituality can influence a greater sense of community and connection to the world. In addressing the possibilities of spiritual education, we are particularly engaged with the ways in which the body, mind, and soul are implicated in formal and informal educational sites. In writing this chapter, we present a perspective that articulates spirituality in education within a critical integrative framework. By opening up discussions, and in interrogating multiple strategies for inclusion, it is our hope that the discussions in this chapter will encourage schools to embrace the promotion of spirituality in curricula and in the culture of schooling.

SPIRITUALITY AND SCHOOLING: TOWARDS A WORKING DEFINITION OF "RELIGION" AND "SPIRITUALITY"

The ways in which we understand spirituality and religion are varied and often contradictory. For this reason, any discussions about taking up spiritual frameworks within mainstream education must first begin with a clear interrogation of how we interpret and understand the concept itself. The word religion typically refers not only to institutionalized structures, a community of "believers" and their doctrine or rituals, but also implies an awareness of a divine or transcendent presence in our lives and the natural world that surrounds us. In an effort to unpack and conceptualize religion in a way that is useful for this discussion, it is important to identify the difference between religion as a theoretical construct and religion as an institutionalized practice.

Religious theory and/or systems belief are intrinsically tied to the ideas, principles and tenets that help to explain our relationship to forces beyond our known world. Religious questions express our desire to understand and know that which is unknown or unknowable. Our responses, ideas and formulations in relation to these theories are played out in our behavior or religious practice.

Religion is often framed as an oppressive tool used to maintain or enforce conformity. While we would not argue that it is not sometimes adapted to these ends, we must also be able to acknowledge the benefits that come with it. For example, religion is often used as a moral compass. Religious guidelines can help individuals and groups to problem solve. Religion is often used as a lens, through which practitioners see and interpret the world. In this context, it is a spiritual or religious framework that guides one's understanding of human behaviour (e.g. how we should act, what we should strive for, how to best raise our children). Ackermann (1985) suggests that, at its core, religion is potentially critical rather than functional or accommodating, and that "the main thread of religion may be one of potential opposition or criticism of a surrounding society by the development of a picture of life as it should be lived" (p. 24). That being said, if religion is understood as more than "a set of mechanically understood dogma," it can provide the possibility for social critique.

Definitions of spirituality tend to be more varied than religious theories, beliefs and practices, which in many cases are observable and articulated in sacred texts or scripture:

> … the essence of spirituality is difficult to comprehend because it cannot be perceived by our physical senses or proven by our intellectual powers. We use our physical senses to experience the physical world and our mental powers to access ideas, but spirituality eludes these faculties. While it manifests itself in a

person's mental and physical activities, the spirit itself cannot be seen, heard, touched, analyzed or proven. Yet from the dawn of civilization, some form of spirituality has been inherent in every culture that is known (Wolf, 1996, p. 20).

The Western definition of the word spirit is derived from the Latin word *spirtus*, which refers to the breath. Spirit is defined in Webster's dictionary as "the life principle" originally regarded as an animating vapour infused by breath or as bestowed by a deity. According to the Faithkeeper of the Onondaga Nation of Native Americans:

Spirituality is the essence of our lives. It's what makes a tree grow and what makes a bird sing. What makes a human smile. Spirituality has its own force and has its own being, something you can't see. It's the power of the universe (Quoted in Wolf, 1996).

Members of the Summit on Spirituality (1995) assert that it is a capacity both innate and unique to all people regardless of religious affiliation or spiritual leaning. In this perspective, spirituality is seen to be a naturally occurring aspect and function of life, rather than lifestyle. They maintain that spirit or spirituality is what moves us in our everyday lives. That it is the engine that fires our search for knowledge, love, meaning, hope and transcendence. That it is the wellspring of human emotion. It is the cradle of compassion, wellness, wholeness and our sense of connection to the world around us. Also, that it is our creative centre, the basis for morality, and ultimately, that which allows us to grow as humane beings (p. 30). Spirituality has also been described as the way "to release the spirit within the individual" (Kolander and Chandler, 1990, p. 3) and as the guide that makes us more responsive and open to different realities of existence (Vardey, 1996).

While these definitions highlight various aspects, characteristics or the nature and importance of the spirit, they do not help us to make sense of the spirit in relation to our daily lives. One reason for this is that these conceptions are often de-contextalized. Popular notions of spirituality (often devised outside of any religious tradition or through an amalgamation of several of them) tend to imply a certain degree of universality. This is problematic because spiritual knowledge, like all knowledge, is constructed within a specific context, and "one-size-fits-all" approaches are not very useful in a pluralist society. For example, primary differences exist between Eastern and Western spiritual journeys. According to Campbell (cited in Groff and Smoker, 1996):

In the East, where a group identity and culture are more dominant, one is expected to follow a path determined by one's spiritual leader. In the West, however, where individual identity and culture are more dominant, seekers are freer to embark on their journeys and engage in experiences of their own choosing.

Many of the community educators who participated in this study had a strong sense of spirituality as it relates to others. These educators argued that students cannot be viewed as disconnected from their communities, families or the everyday realities of their own lives. Further, they claimed that the combined influence of these factors on the student and their ability to relate to others in part *comprises* their spiritual existence and helped them to inform their values, beliefs and the ways in which they make sense of the world.

THE RELIGION — SPIRITUALITY DICHOTOMY

Today, it is almost "fashionable" to say that one is spiritual but not religious (Haynes, 1999; Marshall, 1998). These two concepts are often presented in opposition to each other as two distinct phenomena. For example, Hague (1995) argues that "spirituality may find expression in religion; religion at its best will be deeply spiritual, but spirituality is quite distinct from organizational religion" (p. 13).

In discussing spirituality in education, religion is often portrayed as something to be avoided, and has been described as "a political organization of like-mindedness and values that separates one group from another" (Kolander and Chandler, 1990, p. 4). However, we must be careful not to confuse the two concepts. In considering the pragmatics of incorporating spirituality within mainstream contexts, we must ensure that religiosity and spirituality are not seen as interchangeable ways of knowing. We must be marked on this point: Curricula designed to highlight spiritual perspectives and understandings need not touch on religious concerns (Dickman, 1980, p. 8).

The language used to describe these terms is also significant, and needs to be deconstructed in an effort to make sense of this dichotomy. One example is the use of general or non-religious characteristics to describe spirituality. Dickman describes the attributes of spirituality as "resiliency, responsiveness, joyfulness, patience, humor, hope, happiness and flexibility"

(1980, p. 8). In a similar tone, Kolander and Chalander (1991) contend that we must look within ourselves to find peace, harmony and contentment. That everything necessary for the attainment of happiness is already inside us. The secret is being able to tap into that inner "spiritual" core that embodies infinite knowledge, being, consciousness and joy. The meanings in these two cases may be described as one's response to an outside force or "breath," but that is not apparent, and statements like "everything we need is already within us" imply a deeper connection with ourselves — or our "true selves" — and not necessarily connection, communication or relationship to others.

Haynes (1999) argues that we must not mute interpretations that see "the transcendent" and "the soul" as being intrinsic to spirituality. Any such oversight would risk rendering the concept itself meaningless for advocates of spiritual inclusion in educational contexts. In fact, if interpretations cease to reflect a deep connection with the metaphysical, then spirituality risks becoming perceived as synonymous with the intellectual and the emotional. Such a step would not only devalue its meaning for advocates of spirituality, its meaning and purpose would be negated altogether. After all, if spirituality becomes relegated to the banal, we would have to question the very use of the term.

Many contemporary efforts to disassociate spirituality from religious concerns often do so by simply substituting "humane" qualities for "divine" ones. For instance, in some cases, notions of "humane teaching" and "spiritual teaching" are used synonymously. But is this enough? Can we simply disassociate the religious from the spiritual? Can we disconnect the two without assigning primacy to one? Who has the power/right to determine how these concepts should be interpreted? Rethinking these issues necessitates that we view notions of religion and spirituality through a lens that does not privilege or legitimate one over the other.

For Elkind (1992), spirituality can be understood in either a broad or a narrow sense. In the narrow interpretation, spirituality is connected to a particular set of religious precepts, and is measured by how strictly those precepts are observed. So a truly devout individual would be considered truly spiritual. However, in the broader interpretation, spirituality is associated with human/humane qualities such as love, forgiveness and generosity. In this interpretation, an individual that exemplifies these qualities might be considered spiritual. These two interpretations remind us that problems inevitably arise when we attempt to establish guidelines for, or definitions of, something that is so intrinsically subjective. Case in point, definitions of what it means to be humane, and the criteria by which humanity is measured, are all subjective and culturally specific. Likewise, understandings of what it is to be spiritual or religious will vary from context to context. In Western culture, religion tends to be related to formal traditions and codes, while spirituality gets taken up as something more personal and distinctive. However, in many Eastern cultures, religion and spirituality are not always differentiated from each other (See, Hague, 1995 and Christ, 1986). It may seem cliché, but when we speak of how spirituality relates to religion, interpretations are always changing, and the only constant is that there is no constant. The relationship evolves and adapts relative to individual and/or group tradition, experience and need.

In looking at Marshall's study of South Asian Women and spirituality (1998), we may note how the line between religion and spirituality is drawn and erased simultaneously. Research participants who acknowledged a distinction between the two terms also maintained that their experience of spirituality, while intense and personal, was not divorced from their religious centre. In fact, many went on to assert that their sense of spirituality was sustained and bolstered by their formal religious practices. Of particular importance, as noted by Marshall, is that their experience of spirituality did not push/pull them away from their religious heritage. Rather, it helped them to re-experience their religious roots, and reclaim a connection to their established traditions. Those interviewees who identified with particular religious traditions described their beliefs as the guiding principles by which they operated on a daily basis. As one participant explained, "It is an entire way of life, and that impacts on everything that we believe in and do" (p. 15). Spirituality and religion are positioned in these narratives as distinct but complimentary. However, we must recognize that some perspectives are more guarded and particular about how these concepts are to be defined.

As noted by Haynes (1999), many organized religions around the world maintain strict guidelines as to the nature and course of the spiritual journey. For some, that journey is fundamentally tied to a belief in revelation through scripture. Metaphorically speaking, within these faiths, scripture is a treasure map, and X marks the divine. However, like the hunt for buried treasure, the quest for enlightenment and the sacred requires discipline, and a strict adherence to the rules of the game. In contrast, for many belief systems, (e.g. Buddhism and Hinduism) spiritual enlightenment is seen as a universal experience that spans multiple lifetimes. In these contexts, grace and spiritual completeness are more related to time and experiential growth, than diligence and piety. That being said, while independent of canonical law, like so many others, they still presume that authentic spiritual growth takes place relative to particular disciplines. In this respect, most religious doctrines interpret spirituality as being inseparable from revelation and practice (Haynes, 1999, p. 25).

In contrast to this perspective, however, Nord and Haynes (1998) contend that religion is multifaceted; and "religiosity" as a way of life, cannot be measured solely in relation to practice, tradition and dogma. This framework asserts that if spirituality affirms a sense of the divine as existing in humanity and the cosmos, then it is fundamentally religious. This distances the concept of religion from traditional orthodoxy and establishes a space where alternative readings might be engaged. Therefore, even if we seek a spiritual life outside the authority of canon and routine, our experience of spirituality may be non-sectarian, but it may also be religious. This perspective points specifically to a distinction between the metaphysical character of religion and the corporeal demands of organized religion.

In interviews conducted during the second phase of our research, one interviewee spoke about growing up in Trinidad and his experience of schooling. While relating that his teachers were concerned for his spiritual well-being, he stopped to clarify what that term spiritual meant to him. He explained, "When I say spiritual, I don't mean it in a religious way. I mean it more in terms of what kind of person they wanted me to be." This narrative suggests an interpretation of spirituality as being connected to morality, and the building of character. In other words, it is a way of life, that if practiced, can lead to happiness and personal fulfillment. Interestingly, several other participants spoke of spirituality as a guideline for understanding. Some maintained that it helped them make sense of the world, while others asserted that it was basic to their sense of inner peace. In contrast, many of the narratives that spoke of religion, described it as institutionalized faith, or as a package through which spirituality is presented. These narratives seem to reflect a perception of religion as established or formulaic, while spirituality is interpreted as more freeform and experiential.

These multiple readings of spirituality and religion suggest that we should be wary of attempting to establish a set of ground rules in relation to these concepts. In the attempt to reconceptualize "spirituality" and "religion" as they relate to schooling and classroom practice, it is important not to privilege or impose one over the other. Pitting religion and spirituality against each other serves only to legitimate one, while relegating the other to the realm of myth and lore.

Holistic Education

A holistic approach to education lends itself well to a critical integrative framework. Not only does it embrace/engage the emotional and spiritual aspects of learning, it also facilitates the incorporation of those aspects within mainstream schooling. Educational approaches that espouse holistic pedagogy and practice must not be confused with traditional parochial models of schooling. As suggested by Miller (1996), holistic education must be understood in the broad context of spiritual growth and social reformation. *Holon*, the Greek root of the word holistic, embodies an understanding of the universe as made up of integrated wholes. That is to say that the universe might be seen, not as a totality unto itself, but as a collection and an interplay of multiple totalities that cannot be reduced to the sum of their parts.

In *The Holistic Teacher*, Miller (1993, pp. 20-24)) outlines key assumptions about learning and knowing from a holistic perspective:

1. Learning involves physical, emotional, intellectual and spiritual aspects;
2. There are many ways of knowing and learning;
3. Intuition is a valid form of knowing;
4. The individual's journey to realize the "self" (self-knowledge) is part of holistic learning;
5. Learning is facilitated in an environment that is psychologically safe, where individuals feel free to take risks;
6. Learning involves both the struggle to understand and integrate new understanding (effort) and a playful element that often comes after the individual has gained proficiency and confidence;
7. Learning is facilitated when it is related to real-life contexts;
8. Learning involves letting go of prior conditioning;
9. Growth and development continue through adulthood.

These key assumptions are not unique to holistic education and most learner-centred or constructivist approaches share many of the same tenets (see, McCombs and Whisler, 1997). Although holistic practice would include various forms of educational orientations and strategies (e.g. transmission and transactional), the transformational perspective specifically acknowledges the wholeness of the child, and the intimate connection between curriculum and the child's lived experience. Holistic educational models work to embrace and operationalize the relationships that exist between the "living child" and the process of schooling. To these ends, holistic curricula would focus on the connections and interactions that exist between:

- linear thinking and intuition;
- mind and body;
- various domains of knowledge;
- self and community;
- self and the Earth;
- self and Self.

These connections echo much of what has been proposed in this chapter, but we would suggest that the "self and Self" connection needs to be problematized in order for it to be meaningful in a plural, political and just society. In *The Holistic Curriculum* (Miller, 1996) this relationship is described as follows:

> Ultimately, the holistic curriculum lets us realize our true nature. For centuries various philosophic and spiritual traditions have discussed the two selves of human nature. One self is our ego, which is our socialized sense of who we are. It involves all the roles we play such as wife/husband, father/mother, daughter/son, as well as our job identity. Beyond this self is what has been called our "Higher Self:, our "Buddha nature" or what Emerson called the "big person." This original Self opens to us in moments when we hear a piece of music, see a child at play, are deeply involved in our work or are simply present to nature. Our ego sees our self as separate from everyone else and often competing with others in a never-ending struggle. There is no struggle for the Self since it senses a deep connection to others and all life. It realizes separation is an illusion exposed by a fundamental unity. (Miller, 1996, p. 9)

Notwithstanding the "fit" between this educational approach and a more critical integrative one, there are some aspects of holistic education, as illustrated here, that need to be addressed and challenged. For example, Miller suggest that holism is based on the "perennial philosophy" which holds that all things are part of an indivisible unity or whole (Miller, 1996, p.

20), and outlines the basic principles of this philosophy and holism as the following:

1. There is an interconnectedness of reality and a fundamental unity in the universe;
2. There is an intimate connection between the individual's inner or higher self and this unity;
3. In order to see this unity we need to cultivate intuition through contemplation and meditation;
4. Value is derived from seeing and realizing the interconnectedness of reality;
5. The realization of this unity among human beings leads to social activity designed to counter injustice and human suffering.

Miller writes that

these principles have been articulated in different spiritual and intellectual traditions in both the East and West through the philosophy of Pythagoras, Socrates and Plato and in religions such as Hinduism, Western Idealism, Transcendentalism and some forms of Existentialism and Christian Mysticism.

However, the extent to which these five principles are taken up have a great effect on the actual "doctrine" that they have produced.

Similarly, this philosophy suggests that contemplation and mediation work to reveal and communicate our unity with the universe. In holistic classrooms these two methods are usually translated into practices of visualization and group meditation. However, Kesson (1993) has argued that practices such as visualization are not neutral and can "either work to emancipate consciousness, sustain the status quo, or open us up to even more subtle forms of domination (p. 103). Holistic education must become more critical in order to allow students to examine institutions and social practice that separate and oppress people. This call for increased critical thinking within holistic approaches is partially related to the dangers of appropriation. While these practices are culturally specific and tied to long standing traditions, they may find themselves co-opted if incorporation into the mainstream is not brought about in a meaningful and respectful fashion. Furthermore, Kesson's assertion that holistic practice is not intrinsically neutral serves to remind us that oppressive discourses do not only speak *to* the marginalized, but *through* them, (see Chapter Five for more on discourse). Critical thinking must be incorporated as a fundamental part of any educational model that works towards equity and social justice. These concerns reflect the anti-racist maxim — "good intentions are not enough." Schooling, whether holistic, spiritual, religious or otherwise, must accept and reinforce the relationship between critical thought and emancipatory social reform. On this point, several traditions outside educational contexts have sought to marry spirituality and/or religion with the critical call for social justice.

The creation theology movement is an explicit attempt to connect social, political, moral and economic agenda, with religious thought. The emphasis here is on collective and responsible action designed to transform, not just ameliorate, ecological concerns. This movement is a blend of new-age cosmology and contemporary political theory. It is based in the Christian tradition, but has reformulated this theology to place greater emphasis on joy and compassion and the connection between the mystical and human concerns (see Fox, 1979 for greater discussion).

Liberation theology emerged out of the Latin American struggle to resist and overcome centuries of poverty, exploitation and oppression. In this tradition, the first priority of the religious community (in this case the Catholic Church) is to feed the hungry and to provide shelter for the homeless. The approach involves the construction of alternative communities where the poor, the clergy and volunteers from outside the community discuss connections between their practice and biblical thought. Neither of these movements are universal or neutral.

One might also expect to find a similar commitment to social justice within New Age thinking, which has demonstrated an openness to spiritual experiences and to untapped human potential. In attempts to combine rationality with intuitive and non-rational processes, many New Age theorists employ scientific research to confirm their intuitive notions about the nature of the universe. This willingness to engage both the intellectual and the metaphysical could be a source of great insight and strength for New Age theorizing (for more on New Age theology see, Haynes, 1999; Purpel, 1989; and Nord, 1995). However, while extremely eclectic, this philosophy's attention to spiritual and holistic concerns seems to preclude the examination and/or inclusion of critical political thought. In fact, unlike the aforementioned Liberation and Creation theologies, New Age philosophies commonly seeks to engage spiritual growth irrespective of social inequity and systemic oppression's affects on the individual. This theoretical position reflects an uncritical reading of social change as paralleling changes in underlying human consciousness ... what Purpel (1989) calls a "trickle up theory."

Notwithstanding these concerns, holistic and spiritual approaches to education do carry the potential to infuse educational sites with a sense of connection and responsibility to a greater purpose and vision. However, we would draw specific attention to our use of the word "potential." We do this to emphasize that the implementation of superficial or haphazard initiatives is not a sufficient condition to improve education and affect positive social change. For "transcendent" knowledges to have a critical/political meaning for, and impact upon educational reform, they must be accompanied by pragmatic strategies for inclusion. Such strategies would have to originate within a framework that is open to, new ways of knowing and new ways of doing.

How Do Children Learn?

Despite years of research in educational, development and child psychology, there is still much to be learned about the ways in which students learn. Of the various theories and approaches offered, some are more useful than others in the effort to understand learning as a dynamic, interactive and a culturally mediated process. Mezirow's (1997) discussions on formal and informal socialization help us to understand education as a dialectical process that is developed through interactions with people, objects and events. Therefore, with respect to the process of schooling, children must be understood to learn in and through multiple sites. In fact, he goes on to contend that students are usually trying to master several environments at once. So if mainstream education establishes a greater overlap between the spheres of school and community, intellect and emotion, the secular and the spiritual, then the schooling experience may become more enriching, challenging and engaging for students. This type of inclusive and open framework moves beyond traditional devotion to the three Rs and promotes the development of independent thought and the ability to problem solve. Mezirow's assertions suggest that "open" or inclusive educational models will stimulate learning skills while encouraging students to:

1. Recognize cause-effect relationships;
2. Use informal logic in making analogies and generalizations;

3. Become aware of, and control, their own emotions;
4. Become empathic of others;
5. Use imagination to construct narrative and;
6. Think abstractly;
7. Think hypothetically and;
8. Become critically reflective of what they read, see and hear.

(Mezirow, 1997, p. 9).

The principles of anti-racist education (see Dei, 1996) offer another way to understand the learning process by focusing on knowledge production. This perspective acknowledges that the body is critical to the learning process and imbued with meaning. In schools, teachers and students negotiate social meanings and engage in daily practices implicating bodies along the lines of gender, class, ethnicity, age, ability and sexuality.

The body, mind and soul are implicated in the formal learning process, along with personal knowledge and that which is developed in the home and community. Experience is part of the knowledge students bring to formal education and is relevant to how students construct and make sense of schooling. Either by defining or imagining the self, students, parents and educators are able to define their roles and place in the politics of schooling. Radicalized identity politics is embedded in understandings of our individual and collective existence within a social order. An inclusive pedagogical approach recognizes that students come to school as embodied beings and bring their experiences to bear on the learning process.

Finally constructivist approaches are useful in trying to understand how students learn. Like holistic approaches, they lend themselves well to practices that attempt to be responsive to the spiritual dimension of students. McCombs and Whisler (1997) describe the premises behind the learner-centred model, and even though they are similar to those presented in the holistic approach, they are worth listing because they take a more commonly accepted approach to describing the learning process. The five premises have been described as follows:

1. Learners are distinct and unique: their distinctness and uniqueness must be attended to and taken into account if learners are to engage in, and take responsibility for their own learning.
2. Learners' unique differences include their emotional states of mind, learning rates, learning styles, stages of development, abilities, talents, feelings of efficacy and other academic and non-academic attributes

and needs. These must be taken into account if all learners are to be provided with the necessary challenges and opportunities for learning and self-development.

3. Learning is a constructive process that occurs best when what is being learned is relevant and meaningful to the learners and when the learner is actively engaged in creating his or her own knowledge and understanding by connecting what is being learned with prior knowledge and experience.

4. Learning occurs best in a positive environment, one that provides positive interpersonal relationships and interactions, comfort and order and in which the learner feels appreciated, acknowledged, respected and validated.

5. Learning is a fundamentally natural process; learners are naturally curious and basically interested in learning about and mastering their world (p. 10).

HOW DOES SPIRITUALITY ENHANCE LEARNING?

The development of the spiritual dimension of students' lives can enhance and promote learning in various ways. In this book, we suggest that when teachers and their students are engaged in the development of this dimension, they will begin to realize that:

1. *Spiritual knowledge is socially constructed and changes as new knowledges and understandings are generated.*

Teachers do not "give knowledge," but are contributors, critics and collaborators in the process of knowledge generation. "Any civilization or any culture is a human construction and it is a human responsibility to create and re-create culture; thus, it is intellectually unsound to encourage the notion that cultural institutions, values and beliefs are given" (Purpel, 1989, p. 115). Every knowledge offers a gendered, classed, ethnicized and historicized reading of reality as intersecting and interlocking experiences. Inclusive schooling supports a dialectic view of the world that moves students away from dualistic ways of thinking and addresses the challenge of integrating social and cultural values that promote alternative and multiple readings of the world into classroom pedagogues, instruction and school curricular.

In schools, some knowledges are more privileged than others, and while some are considered to be subjective, mythical or lore, others are viewed as objective, true and scientific. This is evident in the curriculum, the types of teachers that are hired and the administrative practices of schools. Additionally, in Ontario, the teaching of certain religions is sanctioned and financial supported by the state (i.e., Catholic separate schools) while others must exist outside of the public school system and sustain themselves through the support of their religious communities as is the case, for example, in Muslim and Jewish schools. Various policing discourses within schools exist in order to establish discursive regimes of truth and to construct a reality that becomes taken-for-granted.

"Spirituality requires knowing, constructing and composing by individuals in order to understand their relationship to that which is greater than themselves" (Fowler, 1981, p. 24). Before embarking on the journey, it is important that teachers help students establish what they know and understand by spirituality starting from a self-referential knowledge base and one that recognizes the habits of mind that they bring with them. Inclusive teaching requires an emotional investment in all students and a commitment to involving them in the process and act of knowledge making.

It is possible to link knowledge and imagination by seeing knowledge as constructed and problematic. Knowledge is not something that is static and "out there," but instead relies on our ability to interpret and make meaning.... By linking knowledge and imagination we enliven knowledge and ground imagination in a specific context. (Miller, 1996, p. 4).

The interrogation of issues surrounding spirituality and religion can be used to problematize the marginalization of certain voices in society, specifically the delegitimation of the knowledge and experience of subordinate groups in the education system. To speak about power in anti-racist discourse, is to speak about the social construction of knowledge (Dei, 1996, p. 30).

2. *Spirituality promotes initiative and self-reflexive thought.*

In exploring the differences between "intuitive" and "scholastic" learning, Gardner (1991) specifically addresses critical education in relation to the challenges of oppressive discourse and subjectivity. Of paramount importance in his discussion is an appreciation for the deep seeded conceptualizations that students bring with them to their experience of schooling. He recognizes that, a student's lived experience and understandings of the world are not simply placed aside when they walk in the school doors. Rather, these "scripted interactions" speak through us. They regulate our understanding of how we fit into the world and our understandings of the world itself. And, it is important to note, that life-knowledge, however internally oppressive and/or restrictive, cannot be easily reshaped (see Chapter Five for further discussions of discourse and subjectivity). Some theorists assert that these problems might be taken up through the implementation of strategies for spirituality and "intuitive" learning.

Intuition is the most common term for inner knowing where we process information simultaneously (Miller, 1993, pp. 24-5). It is the immediate knowing of something without the conscious use of reasoning. Working with intuition necessitates focusing on the inner life of thoughts. That is not to suggest that we might remove oppressive discourse and "script" from our experience simply by focusing on the "intuitive." Any such assertion would be fundamentally flawed. However, we do contend that an attention to emotion, feeling and "the imaginary" might allow us greater access to a spiritual centre that stands distinct from these external pressures and perceptions. Miller (1996) maintains that a synergistic use of rational and intuitive/non-linear thought, will serve to enrich the schooling experience for all youth.

Clark (1973) identified three levels of intuition: Physical intuition, where we react to different situations physically through the body; Feeling, where we experience "vibes" about other people and mental level where we have hunches about how to solve a problem or some other intellectual insight into a situation. This level is also said to be transforming because we can begin to see and understand at a deeper level. Spirituality is described as "the highest level of intuition" (Miller, 1996, p. 90) and is said to be free from physical sensations, emotional feeling or thoughts.

3.   The development of a spiritual consciences can help students understand the relationship between the self and the community.

Notions of "self" are not universally understood and different cultures/ religious traditions have devised various ways of explaining what the self is and how it is (or should be) connected to the "spirit," "higher power," or "self." In his explanation of the *transpersonal self*, Miller (1996) explores the concept of the self in major religions, and suggests that in Christianity the self is not God, "but the point within us where God touches us." In other words, it is where we and God meet (p. 36). Kabbalah, a mystic strand of Judaism acknowledges that there is a part within us that is connected to the Divine, and that there are three aspects to every person: (1) *nefesh*, a biological energy, (2) the *ruah,* one's spirit or psyche and (3) *neshamah,* the self which unites us to the universal divine essence. Generally, Buddhists do not see self-nature as something separate or identifiable. Instead, self is empty and is interconnected with all things and all life. In this case, in order to find the self, one needs to look inward. Similarly, in Hinduism, the purpose of spiritual practice is to discover the Atman (the connection between the individual and the universal consciousness) within oneself. In Sufism, a mystic form of Islam, this connection between the individual and (in this case) Allah, is known as Tawhid and has two main stages (1) *Fana*, where one relinquishes the ego and (2) *Ba'qu* where one is reintegrated in God.

Notions of identity are connected to the process of knowledge production because it effects ways of knowing and how people make sense of the world. It is important that teachers understand how identity effects the process of teaching and learning. We would suggest that this discovery begins with themselves through an exploration of the ways in which their own personal identity effects them professionally, personally, socially, emotionally and most importantly for our purposes, spiritually. Individual and group identities intersect and help students make connections between themselves and the groups they identity with.

Most of the community educators who participated in this study agreed that providing a spiritual dimension to mainstream education demands a holistic approach to students. These educators argued that students cannot be viewed as disconnected from their communities, families and everyday realities or "their own selves."

Community educators who participated in this study described education as an emotional experience, and were attempting to deliver programs with an educational philosophy that included and recognized the importance of the emotional and spiritual dimensions of students' lives, parental and community advocacy and youth empowerment. There was general agreement that schools were not doing enough to address and nurture the spiritual lives of students.

4. *Teaching practices are most effective when learning is viewed in holistic manner.*

The struggle to recognize the spiritual dimension in students' lives and their learning can provide for a holistic understanding and appreciation of the human experience, comprising social, cultural, political, ecological and spiritual aspects (see Leah, 1995). The philosophy of family/home-based prior learning and community education is anchored in a broader definition of education that encompasses the emotional and spiritual dimension, parental and community advocacy and youth empowerment. Research demonstrates that even very young children are capable of abstract thought and expressions of their own spirituality (Wood, 1995). A personalized, subjective identification with the learning process makes it possible for the learner to be invested spiritually and emotionally in the cause of educational and social change. Practices that recognize and enhance the students' potential for spiritual development, if introduced and maintained within a holistic, constructivist and anti-racist framework, can also enhance educational experiences and help students to fully develop as human beings.

TEACHERS AS FACILITATORS OF SPIRITUALITY IN EDUCATION

Transformative Learning Theory

The tenants of transformational learning theory that were developed by Mezirow (1991, 1995, 1996) and Cranton (1994, 1996) come out of the adult education tradition, but many of their ideas are instructive when considering ways to rethink the notion of spirituality in education. In *Transformative Learning: Theory to Practice*, Mezirow (1997) explains that "transformative learning is the process of effecting change in a *frame of reference.*" These frames are developed through one's experiences, and are the "structures of assumptions through which we understand our experiences."

Frames of reference are composed into two dimensions. *Habits of mind* are broad, abstract, orienting, habitual ways of thinking, feeling and acting influenced by assumptions that constitute a set of codes. These codes may be cultural, social, educational economic, or in the case of our interest, religious or spiritual. Habits of mind become articulated through the second dimension, *Points of view* as belief, value judgment, attitude and feeling that shape a particular interpretation. Points of view are subject to continual change as we reflect on either the content or process by which we solve problems and identify the need to modify assumptions. According to Mezirow (1997), "frames of reference are transformed through critical reflection on the assumptions upon which our interpretations, beliefs and habits of mind or points of view are based" (p. 7). Points of view are more accessible to awareness and to feedback from others. Habits of mind are more durable than points of view. (Mezirow, 1997).

Transformation theory suggests that growth and learning is facilitated by the ways in which individuals make meaning. Therefore, as "meanings" are always situated in contested space, critical approaches to education require that we actively question them and the assumptions through which they are informed. The goal of teaching then is not to "give knowledge," but rather to help students integrate new learning within the cultural meaning systems which sustain them, and to incorporate information about their habits of mind as a way to influence their points of view.

Teachers who provide a space for students to express and develop their spiritual selves are accommodating and demanding, compassionate, questioning and accepting. In *Spirituality as a Force for Social Change*, Miranti and Burke (1998) argue that counsellors must respond to major problems and injustices that infringe upon human dignity if they are to become a force for social change (p. 163). However, they point out that some may be reluctant to do so because of: (a) fear of imposing their own values on their clients; (b) they themselves may hold negative attitudes towards spirituality and organized religions; (c) they may lack specific in-depth knowledge of spiritual concerns; or (d) they may lack a model (Burke and Miranti, 1995). These writers recommend strategies that may be useful for teachers who find themselves in similar situations, and they suggest that they become familiar and comfortable with their own spirituality and became able to articulate what spirituality means in their own lives.

Finally, it is critical that we understand and appreciate varied cultural expressions of spirituality and examine our own biases and prejudices toward organized religion as an institution or particular tradition. It is especially important that teachers be familiar with the religious traditions of their students, especially those for whom religion is a significant part of their identity.

BEST PRACTICES FOR INCORPORATING
CONCEPTS OF SPIRITUALITY

Given the plurality of our modern day society, it is imperative that students' differences be taken into account. These include, but are not limited to their stages of physical, emotional, social and intellectual development, their talents and abilities, learning styles, ethnocultural background, sexual orientation, and religious and spiritual orientation. Inclusive and multi-centred approaches to curriculum and instruction offer concrete and practical ways in which teachers and schools can begin to pay attention to making accommodations for the distinctiveness that all children bring with them to school and formalized learning.

What prior knowledge and experiences do students bring to school? How do we tap into what they already know and believe when they enter our schools and classrooms? How can teachers collect and synthesize this information for classes with as many as 35 students? These questions are somewhat daunting, but the answers are specific to different teachers and do not appear as a checklist or recipe to follow. Because every classroom is different, it is not only impossible, but problematic to prescribe ways in which teachers should operate, the ways that classrooms should be constructed or the topics that should be broached with students. Any attempt to provide an outlet for spiritual expression must take into account the bodies, minds and souls present in the classroom. Teachers need to be reflective about their own practice before attempting to add or change things to support the spiritual lives of students. If we believe that students do not come to us as "blank slates," void of prior understandingss, beliefs and dispositions, getting access to this information is of great importance. Families and members of the larger community can be instrumental in the process of figuring out who the learner is in an attempt to make learning meaningful and relevant. Asking questions in an attempt to uncover information about how issues of spirituality are taken up in the home may be a good place to begin in an effort to create practice that is contextualized and specific instead of prescriptive and generalized.

Best practices create different and integrative centres of knowledge rather than mainstreaming marginalized discourses within the current educational and cultural framework. They are intended to promote effective learning outcomes for all youth by dealing with the issues and dynamics of race, class, gender, sexuality and their implications for youth schooling. In the promotion of spirituality in education it is suggested that schools too become active and cognizant of their role through a recognition of the traditions, values and practices that students bring with them to school and "make room for," or accommodate these things in their educational programs.

The Inclusive Learning Environment

> Holistic education should allow for the development of the student's inner life. This cannot be programmed and cannot even be taught in the conventional sense. It can only arise in a trusting climate and through certain activities that allow for reflection and contemplation (Miller, 1993, p. 29).

Students learn best in positive and supportive environments where they are appreciated, acknowledged, respected and validated. These environments can be supported through a recognition of individual difference that moves beyond "celebration" and "tolerance" towards accommodation and inclusion. The school and classroom need to be places where those with strong religious convictions and traditions can feel safe, if not supported, by their choices and those of their families. Similarly, students without connections to traditional or formalized religious traditions who consider themselves "spiritual" should be encouraged to explore and respect the choices of others. Those who do not find themselves in either of these categories should also feel like the school and the classroom are places where they will be able to express their thoughts and ideas without condemnation or ridicule.

The Incorporation of Diverse Knowledges

World Religions

Excluding or barely mentioning religion is hardly neutral or fair. In an effort towards inclusion, there have been several suggestions that teachers teach *about* world religions with an emphasis on the spiritual practice of the religion or an exploration of how the faith is lived out on a daily basis. Here we are suggesting that religion be viewed as a way that people make sense of their reality and as a way to connect to a "higher power" or life force outside of themselves. It is also critical that students understand that religions are not static collections of dogma, explanations and rituals, but practices that have been redefined over time. Students should also be encouraged to wrestle with the issues surrounding the various religious dilemmas and conflicts that permeate our world.

Diverse Spiritualities

In an effort to counter the trend toward the dualistic thinking so prevalent in our Western society, greater emphasis should be placed on Eastern, African and Native spirituality and the literature from cultures that emphasize holism and connectedness. This literature can also be used to expose students to ideologies that acknowledge a more "universal oneness" and can be useful in helping to expand students' understanding of the interconnectedness and interdependence between the Earth and its inhabitants.

Traditional Religious Practices

The practices of visualization, prolonged silence, yoga and meditation are generally linked to, and arose from, Eastern spiritual and religious traditions. These techniques may be employed in educational contexts for multiple purposes including intellectual stimulation, health and relaxation. Furthermore, presenting these practices/techniques in a cultural context generates opportunities to incorporate non-Eurocentric cultural knowledges into the classroom. However, we would caution that to avoid issues of appropriation and co-optation, these practices should be introduced relative to their cultural, spiritual or religious specificities.

In one interview, a university professor cautioned against the appropriation of Aboriginal practices, which she described as "making yours what belongs to someone else without giving credit." In describing the use of smudging she suggested that "if smudging is done and explained in the way it's supposed to be explained, I have no problem with it happening in the classroom if it helps the students centre." Fitznor (1999) explains that:

> There is a teaching that goes with the smudging, the acknowledgment of the gifts that we get from the Creator and they are all related to the seasons, the minerals and all the things that make up the Earth ... People give thanks to the Creator for the gifts we received from the East — and they list all the gifts because those are memory devices. It's like a book to help you know what comes from the East. In the East the sun rises, so it's symbolic of

the new dawn, newness, new knowledge, youth, the babies. Then you go to the South and you acknowledge the gift that you get from the South. Then you go to the West and then the North. Each of the direction has with it a knowledge base that is interconnected with the sacredness of the teachings of the Earth. You constantly talk about that and you bring that in the classroom as the opening of the smudge so that's what they learn. In this case the teacher might say "We give thanks to the Creator for ..." (she would fill in the blanks) and then the students would repeat it.

However, as a corollary to promoting the use of such practices within the mainstream, Fitznor also asserts that if teachers want to use Aboriginal knowledges and practices within their classrooms, they should incorporate those practices into their daily lives and make them their own. She advises that if teachers don't know the teachings that accompany traditional practices, or the knowledge base surrounding the practice the effort will be a superficial one, lacking "soul." She, like others, suggest that teachers should draw on the knowledge of the elders and traditional teachers spend some time with them and be willing to get involved in the work of the community.

Incorporating the Prophetic Voice

Including prophets who emerge from different religious traditions and led political movements for liberation (e.g. Gandhi, King, Romero, McClung) can help students to make the connection between the sacred and the secular and to see these women and men as social critics who judged their society and encouraged others to struggle against oppression and inequity.

Fables, Folk Tales and Myths

Children's literature has become a popular and effective way to teach about issues like morality, values, diversity and environmental concerns. Fables, folk tales and myths from various countries and time periods have also been used to teach about cultural practices and traditions. These materials need to be selected in a careful and critical way. Images, language and the manner in which conflicts are resolved are just a few of the things that deserve close consideration when selecting books for children and youth. It is also important to engage students in an awareness of which stories get categorized as "myth" and to interrogate the implications of these classifications in relation to the legitimization of some knowledges over others.

Family and Community Involvement

Community service projects have often been framed as a way to help students see themselves as global citizens, but they are also an important way to help students learn about the distribution and use of power, the impact of local communities on schooling and the interdependence/interrelatedness between members of geographic societal groups. This involvement may also help them to understand that oppression and injustice are collective concerns.

Parents need to be, not only *informed* but involved in practices that suggest religious behavior. In *Starting Over*, Petrash (1992) suggests that because "gratitude is an important part of what children should experience from a young age" that at meal times "it is appropriate for the children to stop and give thanks for the food they eat. This simple routine helps to turn children's hearts not only towards that which is larger than humanity, but also to an appreciation of all that is given to us from the bounty and beauty of our Earth and even from the efforts of our parents (p. 29)." This "simple routine" may appear to be harmless, but this practice of "giving thanks" may be culturally loaded for some children. Activities like this one need to be contextualized and presented through the traditions that they are born out of. Like the "mind-body" exercises mentioned earlier, they need to be presented as what they are, and parents need to be involved in the decision to have their children participate or not.

SUMMARY

In order to rethink spirituality in education for the inclusive school, it is necessary to conceptualize it both within a curricular framework and as a philosophical or ideological approach to education and schooling. Rethinking spirituality in education for inclusive schooling requires a pedagogy that can tap into the religious norms and values of students, their families and their communities, and appreciate the sacred and spiritual dimensions of human experience. This is not to imply the enforcement of any particular religious tradition or value system, we suggest that it is imperative that teachers acknowledge and respect the beliefs that guide students' individual and collective actualization, as well as their relationship to their communities and the environment. Further, spirituality in education should encourage and support student empowerment and move students toward a vision of the world that challenges oppression and inequality.

Parker Palmer (1999) describes spirituality as "the ancient and abiding human quest for connectedness with something larger and more trustworthy than our egos" (p. 6). The description of spirituality as a journey or quest lends itself well to the notion of spirituality in education put forth in this chapter. Given this conceptualization, spirituality — "the human quest for connectedness" — is not something that needs to be "brought into" or "added onto" the curriculum (p. 8).

It is also important to come to terms with the fact that on this journey towards new understandings about spirituality, educators will *not* have all the answers. However, because Western educational discourse places significant value on positivistic knowledge, many teachers are profoundly and understandably uncomfortable with reforms that call for spiritual education. In an effort to create an inclusive learning environment where every child is involved in the process of knowledge production, it is important to realize that there will be times when there won't be definitive answers to the questions students may bring up. If we are to open to the spiritual dimension of education, we must understand that spiritual questions do not have answers in the way math problems do (Palmer, 1999, p. 8).

In an inclusive school every student is able to identify and see themselves reflected in the social and cultural organization of the school. This conception of inclusive schooling stresses the idea that socially constructed concepts of race, ethnicity, class, language and sexuality are fundamental to the teaching and learning process. To conceptualize spirituality in education through a critical integrative analysis of social difference is an attempt to ensure that the diverse knowledge and concerns of youth, parents and communities are embraced in school and education in plural contexts. When spirituality is acknowledged in education there is a recognition that there are various dimensions to students' learning beyond the intellectual, and that teaching and learning should encourage parental and community advocacy and youth empowerment.

CHAPTER 5

LANGUAGE INTEGRATION:
FRAMING ISSUES OF LANGUAGE
IN SCHOOLING

INTRODUCTION

So, if you want to really hurt me, talk badly about my language. Ethnic identity is twin skin to linguistic identity — I am my language. Until I can accept as legitimate Chicano Texas Spanish, Tex-Mex and all other languages I speak, I cannot accept the legitimacy of myself, and as long as I have to accommodate English speakers rather than having them accommodate me, my tongue will be illegitimate. I will no longer be made to feel ashamed of existing. I will have my voice, my sexual voice, my poet's voice. I will overcome the tradition of silence.

Gloria Anzaldua[1]

We must ask ourselves, "whose words have merit in mainstream schooling?" Is it those who experience and suffer through the realities of exclusion in their school lives, or is it the person who says, "quality education is better and more important than equity education," and "we can't work for the needs of special interests." How do these dialogues excuse and endorse "privileged" distortions of another's lived experience? How are these "objective" explanations vested with authority, and constructed as narratives of "the real"? As English culture and language are privileged in schooling while others are excluded, we can see the politics of the moment, and we know whose knowledge and culture are meant to be perceived. Yet how do we overcome the tradition of silence? While issues related to race, class, gender and sexuality in education have been taken up in recent years, the question of "language" and linguistic exclusion in mainstream schooling has continued to be neglected. In fact, the often asked question of whether linguicism[2] is a reality for students is in itself fraught with problems. Any such query about the objective nature of oppression can and must serve to silence and devalue "subjective accounts," while challenging the reality of the experience altogether. The emphasis placed by some educators on determining the quantitative value of these circumstances suggests that the reality of "the moment" becomes a function of another's ability to understand it, and name it. When oppression in any form, is not named for what it is, the reality of the experience can always be called into question. So, as schools are not culturally and politically neutral territories, the development of a linguistically inclusive curriculum and environment is imperative if we are to address the Eurocentric/classist/patriarchal/ heterocentric worldviews that persist within mainstream education.

Language must be taken into consideration as a fundamental component of any and all moves towards educational change/improvement in this age of diaspora. Specifically, the languages of socially minoritized and marginalized groups deserve to be acknowledged, respected and validated within mainstream contexts. However, before we begin to advocate for language integration in educational sites, it is vital that we first outline the context in which our discussions are grounded. We feel it important to reiterate our concerns about the false dichotomy that often separates theory and practice with respect to the use of multiple languages in education. In addressing the realities of linguistic integration in our schools, we would work to ensure that theory and research combine to produce feasible guidelines for the practical application of "language as resource."

Towards these ends, the framework of this chapter is threefold: first, we take a theoretical approach to understanding language in relation to knowledge, access and power; second, we situate our investigation of language integration relative to past research and modern problematics of identity, space and place; and third, through a critical analysis of the observations and interviews generated in the present study, we explore some of the strategies and practices of language integration that are currently being employed in both mainstream and local contexts. In attempting to marry theory and practice in this manner, we hope to address the claims that language integration is an unnecessary and problematic step towards educational improvement. We would show that language integration is not only feasible, but basic to educational improvement for all students.

THEORETICAL PERSPECTIVES ON LANGUAGE, POWER AND EDUCATION

In the writing of this book, we have continually found ourselves questioning not only why, what and how we write, but who it is that we are writing for. These questions are particularily important for anti-oppression workers/ activists in the academy who feel the constant pressure to write so that their words might be heard by those in positions of power. In many respects, our survival in the academy is dependent upon our willingness to work within environments that are scripted for us in tradition, and by "privilege."

Our decision to examine these issues, in this space, and in this moment, developed not only out of academic interest, but out of personal necessity and a sense of social responsibility. That being said, these social-psychological dilemmas beg some larger questions that are of particular interest here. If the dynamics of these "moments" are framed such that we, as oppressed people, are cognizant of what can and cannot be said, it is because we have been "educated" to know that there are rules by which we must abide in each given context. These are internalized controls through which we "discipline" ourselves. These self-enforced restrictions frame our "moments" in as many ways as the words/actions/rules of our oppressor. The language/discourse that teaches us how, when, where and what to do, also structures our subjectivity; it speaks through us.

In Chapter Three, we alluded to the significance of the Foucauldian conception of "knowledge and power" in relation to the experience of schooling in North American contexts. Foucault's work moves us towards a closer scrutiny of language. In his interpretation, language can be understood to play a role in the social construction of both meanings and subjectivities. Althusser also embraced a more linguistic interpretation of how meanings become internalized, and how we speak and are spoken by forces that exist outside our bodies (actually, his work was part of the revisionist writings on "ideology" that lead eventually, through numerous re-configurations, to Foucault) (Hall, 1986, pp. 29-31). In order to avoid the pitfalls associated with either/or dichotomies, we do not seek to privilege one conception/ interpretation of language over another. Rather, we are interested in engaging various theoretical perspectives on linguistic systems in an attempt to better understand how language functions to oppress minoritized youth in mainstream schooling today. To that end, Scott (1988) posits several questions that are of specific interest to us: How do meanings and subjectivities change? How is it that some meanings emerge as "norms of truth," while others have disappeared? What do these processes tell us about how power is constituted, and how it operates? How, in what contexts, and through what processes are meanings acquired?

Traditional anthropological frameworks tend to view the distinctiveness of nations, cultures and societies as existing within seemingly unproblematic divisions of space. So if social space is imprinted with cultural norms that are both natural and appropriate within given boundaries, then meanings would develop relative to that space. This conception of a "social-imprint" sees space acting as an organizing principal in society; a principle that establishes an appropriate "place" for some cultural attributes, meanings and systems, while marginalizing others. This rigid conception of social space, cultural boundaries and meanings belies the reality of oppression. In this respect, "the power of topography effectively masks the topography of power" (Gupta and Ferguson, 1992, p. 7). That is to say that the "appropriateness" that is ascribed to a standard language form in a particular time and place, serves to obscure the very conditions and contexts through which the perception of linguistic propriety was constituted.

From a post-structural perspective, language, as a medium of thought, is understood to be "multi-accentual," and one's perceptions of the world are always developed with, and within, these "intersecting accents." In seemingly direct opposition to Saussure's concept of "deep structure" in language, and his assertion that the meaning of language could be found in the function of the linguistic system, post-structuralists have set up camp outside a number of different positions (Scott, 1988, p. 35). Some argue that words have *no* intrinsic interpretation; that language must be analyzed with respect to specific historical and contextual meanings. While others assert that words attain meaning only when in relation to other words; that the only "truth" available is that language cannot be taken at face value. The difficulties encountered in any exploration of language and meaning, serve to remind us that we are socialized/indoctrinated into a linguistic system that *appears* to be a completely developed totality unto itself. However, what if language and linguistic forms are not as fixed and natural as they seem? What if language is in fact, a dynamic system that functions both as an effect of, and medium for, social forces? (Scott, 1988, p. 35)

The perception of language as rigid, normative, and appropriate to given spaces, has been the linchpin of status quo arguments against linguistic integration in schools for years. The continued reliance on, and promotion of, majority/standard languages in mainstream schools, has served to establish a benchmark for success, privilege, access, and normalcy in both education and society. As a result, minoritized students, families and communities find themselves gauging the appropriateness/rightness of their own heritage languages, against the standard language of the school in particular, and society in general. This is a process that often consigns the linguistically marginalized to public silence and personal doubt. We must pay close attention to how we are constituted through language, and how meanings are constituted within linguistic systems. Otherwise, we run the risk of perpetuating "common sense" understandings of the world. That being said, it is necessary to address the question of how oppression in schooling is engendered through the promotion and use of a standard language.

Smart (1989), has asserted that the major forms of domination, as per Foucault's theory of power, are best interpreted as "hegemonic effects," transmitted through the complex of micro-power. Further, these "effects" become hegemonic through the practices, techniques and technologies of power that run through the discourse of oppression. Foucault forwards the notion of bio-politics as the "calculated management of life"; the methods in which truth discourses are employed to manage the bodies of subjects.[3] In these circumstances, discourses operate to prohibit who can know the "truth," who can speak the "truth," and what can be said about the "truth." How often have we heard the disclaimers that seek to discipline subjective accounts of oppression? — "The system is fine the way it is." "Working towards equity for some, only dilutes the system for others." — However, we should note that in legitimating oppression and the status quo, such discourses operate in multiple sites. While they work to constitute privileged understandings of the world, they similarly work to constitute oppressed and marginalized views. To clarify, the hegemonic discourses that teach the privileged to question and silence marginalized experiences and voices, are the same discourses that teach the marginalized themselves, to seek privileged approval or acceptance of their marginalized experience. In other words, we must begin to question why oppression is only acknowledged in the mainstream if accepted as such by the voice of privilege. Hegemonic discourses frame the subject in ways that encourage and suppress the "will to truth" (Gordon, 1987).

In drawing a connection between Gramsci's notion of hegemony, and Foucault's notion of discourse, we may suggest that the "power relations" transmitted via cultural hegemony are constituted through language, ideology and the subject. Oppression arises out of a historical complex designed to support hierarchy, power and privilege, while further pathologizing the marginalized. Language use in schooling is one example of how such discourses become seen as "truthful." Cultural hegemony serves to engender a very real belief in the normative/neutral nature of the standard language. That is to say, that proficiency in a standard language is rarely, if ever, associated with privilege because that linguistic facility is understood to be both natural and appropriate in a given space.

For Foucault, meanings are crucial in organizations of the self, social institutions and political practice. It was through his work that the discursive structure of subjectivity was integrated into a theoretical conception of language and social power; a reading that offers both an interpretation of experience as contextualized, and an analysis of its constitutive and governing relationship with individual subjects (Weedon, 1987, p. 126). Foucault employs the concept of discourse to address these issues. He interprets discourse as an organized complex of statements, terms, categories and beliefs structured in relation to historical, social and institutional specificities (Scott, 1988, p. 35). Discourses attempt to organize the very nature of the body, mind and emotional life of subjects. In short, working with/through social, subjective and power relations, the discursive field *constitutes* knowledge.

In constituting the lives of individual subjects, it should be noted that discourses are always relational in nature. They are subject to a variety of interconnected power relations that sustain each other; the stronger their mutual connection, the more stable their foundation. The most powerful discourses in society have firm institutional and legal bases (e.g. family, welfare, the organization of work, racism, sexism, classism, et cetera). Furthermore, the strength of its support structure is what allows a discourse to gain authority and become solidified within a "regime of truth." These discursive domains are constantly overlapping, influencing and competing with each other. Those that have a common ground will find themselves not only affiliated to one another, but they will look to each other for strength, legitimization and validation (Weedon, 1987, p. 108).

The importance of discourse for the study of oppression and for the possibility of resistance has never been more evident. It was Edward Said

(1979), in his writings on Orientalism that first drove home the degree to which European colonial culture had managed to control and constitute every social aspect and meaning attributed to the concept of the Orient. Through both implicit and explicit contrasts, the dichotomy between the Occident and the Orient was drawn and meanings were established. In this respect, we can infer that all "privileged" notions of what is proper, good and beneficial are to be understood in their relation to another repressed or negated notion. This is a powerful realization. It teaches us that any and all analyses of "meaning" must necessarily involve: a critical inquiry of the dichotomies that are operating therein; an examination of the oppositions and negations at work; and an investigation of how these meanings operate in specific contexts. The reality of the "moment" becomes a function of our ability to understand it (Scott, 1988, p. 36). But how do we understand these moments?

This notion of *difference* is a dimension of post-structural thought that has been employed in much recent feminist literature. It asserts that "oppressive" meanings are understood in their relation to an established "difference" and not due to any innate property. As binary oppositions, the primary terms are defined and ascribed "meaning" in direct relation to that which they repress. These dichotomies do not necessarily speak to, or about, the bodies upon which they act. They work to disguise the fact that instead of being oppositional, they are in fact interdependent. Therefore, if dichotomous constructs are understood to explain some of the multiple ways in which "meanings" are constituted, then an investigation into "meaning" must necessarily question the "truth claims" of oppositions, and proceed to "deconstruct"[4] them for the operations they embody and obscure.

The equality vs. difference debate that currently plagues the inclusive schooling movement is an example of how a false dichotomy might serve as a problematic for both theory and practice. Equality and difference have been placed at either ends of the educational spectrum, and we are asked to choose sides. However, upon critical analysis, the dichotomy hides the interdependent nature of both terms. Equality does not preclude difference, and difference does not negate equality. Similarly, discourses that problematize the compatibility of heritage language/cultural retention and transformative educational agendas, do so by establishing a false dichotomy between tradition and insurgency. Deconstruction works specifically to clarify the operations of "difference" within language by revealing the interdependency of these supposedly dichotomous terms as well as their contexts and historical specificities (Scott, 1988, p. 36).

As suggested by Bourdieu (see Bourdieu and Passeron, 1977), mainstream education operates under the faulty premise that if educational resources are made available to *all*, that *all* will then be able to access them equally. Within this perspective, success and failure may be attributed solely on the basis of merit, thereby obfuscating the truth of oppression while appearing consistent with liberal democratic values. Such ideological discourse operates in conjunction with the sheer volume of time that children are forced (by law) to spend in schools, (i.e., six to eight hours a day, five days a week, for between eight and 13 years). The result, according to Althusser, is an educational system that basically amounts to a process of indoctrination in which students are assaulted with ruling ideologies and then "spit out" to take their role within the relations of production (Althusser, 1971, pp. 154-6).

With respect to linguicism in schooling, the use of a standard language variety in any educational site, is tantamount to legitimizing and validating that language relative to, and above all other linguistic forms practiced in the school. That standard language is employed as the normative model against which all other linguistic forms are compared (Bordieu, 1981). Traditionally, within mainstream schooling, attention to the needs of linguistic minorities has been expressed through the promotion of "special education" curricula (e.g. ESL classes), or it has been overlooked altogether. Both policy and practice suggest that the validation of non-standard languages is perceived to be a peripheral concern to the main agenda of schooling. The resulting power dynamic supports the muting or negation of any cultural/linguistic capital that minoritized people might bring to their schooling experience. Further, it establishes a very powerful language/ discourse that speaks through the marginalized.

Actually, the meanings that are constituted through this system, have a profound effect on both the "privileged" and the "marginalized." The forms of power and meaning that develop in and through these micro levels are the very relations of power that make a coercive discursive model of power even possible. In other words, it is through the complex of micro-powers that we discipline, and through which we are disciplined, (Sawicki, 1991, p. 20). Foucault is clear in his assertion that unlike large scale coercive models, the micro-levels of power are both ever-present and inescapable in that they are not articulated in any single point, rather, they are always expressed in multiple locations. These power relations are part and parcel of the hidden curriculum of schooling; an agenda that is informed and supported through misconceptions, prejudice and false dichotomies (e.g. stereotypes, the pathologizing of minoritized families, et cetera). Whether or not we are in the physical presence of our oppressor, oppressive discourses "teach" us. Through this "subjectivity," the oppressed "become" sites through which discourses travel. So our very concept of self is both informed and constructed by discourse. Moreover, we do not only constitute ourselves "relative" to the positions that are made available to us. Rather, we take ourselves up "as if we are" the positions that discourses and "moments" make available to us. That is why it is so important that we subvert/alter the discourses, meanings, and positions that always seek to frame us.

In the narratives generated through this study, the problem of disengagement from schooling is shown clearly as a point of contention for students, families and communities. A theme that arose repeatedly with respect to that sense of disengagement was the absence or negation of linguistic inclusion in schooling. We have sought thus far in this chapter to establish a theoretical framework through which this sense of disengagement might be better understood in relation to language exclusion and the power dynamics at work. The narratives in this study spoke specifically to the challenges faced by new immigrants and racially minoritized peoples; our focus in this chapter reflects that distinction. That is not to say that we do not recognize the importance of addressing other oppressions linked to language. The general silence with respect to issues of gender and sexuality are problems with which we are trying to negotiate. The politics that surround these silences need to be taken up and brought into specific relief. However, such a project is beyond the scope of this work. The narratives in this study suggest that there is a severity of linguistic issues for certain bodies. We have to recognize the special needs of these groups without creating false dichotomies that engender problematic hierarchies of oppression.

That being said, in the process of racialization, ethnicity, culture and other perceived "differences" may be used along with race as a way to marginalize. So in re-evaluating the propriety of mono-lingualism in schooling, and establishing a case for language integration, it follows that we must first address issues of "space" and "place" in relation to identity.

LANGUAGE, IDENTITY AND THE NEED
FOR INTEGRATIVE PRACTICES IN SCHOOLING

In 1963, the rise of Quebec nationalism and the separatist movement compelled the federal government to establish the Royal Commission on Bilingualism and Biculturalism. The purpose of the commission was twofold: to analyze and report on the realities of Canada as a bilingual and bicultural nation; and to develop policy and practice whereby Canada could be further developed on the basis of a partnership between the two "core" groups. In time, however, and with much pressure from "other" ethnic groups, a policy of "multiculturalism within a bilingual framework" was established in Canada in 1971. This approach took the stance that Canada was a nation with no official cultural affiliation (no ethnicity or ethnic group was to take precedence over another), but there were to be two official languages (Cummins and Danesi, 1990, p. 23).

The B and B Commission was clear in its report that linguistic diversity would only benefit Canadian society, and that educators should explore methods of promoting and developing these heritage language skills in the classroom. Interestingly, however, these recommendations were never effectively acted upon through multicultural policy, and heritage language teaching has only begun to expand over the past decade (Cummins and Danesi, 1990, pp. 24-5). The dilemma that exists for minoritized ethnics in Canada is that culture without language relegates multiculturalism to a type of window-dressing policy as displayed in ethnic parades, public celebrations and the "sari, samosa, and tin-drum syndrome." There are a number of persistent ambiguities that exist within the letter and practice of multicultural policy. Of utmost importance is the relative disregard displayed by the educational system with respect to objective identity factors (e.g. heritage languages) and the significant role they play in the survival of ethnic groups in Canada.

As these groups are transformed from traditional extended family communities into urban groups with little to no cohesion, many of Canada's ethnic populations are finding that their "sacred canopies"[5] are undergoing a massive metamorphosis. This is a considerable cause for concern. Research has shown that positive ethnic identity contributes to a strong sense of self, and a greater sense of responsibility to towards community and society (see, Breton et al., 1990; Driedger, 1979, 1996; Isajiw, 1974; and Isajiw, Sev'er, Driedger, 1993).

A review of the literature suggests that there are numerous sociological and psychological factors associated with ethnic identity retention and patterns of ethnicity that develop among minoritized groups. Driedger (1989) suggests that these factors can be best understood in terms of their relationships to three sociocultural forms of identification (territory, institutions, and culture), and three interactionist forms of identification (history, ideology and leadership). Each set of macro and micro forms of identification are interwoven, and serve to strengthen and reinforce each other. In the macro sociocultural interplay, territory acts as a crucible in which ethnic institutions are constructed, and where ethnic culture is sustained. In the micro symbolic-interactionist framework, historical symbols and ideologies are seen as the means through which leaders can establish a sense of ethnic *Gemeinschaft*. These theoretical perspectives constitute a structural-symbolic continuum within which the foundations of identity maintenance are encapsulated (Driedger, 1989, pp. 143-7). As mentioned above, these interconnected factors are integral to the maintenance of ethnic group boundaries (Isajiw, 1974; Breton et al., 1990; Gans, 1994; Edwards and Dourcette, 1987; Driedger, 1996), so we must begin to question multicultural policies that establish initiatives based on symbolic criteria alone. A positive self-concept is crucial for minoritized students if they are to find a sense of place in the mainstream. A positive sense of ethnic identity provides students with a connection and tie to something of importance. Community, culture, heritage and history act in this respect to bolster a child's sense of belonging, validation and importance. So bearing these factors in mind, we should question whether the promotion of subjective ethnic identity retention in and of itself, is enough to encourage that sense of community. The promotion of a happy healthy student body requires that all youth share a sense of space and place within the school.[6]

As minoritized ethnics find themselves being assimilated or acculturated into a core/dominant group, the cultural features that signal their ethnic boundaries may begin to shift. However, while the cultural characteristics and organizational forms of an ethnic group may evolve, a continuing dichotomy between members and outsiders must be retained to some degree if ethnic continuity and identity are to survive (Isajiw, 1974, p. 115). Now, while the saliency of skin colour must be taken into account when we speak of the degree to which certain groups may be absorbed by the dominant group, identity, as a social-psychological aspect of human growth cannot be based upon skin colour alone. One need only look at the dilemmas that plague communities of colour today to see that issues of ethnic identity decline signal a trend towards an ever increasing sense of inadequacy and anomie[7] among racially minoritized youth.

Barth (1969) suggests that beyond a continued sense of group belonging (sustainable through a symbolic or emotional connection to heritage, culture and history), there are no objective components necessary for the continuance of ethnic identity. It is a definition that is particularly applicable to immigrant communities in flux (Edwards, 1987, p. 57). However, this definition of ethnicity differs from others in that it specifically allows for the interpretation of "ethnicity in transition"; that unstable stage of ethnicity that Bhabha calls the "beyond" in reference to the marginalized immigrant generations living in both cultures but belonging in neither:

> The beyond is neither a new horizon, nor a leaving behind of the past ... Beginnings and endings may be the sustaining myths of the middle years ... we find ourselves in the moment of transit where space and time cross to produce complex figures of difference and identity, past and present, inside and outside, inclusion and exclusion (Bhabha, 1994, p. 1).

Rigid definitions of ethnicity and culture cannot encompass the transitory, evolutionary nature of human interrelations as they exist today. With respect to this conception of ethnicity, Isajiw proposes that identity maintenance over generations may be attributed to a form of ethnic re-discovery, or in other words, the development of a symbolic relation to the culture of one's ancestors. He asserts that items from a cultural past such as folk art, music and even literature can develop into symbols of ethnic identity. Isajiw goes on to note that this symbolic rediscovery is not without direction as individuals appear to select which elements of the cultural past are kept and which are discarded or disregarded. He asserts that this selection process appears to dispense with some of the "excess baggage" of ethnic tradition while retaining those items that correspond to immediate or future needs in the context of the society as a whole (Isajiw, 1974, p. 121). However, one must question why certain aspects of ethnicity are considered to be "excess baggage" while others are not.

Isajiw and Edwards in their discussions of ethnic identity, assert that symbolic ethnicity, in its non-obtrusive and private nature, may come to anchor minoritized peoples in their culture and heritage because ethnic identity can thereby be maintained indefinitely and at little cost. This interpretation, however, does not look at the reality of ethnic degradation and decline. An ethnic group that devalues or minimizes the importance of culture, tradition and ritual within its ethnic milieu, relegates its sense of ethnicity and we-ness to a type of residual ethnicity. Importantly, we must note the language used in reference to ethnicity ("cost," "excess baggage," "future needs"), and the difficulties that arise when certain qualities of ethnicity and ethnic identity are deemed to be more "valuable" than others in the context of a privileged/dominant orthodoxy. This picking and choosing of ethnic symbols may result in new hybrid cultural forms, and it may support ethnic identification to a degree, but is it a realistic basis for the retention of ethnic identity?

To suggest that any one facet of ethnicity is more valuable than another based on its economic viability, or on its non-obtrusive nature, is to relegate the purpose of ethnic identity retention to the confines of an assimilationist project grounded in privileged values and norms. The questions remain: Excess baggage based on what criteria? Non-obtrusive to whom? These value sets are expressed most clearly through an interpretation of language as discourse. The words we use, and the ways in which they are employed do more than simply identify or describe who we are, they make distinctions and construct our identities. By promoting symbolic surface-level endorsements of culture, while avoiding practices that work towards real social change, the smoke screen of multiculturalism allows us to side-step these problematics as they exist in racial and ethnic communities (Karumanchery, 1996).

In this chapter, we focus on issues of linguistic integration because language, as a subset of cultural identification, stands as one of the strongest support structures of ethnic identity. If language, culture and other such identity factors could be integrated into mainstream education, the Eurocentric model of schooling practiced today would shift towards an inclusive environment where minoritized students could develop a sense of space, place and belonging within their schools. Traditionally educators are enthusiastic when home and community initiatives work to promote heritage languages, but they are often reticent when similar programs are discussed within a mainstream frame. It should be noted that our present educational structures do little to assist the generations of students, parents[8] and communities that are fighting desperately to retain ties to heritage, culture and people-hood while attempting to access and succeed within the larger society. Language barriers are some of the first and most important obstacles to access and success faced by minoritized people — but how do we define success? Do we cling to white middle-class notions of success as based in quantitative achievement and economic viability, or do we adapt a new definition of success that involves the promotion of social responsibility, self-esteem and a co-operative environment in schooling. (See Chapter Six.)

In a Canadian context, some English language forms have become more admired, marketed and employed as the variety to be learned. To speak of history and power relations in this context is to speak of the processes through which certain identities and ways of knowing have become linked to language and academic achievement. So fundamentally, the question to be asked here is: what role can schools play in the "centring" of previously marginalized voices? Language is a marker of inclusivity. As such, the primary frame of our approach must be to: a) validate, promote and centre multiple languages within schooling; while b) creating an interplay between home and school, a dialogue that will provide home and community with the tools to promote academic, personal and spiritual success for their youth.

Ethnic identity should be understood to extend beyond the mere existence of a joint history and culture, it also extends to one's sense of belonging and place within that ethnic framework. In this respect, the structures and agenda of mainstream schooling today do not work to establish a sense of place within the space of schooling. Rather, generations of minoritized youth learn throughout their school experience that certain cultures, languages and histories are to be valued more highly than others. These daily lessons will have an enormous impact upon what they value and with what they choose to identify. Language integration, as a domain of inclusive schooling, would work against the alienation, anomie and disengagement suffered by racially and ethnically minoritized youth within conventional school systems.

The importance of incorporating "language integration" within schooling does not stop at the level of linguistics alone. It is not enough that students acquire language skills that will allow them to interact and function in society (economically, socially, et cetera). Rather, as language drives human interaction, it is imperative that students learn to communicate on linguistic and interpersonal levels with society in general and their own ethnic communities specifically. With respect to ethnically and racially minoritized youth, the present lack of linguistic integration in schooling will often bolster already existing problems of identity, space and place. A connective concern arises in relation to the realities of generational decline in ethnicity and ethnic identity. Language integration, as a domain of inclusive schooling, is seen not only with respect to how ESL programs facilitate English skills development among students, but also the extent to which schools validate students' first languages, promote first language learning, and work towards parent/community partnerships.

FIRST LANGUAGE INTEGRATION

> ... for the young person, what happens is that if the society and the school and the curriculum cannot, at some point in time, validate the value and the significance and the importance of that culture that the child comes from, and if this cannot be validated either through history class or through the geography class or through something, then what happens is that the child begins to feel that to belong, she or he has got to be like all the kids in the school and all the other environment, you know ... and to belong, mom should be baking apple pie, you know, not the Portuguese pastries ... and to belong, dad should be watching baseball, not necessarily the Portuguese soccer. (Wendy)

Wendy, a volunteer/organizer at the Portuguese Interagency Network, asserts that these types of binary oppositions are extremely problematic for students as they struggle to determine what is right and wrong, what is good and bad. Within the multilingual vs. monolingual debate in schooling we see how "difference" is played out in the binary opposition that hides the interdependent nature of both terms: linguistic plurality does not need to be "set up" as detrimental to the educational access of standard language speakers. However, should we not also be concerned with educational access for linguistic minorities? When linguistic resources and "capital" are made unavailable, the result will invariably be detrimental to students, family and community alike. In a system that normalizes Western culture, differences, whether linguistic, racial or cultural, often become the impetus for ridicule, and mistreatment. The promotion and utilization of heritage languages in mainstream schooling is one of the more innovative ways in which schools can combat these forms of racism and negative representation while promoting success for all students.

Venisa, a seventeen-year-old student of Jamaican background who learned Patois from interacting with her parents, contends that heritage languages can be utilized to fight and eliminate the negative stereotypes that are associated with speakers of non-European languages. She asserts that, as a good student who speaks Patois, she acts as a counter-representation to the negative imagery and representations that are linked to being Jamaican in the popular media.

I like to speak Patois and to show people or let people see me as a good person, but speaking Patois and having Jamaican background, people will see that not all Jamaicans are like what the media tells them. Even though I was born in Canada, I still hang on to that Jamaican identity.

The social-psychological dilemmas faced by minoritized youth are a clear manifestation of the dichotomy that exists between the linguistics and culture of home and school. When a student's sense of belonging is compromised, such that she feels the need to prove the worth of her ethnicity or race, or when a child assimilates in order to be accepted or tolerated by those with privilege, one must question the state of that child's sense of identity, her sense of self-worth and sense of place within the school. The danger that arises herein is that silence, exclusion, and inferiority will often lead to a process of disengagement from school. Issues of voice and inclusion are integral to the education of minority youth, and as language is a fundamental component to identity and a sense of belonging, language integration as a strategy is one method by which many of these issues may be addressed. Given the present state of education, it is not difficult to understand how ethnic identity, or identity in general might be negatively effected or muted in schooling today. However, unlike Venisa, several of the students interviewed employed their heritage languages in school, not in defense of who they are, but because of who they are. That is to say that, in a number of interviews, students found that heritage language acted as a powerful mediator between themselves and their ethnic community. Case in point, Ravi, a fourteen-year-old boy attending the Milliken Mills Saturday School, speaks about how language helps him to retain a sense of his identity:

My first language is English ... I speak English except with [a Guyanese] accent ... I still have it, I don't want to lose it.

Ravi immigrated at the age of 11 and began attending the program soon after his arrival. He suggests that his involvement in the program has helped him to sustain a sense of ethnic identity and pride, a fact that is supported by his desire to keep his accent as a symbol of his Guyanese heritage. All people have a self-image or self-identification, a way of locating themselves socially. The image may consist of personality attributes, status characteristics or any number of qualities. In relation to ethnicity/race/culture/gender or any number of social groupings, that image develops as negative or positive. Research suggests that people need to have a firm sense of identification with their ethnic heritage and culture if they are to establish a secure sense of self, personhood and community (Driedger, 1989, p. 145).

As mentioned before, several factors will tend to interact in the development of that identity and that sense of self. Mashi, an eighteen-year-old girl who identifies her origins with Ethiopia even though she was born and raised in Montreal, asserts the importance of ties to heritage languages and the related connections to culture. Her ability to speak and understand her heritage language (Amharic) not only gives her a strong tie to her ethnicity, but it increases her ability to see the importance of that connection relative to the "larger picture" of schooling.

> I have to say that I would like schools to talk more about our history. For example, I live in a Portuguese neighbourhood and I have grown up in a white community and don't really have much understanding of my ancestry or my heritage, and in that sense I would like schools to have more of a broad subject [base] ... not like Black history month. Just to have a month dedicated to Black people isn't quite enough, specially for students like myself who are born in Canada ... I am more aware of my history and my background and it just boosts my self-esteem. I have something to be proud of instead of the negative aspects I see on the news and stuff like that.

For some, like Mashi, ethnic identity not only strengthens a sense of self, but it also helps students to assess or reassess the difficulties of mainstream schooling relative to the muting of certain voices and knowledges.

Among the more progressive educational practices that promote language integration within schools and communities are those strategies that validate students' first languages and provide support mechanisms to facilitate the development of first language skills. Fernando, a teacher of 28 years from a Portuguese school, explained that, in the beginning, the Portuguese community used to teach math, science, geography and a host of other subjects. However, issues of cultural decline within their youth necessitated that educators focus their time and efforts on teaching Portuguese history, culture and language:

> The Portuguese saw the necessity for opening the school. They saw that they were losing communication with their children, the children were losing their language or couldn't communicate. What I see here at the school is that at the beginning, the Portuguese wanted that link with the Portuguese homeland. They were afraid of [getting] to a degree that they [couldn't] communicate with their children, and vice versa. Parents also go to their homeland almost every year, and they didn't want their children to go there and they only speak English and couldn't communicate with their families there. There is also an interesting phenomenon too … the Father goes to work and the mother goes to work, so they call their grandmother to care for the children. So, if the grandmother couldn't communicate with their children … so it was very important. (Fernando)

The promotion of heritage languages is not a responsibility that belongs solely to the educational system as a whole or to schools specifically. It is also important that families and communities work to ensure that their children do not lose their language. Tammy, a Chinese-Canadian mother of two, spoke about the importance of supporting heritage languages and culture along with mainstream education:

> It's a pretty hard job … after work I have to sit with them to make sure they learn something from school and get the education … they take Mandarin classes, and they have Cantonese heritage on Saturday mornings.

The importance of integrating heritage languages into the mainstream goes beyond the need to support and sustain ethnic identity, and beyond the need to sustain intergenerational ties. In our interviews with Chinese-Canadian parents and community workers, a common thematic developed with respect to the problems faced by newly immigrating Chinese children. Many parents identified Mandarin or Cantonese as the language spoken most commonly at home. In contrast, English was the language of instruction used at school. It became clear that the Chinese community was/is engaged in an ongoing struggle for access. Many of the parents interviewed would make particular note of the linguistic difficulties and resulting academic struggles that Chinese students would face upon immigration. In fact, in order to combat these obvious linguistic barriers, parents would usually send their children to Chinese language classes shortly upon their arrival to the country. Tammy relates how her children struggled in school when they first arrived in Canada, and how they rarely felt comfortable asking questions of their teachers because they were afraid to speak English. With reference to the Chinese community in general, she had this to say:

> I think what I hear when they go to school, where the majority is Chinese, their language is not that good because they're used to speaking their native language instead of English. But it's okay. I think. It's good to learn both languages.

Within mainstream schooling, heritage languages have been traditionally neglected and all but prohibited within the curriculum. Drawing parallels between English language fluency and economic/social mobility, schools spend a great deal of time promoting English facility while disregarding knowledges that students bring with them. The political ramifications of this "silent" policy against heritage languages cannot be overlooked as language has almost become an indicator of status and economic privilege. We must ask ourselves why it is that privileged students are encouraged to take up new languages while others are encouraged to abandon their heritage languages in favour of English. We cannot dismiss the realities of this practice, as they speak to the political atmosphere in which our children are educated. How did the dichotomy between English and heritage languages emerge as a "norm of truth"? What does this process tell us about how power is constituted, and how it operates within the system?

In an effort to confront the existing policies toward heritage languages, many of the communities in this study have established formal educational sites for their youth. Also, along with these formal sites (i.e., programs such as the Milliken Mills Saturday School), there are informal methods of instruction that should not be overlooked. One such aspect of informal education takes place in the home through normal everyday interactions. For example, Abate, an Ethiopian-Canadian father of two, teaches Amharic (the Ethiopian national language) to his children through verbal communication during meals, gatherings, and normal day-to-day conversation. It is important to note, that while such informal home schooling is fundamental to the development of heritage language competence, it is equally crucial that schools and formal educational sites do their part as well. In those situations where youth are able to access heritage languages only in specific spaces (i.e., home *or* school), it is not uncommon to see the development of a hybrid bilingualism among second generation ethnics where in-group language is understood but not effectively utilized in writing or speech.

Linguistic integration within formal educational sites must take into account both the immediate and long-term consequences of linguistic exclusion for students who do not speak the majority language of their school. Iman, a Somali-Canadian mother of two, spoke about the perils that exist for the Muslim community in relation to language and inclusivity in the curriculum:

> Well, the school system ... they talked about concentrating on music ... well, I wasn't comfortable with that ... Christmas is coming up. I wouldn't be comfortable with my [children] singing Christmas [carols] and all that because, of course, we are Muslims, we don't do that. So it is very difficult because my son is in class and the whole class is learning how to sing a Christmas [carol]. The teacher said, "... if you were to tell your son to go, take him somewhere ... We have to have a teacher for him to do another activity and of course we don't have money for that. What do I do, send your son home? Of course I can't do that ..."

The respondent's narrative further reminds us that while educators seek ways to build language competence in English, they must be wary not to ignore diversity. One school that we looked at recently offered Cantonese as an optional subject, and some of the teachers tried to strike a balance between enforcing the speaking of English and allowing students to work in their own linguistic groups for certain activities.

Examples of Best Practices of First Language Integration

- School choirs performing songs in different languages
- The Bilingual Book Project: a project whereby a school acquires books in various languages so that non-English speaking parents can read to their children in their first language. This supports the philosophy that literacy is literacy in any language.
- Creating Bilingual Books: In one school, grade four students were writing short story books in both English and their first language with their parent's help. And parents were invited to a presentation where the books were read by the students.
- "Reading Buddies" with Bilingual Books: A corollary to the "Creating Bilingual Books" project. Grade four students were paired with Kindergarten students from the same ethnocultural/linguistic background to read the stories they had written in both English and their first language.
- Further, some schools go so far as to actually bind these stories and have them placed in the library for circulation.

Case Study: The Milliken Mills Saturday School

This program is not a true example of formalized first language integration as it takes place on weekends, when the mainstream school is out of session. However, it is a fine example of how heritage languages and cultural knowledges can be worked into a system of schooling. Following many of the paradigms of inclusive education and Afrocentric schooling, the Milliken Mills Saturday School, an African-Canadian community based organization, was designed to promote youth success in school. By drawing on the domains of linguistic integration, representation, and family/community partnership, the Milliken Mills Saturday School worked to create a centre for students that will provide a source of strength and cultural capital when they are in the mainstream system.

As a Saturday School occupying space within a mainstream institution, the visual representation of African culture at the Milliken Program was limited. However, while participants of the program found the visual aspects of culture to be somewhat lacking, they did assert that culture, heritage and history were very much represented in other less obvious ways. While tutorial programs act as the main instrument through which the Milliken Mills Saturday School supports and promotes student achievement, other devices are employed as well. One such device is the group pledge that is taken by parents, youth and program leaders alike at the beginning of each session ...

> Today I pledge to be the best possible me I can be ... no matter how good we are. Today I pledge to listen to the beat of our drummer who leads us onward to the rewards of tomorrow. Today, I pledge to reach new goals, new challenges and new horizons.

While visual representations serve as an outward indicator of dedication to cultural knowledges, knowledge representation in the form of the pledge or other such tools (i.e., guest speakers, cultural celebrations) explore those linkages more deeply. Within the symbolism of the pledge is displayed a commitment to Afrocentric values of community and co-operation, social responsibility and justice ... a new way of approaching education that is neither hierarchical, individualistic nor antagonistic, but rather, spiritual and mutually beneficial to students, teachers and the community. Shania, a Jamaican-Canadian mother of three, said:

> I like what I see, I like what I hear, I like the way it started out with a pledge. I like the idea that my children can identify with the teachers and their fellow students on a cultural and ethnic area.

In this program, the integration of cultural linguistics is understood as more than the use of heritage languages alone. Linguistic integration is understood to reflect not only the spoken language of a community, but also the intangible more elusive qualities that shape its culture. Culturally-specific programming such as this are some examples of a holistic approach to inclusive schooling. Focusing on what a school is doing rather than on student deficiencies is an exemplary method of creating inclusive schooling. These types of strategies not only increase student ties to heritage, culture and community, they also validate the student's linguistic culture while building on her/his self-esteem.

Case Study: The Ambassador Program

Whenever a new student came to School B, an elementary/intermediate school, she or he was paired up with someone from her or his class who was of the same racial/ethnocultural background and who spoke the same heritage language. In devising the program, students had input on deciding what was necessary for new students to know about the school. They were also involved in the preparation of a booklet, which Ambassadors used to introduce new students to the school's environment and activities (e.g. photos of school sites and where they are located, et cetera). In addition, the student council (also representative of the diverse racial backgrounds of the student body) developed the idea of a school welcome bag for new students. In the welcome bag are a school planner, school pen, and food coupon. Many of the students interviewed seemed to be proud of the Ambassador Program:

> Ambassador is the name for [the program] because that's what you are; it's something special among students; you get chosen in class to be Ambassadors, and like, whenever a new student comes, in a class or another classroom, we show them around .... (Ebrim)

> ... if there's somebody in the school who is of that race and they understand the language, they will get that person to show them around the school ... invite them to be friends with them, they'll show them around, and stuff like that; introduce them to others, to things, activities around the school. (Alex)

The Ambassador Program is also a good example of co-operative education in that it provides students with an opportunity to identify their own abilities and work toward a common goal with other students.

Case Study: MENTORS — The Muslim Education Network, Training and Outreach Service

Abdul Rahman, a volunteer at the MENTORS program, spoke about some of the initiatives taken to integrate cultural and linguistic aspects of Islam into the mainstream:

> [We will] go into the school system and do research into what kinds of literature are available in the library system of the schools. If we find books that are inappropriate, we will move them, and then provide the schools with the appropriate literature in the area of Islam. [Also] we will be able to help teachers through workshops, to be [more] knowledgeable about Islam, and how to present Islam in a non-Islamic class or even to children who are Muslims.

So we help the schools through workshops to see the alternatives we can provide, such as Quranic recital, or song without guitar or piano. Ask, for example, the child to do some research on these recitals and present it to the class, but also meeting the requirements that are already stated within the curriculum.

Another area is to provide Islamic education to the Muslims themselves. We would like parents particularly [to] come out and participate in these activities and be role models to the children. Some of our youth are so embarrassed to be identified as Muslims, so if you have the visible presence of parents and Muslims in the school system, participating actively in the activities, then the children will feel comfortable to identify themselves as Muslims.

The work of Abdul Rahman and MENTORS attempts to bridge the gap between language integration, diverse knowledges and community involvement in education. By advocating for the inclusion of Quranic recitals in Arabic, and traditional a cappella singing, MENTORS was creating a space for non-standard language and oral communication styles within the mainstream system. This is an example of how diverse styles of communication can be integrated into the everyday experience of schooling. The use of such non-European traditions creates a more culturally and linguistically diverse centre within mainstream educational discourse and praxis.

ENGLISH SKILLS DEVELOPMENT

For minoritized youth, English language facility is another important aspect of the "cultural capital" required if they are to succeed in education. The assertion that weak English language facility is often a basis for differential treatment in schooling is a theme that arose in several interviews. With respect to language barriers, one student found that:

… kids who could speak English well have a better chance to succeed, they have less barriers because the teachers will ignore the kids who may not sound like them and pay attention to the other kids. (Orin)

There is a large body of research that suggests educators need not hold any particular malice for systematically inequitable outcomes to be realized. However, a critical investigation of this polemic reveals that we cannot escape the reality that "schooling" is geared towards engaging some students, while disengaging others (Dei and Razack, 1995, p. 180). In their 1994 study, Cummins, Feuerverger and Lopes addressed the considerable frustrations that ESL teachers expressed with respect to their efforts at implementing a collaborative model with mainstream classroom teachers. One teacher asserted that:

> It is difficult to provide support for classroom teachers who do not understand or believe in the need to modify programs for their ESL students. We don't seem to have the support of our administration to help us connect! (Cummins et al., 1994, p. 10)

At present, ESL classrooms are generally not bilingual in nature. A bilingual classroom would necessitate that both languages are equally practised and promoted; this is not the case in general ESL classrooms. In fact, while it is not uncommon for an ESL classroom to have an aid who speaks one or more languages, thus allowing her/him to translate and explain concepts in certain instances, this does not make a class bilingual or multilingual. What these types of classes do is help establish a working knowledge of English that the student will be able to employ in school. Unfortunately, while these children are working to succeed within this model, they are all too often forced to deteriorate in other subjects because they cannot yet communicate in the language of instruction (Nieto, 1996, p. 191).

Of utmost importance in the delivery of English skills is an understanding by educators that they are all ESL teachers, and that the integration of student/community knowledges is a fundamental aspect of an inclusive school. This commitment to understanding how students conceptualize and communicate is basic to any ESL program. For mainstream educators to develop a student's English skills without also detracting from their progress in other subjects, schools must work to establish classrooms that do not separate languages into different programs. This would suggest that the language of instruction is not the crucial element in reversing student failure. In fact, the key element in halting student failure would be a move from educators and administrators alike towards reversing the institutionalized racism of schools in particular and society in general.

Furthermore, unless bilingual education becomes anti-racist education, we will simply be placing a sugar-coating over the reality of sustained discriminatory structures in schooling (Nieto, 1996, p. 191).

Establishing classrooms in which students may learn in both English and in their heritage languages acknowledges where students are coming from in terms of language and knowledge. It also allows teachers to provide validation and in turn empowerment for ESL students. This type of strategy endorses their first language within the classroom, and it acknowledges the set structures that exist in both languages. Inclusive classrooms work to bridge differences, identify similarities and legitimate the knowledges and language of students. These practices become even more important and empowering for ESL students when they occur within an integrated classroom where their languages and cultures are recognized and validated within the context of the broader school system.

Presently, there are numerous ESL initiatives being undertaken within both schools and communities. While there are always concerns as to the availability of resources and the effectiveness of any given program, in discussing these initiatives, Grace, a community liaison councillor in the Chinese community, expressed a certain degree of confidence in the resources that are presently available:

> [W]e have the ESL upgrading program, for those students who have very little English and lots of gaps in their education, and yet they do have the potential to learn. We also have the booster program which is mainly for the kids who are English speaking. But there are educational gaps in their background and we try to boost these kids up to the level where they can handle mainstream homework. Right now, I think they have eleven classes.... I don't have the most accurate numbers, but we have three or four schools doing upgrading and another six or seven schools are doing the booster programs. We also have the high school booster programs, which eventually help the kids get into mainstream programs.

> [T]here are a lot of parents who are saying I don't have English, I don't know how to help this child at school. It's not like before where the kids come home with the homework book and if the parents have any queries they can phone up the teachers and ask "what's going on." Right now because of the language barriers

they can't do that, so all we can do right now is encourage them to use some of the community agencies. Don't say that you don't speak English so that you're totally outside of the school system … that's why the community agencies are setting up tutoring programs after school. Obviously the South Asians have done that, Tropicana has done that. The Chinese community has lots of tutoring programs, but they are paid programs, but this is one of the communities that are fairly well established and financially that is not a problem for them. So lots of Chinese parents are buying these services outside of the school system.

The tendency of referring to all minoritized communities as being bound by similar experiences of linguicism, cultural boundaries and racism would belie the truth of intersecting oppression. When speaking of the opportunities available to those requiring English skills development, an explicit connection has to be made between education and social class. Connections were made between educational resources and social class throughout the narratives, particularly those in the Chinese community. When asked about ESD resources for the Chinese community, Grace implicated issues of class:

[T]hey have their own private locations. And they advertise, and people shop around and see what they can get, what's the best deal they can get, and they're usually not just for English, but they incorporate math and the computer science stuff like that. In the higher grades, they even have programs that are geared to OAC programs. They really help the kids to understand the concepts in English, math, things like that. So they have some of them that are very specialised programs, not just general tutoring programs. But again they are all paid programs, obviously some other communities are not as fortunate that they have to rely on some of the free programs that the communities are providing. Though some agencies have set up Saturday morning programs and things like that to help the parents. [With respect to parents who can't afford the paid programs] Well, definitely if they are free programs they will send their kids there. But the Chinese parents, as I pointed out, they are very concerned about education. They always want to shop for the best for the kids so they want quality, so they figure

that if they pay for a program, they get quality, so if you're talking
about a volunteer program, yes they may come one day and then
next week the volunteer can't come, then you know there's a gap
there. So ... I have families who can't come up with any money at
all [so] we have to go to agencies. We do have a Chinese agency
right now that has quite a number of volunteers helping those kids
on a one-to-one basis, so I just have to arrange that you know
there are some out there who are in agencies. I have arranged for
some high school students — they have university students there
doing volunteer work — and then we pair them up with a high
school student who cannot afford to pay any tutoring fee. And we
try and arrange their meetings after school, and the university
volunteer student will come over and help, right in their own home.

Examples of Best Practices of English Skills Development

• ESL literacy programs for students who have not had formal schooling
  or who have had interrupted schooling.
• Psycho-educational consultants for ESL students.
• Children's aid reading programs that support those students who require
  more extensive support.

PARENT AND COMMUNITY PARTNERSHIPS

In many of the interviews, one theme in particular resurfaced time and time
again; there was a consistent perception that a division existed between
generations and between home and school. As alluded to earlier, these
perceived divisions are directly related to the social/psychological dilemmas
that minoritized students face as they attempt to fit-in/succeed within
mainstream schooling. As the language, culture and environment of home
becomes perceived as dichotomous to those of school and society, divisions
begin to develop between generations within households and communities.
Wendy, one of the organizers of a Portuguese community group noted that
it was not uncommon to find grandparents and sometimes parents who
could not communicate and/or interact with their own grandchildren and
children:

… so psychologically what happens to the child is that the child starts to move herself or himself more and more and more, from his home situation. So, that's one aspect of it, the other aspect is that the parents feel the opposite. They feel that they begin to lose touch with the kid and for a Portuguese family, like I would imagine for a lot of the other cultures, because of the nature of the extended relationship between grandparents and aunts and uncles, it becomes really, really traumatizing for these people, because it gets to a point where they cease to be able to communicate with their own people.

These concerns should be addressed in both formal and informal educational sites. The same scenario is relevant with respect to the experiences of parents within our present structure of schooling. Language integration also requires that schools work to motivate and include parents in the business of schooling because language often acts as a barrier to parental involvement in education. The implications of these language barriers are that non-English speaking parents are greatly deterred from participating and engaging in the delivery of their children's education. There are several dynamics that develop in relation to these types of language barriers. First, establishing a dialogue with teachers is often difficult for non-English speaking parents, and standard educational policy/practice is relatively non-progressive when it comes to encouraging participation from such parents. Second, parents who are not fluent in English will find it difficult to act as advocates for their children within the system. Third, parents without English facility will find it difficult to take part in their children's academic education at home. Fourth, parents who are functionally illiterate in their own heritage languages will find double barriers to participation in their children's schooling. And fifth, economic constraints contribute to push some non-English speaking parents out of the educational arena altogether. It is important to view these factors as interacting and intersecting barriers to the delivery of education for non-English speakers.

Natalie, one of the organizers of a Chinese Parent's Association, discussed the barriers that exist within the Chinese community with respect to parental involvement in schooling:

From the Chinese parents' point of view, maybe the language is one of the barriers, because when you can't talk to the teacher, you're often withholding your discussion. And also, it's the culture barriers as well. For a lot of the parents who came out of the country, parent[al] involvement is very new to them. My parents were never encouraged to participate in any school decision making. So it's difficult for them because you don't know where to begin.

Wendy also spoke of her understandings about the lack of parental participation from within the Portuguese community, and how in her opinion these participatory deficiencies were directly related to the traditionally formal relationships that parents have with school structures in Portugal.

And also there isn't a background of culture of where they come from to get involved in the system. Because back-home traditionally you left school to the teachers. And so if they still believe that that's the case, they don't see [themselves] as really having the power to be involved, to have a say, you know, so all of those things are playing out, all of these different determinants, variables coming together, it causes a lot of problems.

Iman echoed these cultural barriers when speaking about the troubles that exist for the Muslim community:

I think the Muslim community has just realized the importance of being involved in school because what they thought was, you know, we send our children to school and the teachers will do their work, and that is it. When they come home, they don't have to do what they do in school. But now, they realize the importance of them being involved to help the child be comfortable in school, and also, they know how the system works ... This is a different country. It is not like back home. So it is a whole new world to them.

When asked about barriers to parental involvement in schooling, Stephanie, a Jamaican-Canadian mother of two, pointed to language barriers as a fundamental problem for many first generation parents:

I think for some parents it's probably ... some parents are intimidated. They're afraid to go in. Some of them might [have] a language barrier. I know where my son goes to school, 95 percent of the school [are minorities] ... a large number of Chinese, and you know, English is not their first language. They just don't feel like they can go.

These language barriers carry very serious consequences for non-English speaking parents in that they directly deter parental involvement in educational sites. Natalie also identifies the interaction between identity factors when she notes that language issues cannot be divorced from issues of culture, tradition and history. It follows that this lack of participation can be related closely to the educational outcomes of language minority students, and newly arriving immigrants. Cultural barriers that prevent parental involvement in the delivery of education necessitate that schools move beyond their present practices to ensure that such parents find a comfort level that facilitates a greater involvement in the schooling process. We must remind ourselves that equality of access does not necessarily translate into equity or equality of outcomes. Opening the doors of schools and saying "all parents are welcome" is not a sufficient practice to involve all parents. In fact such policies are directly detrimental to parents without the linguistic/cultural tools to take advantage of such an invitation. Rather, these types of open-door, "colour-blind" policies work within a meritocratic framework that pathologizes the families of non-English speaking parents. Tammy spoke about her involvement in her children's education and the barriers that exist for parents who are not as fluent in English:

Because I'm new here ... I joined the association. So I knew about the educational system, and the school board was there with programs and what we parents can participate in, telling them our concerns and all that. So it's quite useful ... Most of the parents are not very active in attending all these parents' meetings. That's what I hear from them. I think because they're busy and the parents themselves cannot speak good English. That's a problem too.

The arguments put forward by so many parents like Natalie and Tammy support the view that fluency in English continues to be a considerable problem for first generation parents of various racial/ethnic groups. The issues are overlapping and numerous. For those parents that do not speak English, access to the system must move beyond letters home, parent-teacher meetings and other practices that are based on English facility and comfort with the system. For those parents who cannot speak English, the barriers to participation in schooling are obvious. However, for those parents who have a working knowledge of English but are bound by cultural barriers, the lines become muddled and the relative powerlessness and/or cultural "hands-off" practices of some parents become seen as disinterest or general apathy.

Parents that are functional English speakers will find that they are privileged and able to access the system in ways that are impossible for non-English speakers. Like so many other parents that have a working knowledge of English, Iman has always tried to keep herself involved in her children's schooling. She works hard to develop both a rapport and a relationship with her child's teacher. This connection allows her to stay abreast of the key developments in her child's academic and social life at school. Here, she responds to how her involvement creates a space through which she can affect positive influences on her child's school experience:

> I am a member of the Parent Teacher Association. We have meetings once a month ... [and] of course there are always parent teacher interviews. I volunteer if they go for a trip ... if I can, and I do communicate with the teacher ... we communicate through writing ... I should be able to help the teacher, to be able to be a friend to the teacher so that we can discuss what ... help is needed for my son either in his marks or in his behaviour.

Importantly, this relationship also places her in a space where she can work proactively to ensure that her child's rights are always promoted. Parental agency is directly related to language facility and cannot be overlooked as a crucial factor in the delivery of education. However, the role of parents as advocates for their children becomes diminished when they are not regarded as stakeholders and are not apprised of the school's educational policies and practices. Abate spoke of how parents must be kept apprised of what goes on in "their" schools:

> There is not much interaction between parents and educators. There is a barrier ... I think parents should also be much more involved in the education of their children. As it is now, most of the decisions, the policy decisions, are made on behalf of our children, perhaps not in consultation with parents. I think parents should have critical

policy decision making offers from the school boards and from the school community. The policy decisions that parents are involved in are very minimal. I think parents should have more input. As it is now, I think there are very limited interactions between the school community and parents.

When parents are able to access the system and play a part in the educational process they will often be able to work towards a positive change in the school lives of their children. Iman responded to the question of how she addressed some of the barriers that exist in relation to her child's education:

> [M]y older son, he is very hyperactive … So the teacher, of course with the cuts, has a large amount of students in the class … the teacher is not patient with my son. [W]hen we spoke, she said that my son has attention deficit syndrome … because my son is active she … has a name for him: Attention Deficit. So I thought the teacher should be a little bit patient with him … I do not like the way she said, "I think your son has Attention Deficit Syndrome." Just because he is hyper and full of energy. So I was not really comfortable with that.

> I help through talking … I talked to her about it and she said that is what the description of Attention Deficit is — a hyper child — and she told me "Why don't you go to your family doctor and ask your family doctor to send you somewhere else?" I said, "No, I am not taking my son to a psychologist … or a doctor to start telling me he is like that … To me, it is normal, coming from where I come from, coming from Nairobi and Kenya, there are children who're worse than him."

Having a sense of agency about what happens within the classroom and feeling as though she was part of what eventually unfolded in the class was clearly empowering for Iman. Unfortunately, the proactive measures she had taken to ensure that her child's rights were not infringed upon are not feasible to non-English speaking parents. Parents must be able to understand in order to advocate. Without agency and the ability to play an active role in their children's education, non-English speakers will often find themselves relegated to the place of spectator in their children's education. Realistically, we cannot expect culturally and linguistically minoritized parents to stand centre stage and defend their children's rights without a working knowledge of even the basics of the system. Cultural differences have too often been used as a reason for differential treatment. As mentioned previously, it is not uncommon to find well meaning teachers sustaining and promoting existing inequities within the system. Unless parents have the linguistic capital with which to act on behalf of their children, students lose an important resource. Parents should not only have agency, but they should be able to act as advocates for their children within the system. This argument was furthered by Shania, when she spoke about advocacy, and her responsibility to defend and support her daughter within the mainstream system:

> ... from day one right after grade six, she was beautiful academically. Grade seven, she got a horrible teacher and yes, sometimes it is the fault of the teacher that the child fails ... I spoke to the principal about it and he said "Oh no, Mr. so-and-so is a fine teacher, he's a good teacher, blah blah blah." But she couldn't do well. For the first time she got her report card and I couldn't believe the report card. She ... just went down, her marks went down ... everything. I showed it to the principal, and he saw the difference, he couldn't deny it.

The mainstream system must make participation in school understandable and accessible to all parents. It is not enough to employ practices that work towards including those who are already familiar and comfortable with the system. Schools must extend themselves beyond conventional strategies for parental involvement and develop inclusive initiatives that will break existing cycles of failure by effectively encouraging and facilitating participation from non-English speaking parents. One such initiative has been the introduction of community liaison counsellors as a linguistic and cultural link between the home and school. In defining her role as a community liaison counsellor for the Chinese community, Grace clarifies:

> Our basic role is to keep the communication open, the link between the school, community and the home. That is the biggest job where

we are using our language facility to facilitate communication with the ethnic parents that are out there who might be intimidated by the school system. Because they don't speak English, they are sort of hesitant to come in and get involved.

When linguistic barriers establish a material divide between home and school, the perceived dichotomy only widens when cultural and social factors are thrown into the mix. The community liaison counsellors do more than simply translate, or act as linguistic guides for parents such that they might better navigate the wilderness of a new and different school system. The counsellor's job extends also into home relations between children and parents, a position that allows them to act as generational mediators. As one of the most positive initiatives working towards students success, the presence of the community liaison displays a sense of reception to both child and parent, a sense that their culture, heritage and language are of interest to, as well as honoured and welcomed by the school system. Too often, parents are expected to simply avail themselves of the open-door policies that schools espouse. Grace comments on how she as, a counsellor, engages those parents who are less able to take advantage of the system:

[T]hey expect them to get involved, but when they only have one word of English it's very difficult to even cross the door and come into the school ... we have some literature in the schools that has been translated into different languages, so for the initial contact, at least we know the kid arrives at the school with the parents and sometimes they have their own relatives to bring them to the school for the registration, and then the secretary can then give them some information that's in Chinese or whatever language that is available there to at least help them understand the basic routine of the school, what time the kid comes to school, what time they leave for lunch, and what is "PA day," you know things like that. And once they've got that established, if the parents have more questions that they can't answer or the relative has voiced some concern about the child's placement, the school will call us and then we will make the contact with the family and explain what the school's role [is] and how they as parent[s] can help the child to feel more comfortable in a new school. And then we sometimes get called out to the school and look at the documents if they have any, to look at the documents and help the school to place the child accordingly.

Isabelle, a community liaison counsellor for the Portuguese community spoke about some of the methods she employs with her non-English speaking parents:

> ... the work has to do with informing parents how the school system works if you speak the language. If you don't speak [the language], then you hire an interpreter. You would do a lot of ... information sessions with teachers to help [them] to be more sensitive and knowledgeable about the community. So our work was really like two folders: working with the teachers and helping them to understand the new cultures that are coming into the schools, and also to work with the parents, helping them understand how the school system functions, and their role as parents.

Parents with English language difficulties often find themselves unable to follow the homework that their children bring home. So, because they are either unable or unwilling to contact the administration or to challenge the educational system, resources like community liaison counsellors have become indispensable. The liaisons, as an extension of both community and the school, work to help parents understand what their children are doing, and how they can become more involved. Parental involvement is a crucial factor in student success, so community liaisons act as an important resource for parents, teachers and students alike.

Our intent is not to suggest that parental involvement should be interpreted as the last word in student success. On the contrary, parental participation in schooling is only one of many possible methods of improving both the experience and outcome of schooling for students. However, like issues of heritage language integration, parental input and participation act as very important support structures for a child as she/he seeks to establish a sense of space and place within the process of schooling. In almost every student interview, children saw home support and parental involvement as integral to their educational success, be it academic or otherwise. Almost all of the students interviewed assert that the interest, dedication, support and encouragement displayed by their parents translates into an immeasurable personal resource. The following two students, Biju and Arun, respectively underline the basic themes that arose throughout almost all of the student interviews with respect to their feelings about the importance of parental involvement in schooling:

Biju, a nine-year-old African-Canadian boy, asserts that among the most important factors contributing to his educational success is the deep interest and dedication shown by his parents with respect to his schooling and his academic future. And Arun, a seventeen-year-old African-Canadian student, firmly believed that parental input, support and participation were all pivotal in his success as a student. When asked about his parents' contribution to his success in school he replied:

> Yeah, not really the help, but just their involvement in the school ... Knowing that there's a close relationship to school and my parents ... My dad is on the PTA, and my mom would just help out ... Teachers know my parents because they'll come in for interviews and stuff like that ... so if there are any problems, they'll communicate, so there's good communication. Like they know that if [my] grades are dropping or anything, they can go talk to [my] parents. So if anything happens at school, they'll talk to my parents with no problem.

Presently, English language facility is basic and necessary if parents are to involve themselves as participants and advocates within formal structures of mainstream education. However, we must not overlook its importance within the educational process at home as well. There are informal methods of instruction that take place in the home that should not be overlooked. Ryan explained in what ways he is involved in his children's education at home and in relation to the school:

> Of course there is the interaction in the house with respect to whatever they have done on a daily basis ... help them in their assignment and look at what exactly they have achieved, look at their strengths and look at their weaknesses and see where we can help most, their mother and myself. Besides that of course, we are involved with the parent-teachers meetings, where we go from time to time, interact with each teacher of each subject matter ... and look at ways and means of helping them at home to complement what they are doing at school.

This narrative recounts a theme of parental support and encouragement when language does not act as a barrier. Often however, language and culture will prevent even the most interested, devoted and determined parents from effectively assisting their children. A case in point would be Tammy, who felt that helping her children with their schoolwork was not always feasible.

> I think for new immigrants there's a language barrier. And I think the most that things that I'm not used to is that you have textbooks to bring home. So I have to really ... have an idea of what they're learning when they bring back their homework in case they finish all homework at school and didn't bring anything back ... I don't know how to help them ... Actually, I remind them to write down everything they don't understand at school ... What they remember, they tell me and I try to help.

Schools and educators should make every effort to support parents in their efforts to aid their children at home. Quite often parents, even those with a functional level of English, will not be able to assist their children at home. As primary stakeholders in their children's education, parents must develop the resources with which to promote and facilitate student success. The development of parental resources must not be placed solely on the shoulders of parents, but must also be taken on by the system itself. Importantly, we should seek to avoid the existing rhetoric that suggests schools and educators can only do so much. As education and the promotion of success for students are the primary goals of schooling, we cannot continue to sustain and support irresponsible policies and practices that seek to promote success for those students best able to take advantage of the system. Such short-sighted perspectives should be replaced by efforts that work towards the success of all students. Bearing these issues in mind, we can no longer afford to avoid the social imperative to involve non-English speaking parents in the process of schooling. Inclusive education theory reminds us that while literacy in any language is still literacy, literacy is not always a mutual starting point:

> We have to understand that they have difficulties with their own mother tongues. [M]any of them did not attend school in their own country, and we are talking about the people who are so poor in the

rural community of the Azores, you know, many couldn't attend school ... we're talking very very economically depressed communities. (Fernando)

Educators and school administrators would do well to remember that some of our parents are not functionally literate in either English or their own heritage languages. This reality paints a different picture of what we need to do in terms of inclusive practice. Existing models of schooling that encourage parental participation are even less equitable and inclusive in these situations than with respect to parents who at least speak their heritage language. One example of how schools may work to affect changes in these situations would be the development of ESL programs for adults. These programs would, at the very least, work to establish a common frame of reference for parents and children as they work to develop mutually necessary language skills. We must be explicit in addressing arguments proposing that the education of adults is not the primary business of schools. If educating non-English speaking adults promotes success for their children, then it is indeed essential to the main business of schooling.

Importantly however, these types of literacy issues are not the only barriers that first generation parents find themselves dealing with. As asserted by Gail, a community liaison counsellor in the Caribbean community, poverty is also an issue:

... people who came and who had an enormous difficulty trying to survive, let alone flourish, in economic terms. So, people whose priorities were survival ... and who came and perhaps were ill-equipped to deal with the development of their children .....they were spending their time trying to feed them. So, when you put it into those perspectives ... when you look at the socio-economic[s] of people, you can see how pretty easily a generation of students was created who didn't have mommy reading ... I mean you just don't. You know, life in Richmond Hill is what we would all like ...

Economic factors will also play into whether or not parents are able to participate in the process and structure of schooling. Poverty is enough of a detriment and deterrent to English speaking parents but when you combine these factors with a lack of ability to function in English, the result is too often disengagement from the educational process. The problematics of economic survival are prominent inside various communities, and can have a significant impact on children's academic achievement. There is a double edged sword here: the ability to involve oneself in the processes of schooling is a function of time, and time is too often a luxury; also, when survival itself is one's first priority, education may find itself lost in the shuffle.

For these parents and their children, English language facility is an important aspect of the "cultural capital" students require to succeed in education. Also, it is important to make a special note here with respect to who is affected by exclusion and inequity in schooling. The reason for the great feeling of urgency that resonated in many of the interviews becomes clear when we reflect upon the purpose of inclusivity. Student success and/ or failure is not simply an issue of the moment. Student success and/or failure will, in many cases, directly impact upon future generations. Success gives rise to success, and failure all too often engenders failure.

Breaking free from a cycle of failure can be incredibly difficult. Case in point, a second generation of parents in Toronto's Portuguese community continues to struggle with many of the same issues tackled by their parents. They are raising their children in much the same way that they themselves were raised. Some were low achievers who were unable to break out of the cycle, and now, many of their children face the same dilemmas. Diego, a counsellor in the Portuguese community spoke about these problematics:

> So, sometimes [we] say there are very real issues in our community and people say your community is well established. Well no. You have to understand … the second generation … the only thing that they are not going through is some of the language barriers their parents went through. But, these are the people that even in English, they are not necessarily literate in the [true] sense of the word.

Unfortunately, while these dilemmas continue relatively unchecked, generations of students find their languages and cultures to be placed in direct opposition to everything that is mainstream. These are fixed oppositions that speak to the bodies upon which they act. Bearing this in mind, the knowledge base of student/parent/community must be incorporated into even our most basic conceptions and understandings of schooling excellence.

Examples of Best Practices of Parent and Community Involvement
* Children's Aid reading programs that include support for ESL parents
* Multilingual communications that take form in:
  * Information videos about the school in various languages
  * liaison officers employed for interpreting and translating letters for teachers to communicate with families
  * translation of student handbooks
* Home-Based Learning Strategies
  * reading books together, learning together in a co-operative environment
  * sharing stories; both contemporary and heritage

Case Study: Pais e Filhos
> If you have 10 percent of parents who are involved, and if you can use whatever means available to you to reach more parents and make 20 percent of the parents involved, then more and more you have communication with the parents and they will understand the system. The ultimate is to reach 100 percent and then you can talk about partnership between schools and communities. The parents would know what the children are doing and then we can reach the ultimate [potential] of the child. (Diego)

The Portuguese community initiated a coalition called Pais e Filhos (which means Parents and Children), an umbrella organization whose purpose is to encourage, promote and support any and all groups whose intent is the betterment of the Portuguese community. Their priority is to reach all of the Portuguese community and help parents to help their children to reach their ultimate potential. Because the first wave of Portuguese immigration mainly consisted of people without extensive education, many of these people were unable to follow and/or understand their children's homework. They found it difficult to contact the administration and/or challenge the educational system on behalf of their children. This community organization exists to help parents understand what their children are doing in school, and how they can help their children succeed.

One of the initiatives that Pais e Filhos has spearheaded is the production of a Portuguese booklet that helps parents to understand what it means to grow up as a child in Canada. This involves issues of parenting, youth social behaviour, schooling in Canada and parent-child relationships. The organization is trying to promote a partnership between parents and institutions such that they can help to break down the language barriers that prevent some parents from contacting schools and understanding their children's academic situations.

Another initiative produced by Pais e Filhos is the media literacy program for parents. The Portuguese community uses media literacy to encourage the use of Portuguese language radio and newspapers in order to help parents learn and understand English. By encouraging the reading of newspapers and other media sources, the media literacy program attempts to reach and educate parents. The first goal of the program is to promote reading and comprehension skills among Portuguese parents, and the second goal of the program is to provide parents with the skills to involve themselves to a greater degree in the lives of their children, their families and their communities.

FUTURE CONSIDERATIONS

In recent years it has become painfully obvious that systemic change/ progress can be short-lived, and is ever at the discretion of those in power. Over the last few decades, we have seen marginalized groups fight to implement anti-racism initiatives, AIDS related education, and numerous other inclusive measures into schooling. The progress, while slow, was encouraging. However, under the banner of the "common sense revolution," Ontarians have seen the removal, reduction and/or "re-focusing" of many of these programs. Evidently, the conservative government felt/feels that such initiatives were/are irrelevant to the "main business" of schooling.[9] These backslides in Ontario's educational system have demonstrated very clearly that we work in spaces that are scrupulously policed. We may win a "victory"[10] for equity here or there, but they are always carefully regulated victories, because programs adopted in these "moments" remain in constant danger of removal or "re-focusing." As noted by Hall, "… what replaces invisibility is a type of carefully regulated, segregated visibility" (Hall, 1996, p. 468).

This chapter has addressed some of the numerous strategies adopted by parents, communities and educators in promoting language integration within their respective and interconnected spaces. There are important lessons that can be learned from these strategies, and future considerations for research would do well to address the realities of systematically integrating these strategies into mainstream schooling. We would note that while many of the best practices proposed in this chapter appear designed to increase access to "diverse histories, experiences and viewpoints" and to *open* space for new insurgent ways of knowing and acting within school settings, one must not underestimate their transformative and potentially disruptive nature.

Resistance can take many forms, and like all relations that take place within the "moment" they are conjunctural, complex and contextual. "Strategic allocation of resources" would suggest that we reserve our efforts for use in those areas and those moments in which they might be best employed, a "moment" that would be less draining upon us, and more fruitful in the long run. Many of the best practices noted in this work, and in this chapter in particular, reflect beginnings. That is to say their implementation may not lead to immediate systemic rupture or change. However, simply because these strategies exhibit no immediate material consequences for the hegemonic structure, it cannot be taken to suggest that there was then no worthwhile activity. The political strategies taken up in this work may constitute the development of a symbolic or emotional authority over oppressive structures, an achievement not to be overshadowed by calls for overt political action. As both Gramsci and Foucault would point out, "insurgency" and social change are best approached as long term goals, this is not a "winner takes all" game.

That being said, much of this chapter has dealt specifically with the delivery of education and how it impacts on students and parents. There are, however, other issues that arise in relation to language as well, problems that have less to do with the delivery of education and more to do with how educators are educated. The issue that arises when addressing pre-service teacher education in relation to language integration in schooling, is that discussions often begin and end in relation to the numbers of bilingual and ESL teachers that are being graduated from teacher's colleges around the country. The issue of numbers is indeed a salient matter in that we do not have the necessary number of teachers to service our ESL population. Nevertheless, we must begin to take into account issues of teacher education and ask ourselves what it is that we teach our teachers.

As suggested by Cummins (1989), it is not enough to simply teach language. The methods through which we instruct are also of paramount importance. Today's educator is ill-equipped to deal with the realities of a multicultural/multiracial/multilingual school system because she is not taught to analyze and address the shortcomings of the system as a whole. Over the last thirty years of immigration within what is considered to be a multicultural framework, teachers have continued to be educated in basically the same manner, and with basically the same materials that were used up to that point. The reality of education today is reflected in some of the previous narratives that show some non-ESL teachers to be less than enthusiastic about integrating their classrooms and restructuring discriminatory curriculums with which they have become comfortable. We envision this to be the future mandate of pre-service education: to ensure that integrative inclusive educational methodologies become the norm and not the "special interest" concern that they are seen as today.

ESL students should be integrated into mainstream classrooms, but before that can happen teachers must be equipped with the tools to teach these students and support/communicate with their parents. At the pre-service level, modifications must be made to instruction and curriculum such that TESL stands at the forefront of all teacher education. This does not necessarily mean that all teachers must be bilingual. It does, however, infer that all teachers should be able to teach all children. Therefore, traditional strategies, policies and environments within schooling should be reassessed, and heritage languages/cultures need to be taken out of the auspices of the ESL classroom and brought into integrative inclusive environments within schooling in general.

If language is to play a significant role in the transformation of dominant Eurocentric notions of education and communication, how can teachers make use of students' practiced linguistic norms? How do you make use of ESL in the ideology and practices of inclusive education? How do we incorporate the linguistic knowledges of parents and community in schooling? How can the definition of competencies in language be broadened and/or transformed? What are the further implications for pre-service teacher education? It is imperative that a critical examination of these questions be conducted.

NOTES

1   Anzaldua (1987), is cited as in, H.A. Giroux. *Resisting Difference: Cultural Studies and the Discourse of Critical Pedagogy*.

2   Skutnabb-Kangas coined the term "linguicism" in reference to "ideologies and structures which are used to legitimate, effectuate and reproduce an unequal division of power and resources (both material and non-material) between groups that are defined on the basis of language" (Nieto:1996, p. 203).

3   See, Michel Foucault, "Body/Power" in Colin Gordon (ed.), *Power/Knowledge: Selected Interviews and Other Writings 1972-1977* (New York: Pantheon, 1987).

4   Deconstruction is a valuable tool for the activist, and must be understood to be essential if we are to address critically the underlying patterns of "meaning" that seek to sabotage our work. Deconstruction works specifically to clarify the operations of "difference" within texts by reversing and displacing these binary oppositions. This methodology allows us to reveal the interconnectedness of these supposedly dichotomous terms as well as their contexts and historical specificities. See, Joan Scott. "Deconstructing Equality-Versus-Difference: Or, The Uses of Post-structuralist Theory for Feminism" *Feminist Studies*, 14, 1 (Spring 1988), pp. 37-38. See also, Jacques Derrida, "Of Grammatology" (Baltimore: Johns Hopkins University Press, 1976).

5   Berger's concept of the *sacred canopy* establishes a foundation for the development of ethnic identity and identification by bridging the gap between the macro and micro realities of ethnicity. Theoretically, the *canopy* is merely a large blanket held up by a series of stakes attached to its four corners. The canopy is a symbolic shield used to protect those under its roof from the influences of the outside world (i.e., with fewer or weaker stakes, the stability of the canopy decreases). There are four main stakes that support the canopy: 1) religion or ideology; 2) community; 3) ethnic culture; and 4) ethnic territory. All four components exist as part of a symbiotic relationship, each drawing strength from the other (Berger, 1978, pp. 13-6).

6   By subjective ethnic identity we refer to those images, ideas, attitudes, and feelings that symbolically or psycologically define an individual. The term objective ethnic identity would refer to external or observable cultural and social behaviours. For example: 1) speaking an ethnic language and practicing ethnic traditions; 2) participation in personal ethnic networks such as family and friendships; 3) participation in ethnic institutional organizations such as churches, schools , media, et cetera; 4) participation in ethnic voluntary organizations (e.g. clubs, societies, organizations); and 5) participation in ethnic functions (Driedger, 1975, 1976, 1996; Isajiw, 1974; Breton et al., 1990).

7   Durkheim's (1965) original definition of anomie comprised notions of normlessness and social isolation. Robert Merton (1956) limited the concept of anomie to encompass only issues of normlessness. Regardless of the debate, one constant in discussions on the topic are the feelings of isolation and lack of power that anomie represents (Sev'er, Isajiw and Driedger, 1993, p. 84).

8   In exploring strategies for new and alternative modes of schooling, we have specifically looked towards initiatives that would address the particular concerns of minoritized educators, students and their families. Considering the great deal of emphasis that

we have placed upon family and parental involvement in this work, we would take particular care to ensure that the neo-conservative rhetoric that currently views education as a private personal concern is not bolstered in this work. Specifically, in our focus on parents and primary caregivers as the principal stake-holders in their children's education, our intent is not to take away from a view of education as a public/social responsibility.

9   In June of 1995, Ontarians saw the election of a progressive conservative government in their Province. This shift in power brought promises of a "common sense revolution," a revolution that sought to *open Ontario for business* by conducting a vicious attack on any and all who did not fit into the conservative's economic agenda. Couched in a language of democracy, self-reliance and family values, the new government's restructuring campaign began with the muting or negation of several policies that sought to improve the social condition of society (i.e., employment equity legislation, affirmative action, human rights policies, et cetera). See, Kari Dehli, "Between 'Market' and 'State'engendering education change in the 1990s" *Discourse: Studies in the Cultural Politics of Education*, Vol. XVII, No. 3, pp. 366-369.

10   We use the competitive language of "victory," "game," and "ballpark" relative to the combative/oppositional language employed by Gramsci, Hall and others in relation to culture as a contested space. (i.e., Gramsci called culture "a war of maneuver" and Hall referred to it as a "war of position.")

CHAPTER 6

ACHIEVING SUCCESS THROUGH INCLUSIVE EDUCATION: FULFILLING THE NEEDS OF ALL STUDENTS

INTRODUCTION

School is not a voluntary, ad hoc gathering of strangers, but a selected collection of individuals grouped by and required by an unequal power structure to act as if alone while in the presence of others, for the purposes of evaluation. The classroom, from the perspective of the antiracist educator, needs to reflect the learner's needs. Being learner centred, the setting for the educational experience must be realistic, uncontrived and include trust and respect (Rymer and Alladin, pp.163-4, from Jackson, 1968).

"Children have a right to a quality education." This is a common refrain among educational reformers, but the axiom should not end there. In fact, children have a right to a quality education that centres, engages and motivates them. Throughout our research, the youth, parents, administrators, community liaison officers and community organizers agreed that the traditional education system is failing many of its most vulnerable students. "Success needs" is a term that we have adopted to signify the psycho-social/pedagogical imperatives that a student requires to survive and thrive in her or his educational context. That is, once the basic needs of food and shelter are addressed, a student still must gain a sense of belonging, hope, validation and competence that fosters a greater ability to concentrate on the task of learning. As noted throughout this text, the educational system in North American contexts speaks to a middle-class Eurocentric experience.

While this study by no means intends to represent the views of all stakeholders, several key points did reoccur. In this chapter we will discuss:

1. An integrative definition of "school success";
2. The benefits to *all* students of a more inclusive definition of success;
3. Specific areas and examples of a broader definition of success;
4. A reconception of traditional school practices;
5. The role of stakeholders in this re-conception and;
6. Recommendations for stakeholders working together towards a more inclusive school system.

It is no longer sufficient that we, as parents, researchers and observers of the school system, endlessly debate the "what ifs" of student engagement and achievement. To paraphrase Giroux, it is time to develop a language and practices of "success" based on the needs of diverse youth, and the individual/collective responsibilities of educational stakeholders (Giroux, 1988).

HOW DO WE ACHIEVE "SUCCESS" FOR MARGINALIZED STUDENTS?

Towards understanding the concerns of marginalized students, their parents and educators, one teacher in the study noted how the issue of individual attention and learning extends to student assessment. Ron compares the context of the traditional school versus the Caribbean community focused Saturday School in addressing the specific realities of his community's youth:

> [The] Saturday School has a smaller group, sometimes one on one and sometimes one to three or five. Many of our kids do not function well in the large group. They need more directive type counselling. They are told what to do, rather than left what to do. They need more structure. So what we try to do is to provide more structure. My theory is that children need four main things in order to be successful: a) they need love and caring; b) they need security; c) they need stability; and d) they need positive role models. If we

can provide these four things, no guarantees, but we have a good chance of success.

Ron's commentary speaks directly to the inherent benefits associated with holistic approaches to education. Again, the issue is not necessarily which approach works best, but rather, how we can best employ multiple frameworks to fill in the system's existing gaps. Addressing only the academic components of education fails to support many students whose everyday realities prevent them from focusing on the task on hand. The abstract alpha-numeric exercises lose importance when a student can't access the "hidden curriculum," mastery of which allows white middle-class students to obtain a comfort level on the road to academic, and later, socio-economic achievement. This community based program examined and recognized the importance of viewing the student in a holistic way by validating social, emotional and spiritual experiences as valuable clues to improving achievement. Strategies addressing the "learning needs" of students, therefore, seek to integrate issues of belonging, security, understanding and acceptance with school curriculum, instruction and pedagogical practices. The personal subjective identification with the learning process makes it possible for the individual or group to invest in transformative educational practices. The concept of holistic education emphasizes that the acquisition of knowledge is a process of interactions among the physical/ received body, the learner's adaptable/adaptive mind, and the power of the human spirit.

Yet many still question what a "holistic" education or framework has to offer a public school system that aims for all its students to excel. The difference lies not just in interpretations of terms, but in the application of inclusive practices. In an assessment of such practices, one cannot avoid the complex and often misinterpreted notion of success. The idea of "success" is often discussed in the literature on inclusive educational practices. For example, in the Euro-American school setting, "student success" and its nemesis "student failure" are sometimes narrowly defined to the extent to which the student adapts to dominant norms and expectations. Many researchers, in Canada and internationally, have found that "unequally structured material and social conditions" (Dehli, 1996) contribute to the success of middle-class white students over that of "other" students — "othered" in that they are not in the dominant group, and "othered" in the subaltern sense of being made foreign and being classified as marginal. Thus poor and working class, visible minority, differently abled, Aboriginal, recent immigrant and sometimes, the female child is left behind in the project of learning before the first textbook is opened, or the first lesson is taught (see Dei et al., 1997; Darder, 1995, and others).

In light of the educational dilemmas faced by minoritized youth, community strategies often focus their efforts on more than simple academic goals. Beyond encouraging improved academic performance in their youth, many community-based organizations work with a broader definition of what it means to be successful. A "successful" student is considered to excel in non-academic proficiencies in areas such as pyscho-social development, the ability to access the cultural knowledge of their "in-group," and competence in the "cultural capital" of the dominant society. Of course each program emphasises different aspects according to ethno-cultural background and the cachement area of students, teachers and community organizers. Thus a teacher in a transitional school setting, such as the Nighana Program, may actively need to build a student's sense of belonging and competence in an alien school system while a community organizer in the Millikin Mills Saturday School Program may concentrate on interpreting and reinforcing skills taught through the dominant school system. This educational approach helps to improve and/or sustain the individual learner's self-esteem, pride, and sense of identity. Moreover, it plants the seeds for lifelong learning by helping to instill a sense of ownership over education. In other words, children who feel a connection to their schooling experience are more apt to view education as relevant and vital to their future.

By extending local "definitions of issues" to include the fulfillment of both rights (i.e., equal learning opportunities, owed by the dominant system) and responsibilities (i.e., community service, given by community organizers and concerned parents) community teachings draw on the interconnections between individual rights of membership and a responsibility to "give back" to the collective project of education. Individual success is not simply the result of one's talents and accomplishments. Due credit must be afforded to members of family (home learning practices), community (community schools) and dominant society (the best practices of regular schools) who put so much effort into student success. Therefore the rights of success are accompanied by reciprocal obligations and mutual interdependence. Community based teachings often privilege voluntarism, collaboration, acts of empowerment or rights demands, and the promotion of collective as well as individual learning. Multiple forms of knowledge are validated in the effort to create new ways of understanding, validating and evaluating achievement.

Often, community influences will move adult learners and students towards a greater involvement in schooling. The co-operative interplays that develop in these "moments" are some of the first steps towards shared decision making, the resolution of home-school conflicts, and greater educational success. Farah, a tutor from MENTORS, observed that these expanded notions of "success" result in greater learning potentials for students:

> Student success? That would have to be a child that is not having problems in the school in the sense that they feel that they are a part of the school. They feel like they're a part of their class. They feel like they're contributing something to their class. They feel like they're being encouraged by their peers, by their teacher, by their parents to participate. And then, because of that, they have an open mind and they learn, and they're more enthusiastic, and they want to contribute more, to help out, and they feel they're being encouraged to do so.

From this description, educational success is defined as a sense of belonging that empowers students to make more effective contributions. It was clear from the stakeholders we interviewed that understandings of educational success are still attached to notions of hard work, achievement and encouraging students to try their best to reach their respective goals. However, although parents have high expectations of their children, they also recognize the importance of affirming the individual efforts and capabilities of students within a setting of marginalization. This responsibility for student achievement is shared. Such a philosophy is also evident in the community school programs that we visited. In many of these sites, educational achievement will commonly be taken up relative to personal growth as much, if not more than academic growth. That is not to say that academic achievement takes a back seat to intra/interpersonal development. Rather, it emphasizes the importance that is placed on emotional and psychological well-being. After all, if children are not centred in themselves, how can they hope to find a centre in their educational experience? Another member of MENTORS, Asim, said:

I don't think I have a sort of traditional definition of success in the sense of either [money], wealth or education. I think it's something that empowers the student to become active or, I don't know ... proficient? in whatever area or however they choose to follow through in their lives, whether it is through education or if they decide that they want to work or [do something] non-traditional ... if they don't decide to go to school. And I think it really depends if they're happy and they're fulfilled. For me, I think success has to do with ... if you [have] an intention and you're working towards that. You might not get to that objective, but you're working towards it, and you're trying to better yourself constantly. I think that's really what defines success for me. That you might face obstacles along the way, that you've been challenged ... And I think it's also inner peace, it has a lot to do with inner peace.

The above excerpt reflects both pragmatic, and personal and spiritual aspects of a parent's understanding of success, his notions of both socio-economic security and personal growth. Thus monetary rewards or the status that education brings are by-products of the hard work in overcoming challenges, and not the goal itself. The tension between notions of success, "Western, capitalist, material" verses, "non-Western, co-operative, spiritual" is noted by Asim, but is reduced in significance when compared with the true measure of prosperity as learning in the general sense, and not the status of education, happiness and not the superficial trappings of wealth.

THE ARTICULATION OF POWER PRIVILEGE AND SUCCESS

Those with power in the school system who do not wish to acknowledge their own relative privilege or the systemic nature of discrimination may instead concentrate on relative disadvantages of the student and her/his family. The teacher or administrator decides whether the student and his/her community possess the "right profile" within the actual social context that contributed to his/her disadvantage in the school system. Thus poverty, single-parent family situations, and English language difficulties are not seen as possible signals for extra support and a greater drive for school success. Unfortunately, they effectively reinforce some stakeholders' conclusions about the "natural" (normalized) achievements of students and communities of privilege who have traditionally held the most faith in mainstream schooling. Schools routinely engage privileged students with "cultural capital." That is to say that these students enjoy the psychosocial and material benefits that facilitate school success. Their parents understand the workings of the system, having succeeded in the same or similar system. Teachers who are almost entirely from the dominant group, understand and validate their culture, as normal and invisible. They hold higher expectations of students who have may have a relatively higher level of English fluency, greater access to "quality" lifestyles, health care, and a steady access to a socially reinforced sense of normalcy and belonging. In short, the requirements of success for these students, or their *success needs* are consistently being met, in nearly every aspect of home, school and community life. For most minority students, especially those with greater disadvantage, the same may not be said. Dan, a teacher and parent educator remarked:

> ... the news portrays Blacks in a negative manner, but there are a lot of Black role models out there. For example, we always see white faces when it's related to computers. But here are a lot of young Black people involved in the computer industry that you've never heard of and there are a lot of success stories among Blacks, other than football stars and basketball stars. The news media does not portray the success of Black people. I think we need a better distribution of the community based news media. Use the internet to portray Black people. I think such portrayals of Black people in the mass media can have an impact on the attitudes of Black children toward themselves and toward others.

In discussing oppression, we need to address issues of power and privilege. When taking up these problematics, anti-racism works on multiple fronts to develop agency within marginalized communities and to develop awareness/acceptance of privilege among "the privileged." However, in recent years there have been major conservative backlashes to these anti-racist efforts (most notably, the extinction of employment equity legislation, the dissolving of the Anti-Racism Secretariat in Ontario, and the proliferation of Canadian-made hate propaganda). While damaging to the anti-racist project and problematic for the immediate future of school reform, these moves signaled a far greater, far more troubling possibility. These seemingly strategic attacks to anti-racist initiatives would almost suggest that there was a "collective will" at work, and that these moves were part of an oppressive agenda.

McIntosh (1990) argues that the dominant group is "made" to deny its privilege. However, from an integrative anti-racist perspective, we would interrogate this well accepted conclusion as problematic and only partial in scope. In the production and reproduction of oppression, the dominant group is taught to employ and justify its power, just as racialized and minoritized people are taught to recognize, fear and sometimes appropriate it. In asserting that equity and affirmative action programs were targeted by the privileged in order to secure a hold on existing power dynamics, this perspective would at least begin to make sense out of the closures and erasures mentioned above.

THE NECESSITIES FOR CHANGE: AN ANTI-RACIST PERSPECTIVE ON "SUCCESS"

Aside from the obvious material gains, minoritized peoples, need to ask themselves if they are willing to pay the price to "access the knapsack," to live in fear of "others" and to constantly contend with the loss of their new-found relative privileges. Of course we should strive for equity, to have equal opportunities and equal outcomes. Cultural capital is extremely important to the psychological well being of marginalized students struggling within the mainstream system. Those without it, or with less of it, will often find themselves fighting to meet their most basic success needs. These students in particular deserve to have an equal opportunity to engage the system fully, but this is not the case. For example, in dealings with the educational system, immigrant and ESL families often experience a lack of empowerment and a limited access to social services. Research by Carol Tator (1990) and Tim Rees (1987) conclude that many service providers continue to refuse to even recognize how systemic racism disadvantages their clients, or to interrogate their own complicity in continuing the cycle of disadvantage. When considered with the similar reluctance in many traditional educators, the gravity of the situation reveals that our system is more in a state of chronic shortcomings, than a situation of crisis. Generally, issues of disadvantage and relative privilege have been omitted from the discussions. It is a political "negation" or oversight that allows such disparities to go on unchecked and unchanged (Desai, 1996). While these problems are not easily repaired, their influence on the minoritized can be mitigated, compensated for, and eventually overcome. We feel that anti-racist reform and the re-articulation of "success" will go a long way to ameliorating many of the present educational dilemmas. Even groups who are traditionally well-served by the school system express wide-spread dissatisfaction and a growing fear that Canadian students will be ill-prepared for the consequences of globalization and a technology driven society. Redefining success must be informed by integrative anti-racism so that teachers will be supported in their efforts to teach diverse classrooms. Parents will be empowered to participate actively in a school system that is reflective of their values and respectful of their cultures. Effective community partnerships could become normal, not novel, as resources and knowledges are shared. Most importantly, students will be more confident that they will be prepared for their future, and hold a valued place within society.

In "The National Report of Exemplary School Projects," the authors argued that there should be numerous ways of achieving success, and further, that success should be a local measure that is defined by each community. They went on to assert that thoughtful efforts are needed to teach students to make decisions about learning rather than how to simply consume courses and earn credits (OPC News, February 1996). Success should be defined such that the learner's expectation, the extent of community involvement, non-academic proficiencies (i.e., psycho-social development and the ability to utilize culture knowledge) are recognized and valued by educators. This educational approach helps to improve and sustain the learner's self-esteem pride and sense of identity, while also encouraging a belief in the relevance and utility of education for the individual student, and for the benefit of her/his community. It allows the learner to develop an important sense of ownership of her/his learning and education. An integrative definition of success should inform the redefinition of such commonly understood principles as discipline, measurement and evaluation, good behaviour, learning expectations — the very criteria of success.

A well-versed understanding of the "hidden curriculum" and its related rules may not ensure academic excellence, but it will, at the very least, provide marginalized students with a firm grounding from which to engage their schooling experience. Zine (1999) expressed concerns that the Grade 3 standardized math test included references to Anglo-Franco Canadian pastimes that would be unfamiliar to a student new to the Ontario school system, and/or unfamiliar with such mainstream activities. She asked the rhetorical question, "what was being tested, knowledge about snowmen or problem solving." Without ownership of the appropriate "cultural knowledge," immigrant and minoritized students may find themselves unfairly "penalized" for being who and what they are. In effect, this type of test is less a diagnostic tool than a sorting tool.

Recent changes to Ontario's high school requirements now mandate that students must perform a specific amount of community service in order to graduate. While on the surface, this might seem like an ideal method to bolster home-school-community interactions, like many of the other reforms to Ontario's school system under the Harris regime, these efforts seem ill conceived (See Dei and Karumanchery, 1999). After all, how do they define "community"? Are services limited to social and political efforts? Or do they extend to apprenticeships and other methods whereby business may take advantage of a cheap, or in this case, free labour? We do not want to be too cynical, but at the same time we cannot afford to keep our eyes closed to reforms that would "marketize" public education.

As noted by Dehli (1996) the invasion of market forms, relations, and concepts into schooling usually results in the marginalization and muting of other dimensions of education. For example, issues about equity, educational inclusion, morality and social justice become trivialized as schools are taken up as gender, class and race neutral. Hatcher (1998) argues that the new Labour government's policy of "School Improvement" promotes a reformist vision that does not take race, class, and gender into consideration.

Unfortunately, the Ontario government's overriding concern for money management and the bottom-line has resulted in cut-backs to guidance departments, community services and a host of other programs that were particularly relevant in serving the needs of the marginalized. Under the smoke screen of current conservative reforms, students may pass all the standard requirements for "educational success" without a connection to community, without a personal relationship with educators, and without the skills to apply community based/Indigenous knowledges. Minoritized youth who do not receive a relevant and encouraging education may lack the tools to obtain social success, a post-secondary education, or stable, full-time employment (Winzer, 1997; Dei, 1996).

A critical anti-racist framework asserts that an education must be understood in relation to more than the sum of a student's report cards and attendance record. However, under the new educational guidelines, respect for, and the utilization of a student's multiple knowledges, individual learning styles, and sense of identity, remains a function of individual teacher agendas and not school policy.

Being educated for success, then involves the opportunity to engage in a variety of learning experiences which often take place outside of the traditional classrooom. Education articulated within such a broad context is rooted in a sense of one's community, home and relationships to school systems and society. The experiences and knowledges acquired within these various educational sites should be integrated into an anti-racist approach to learning that engages the cultural knowledge of traditionally marginalized groups in society. This approach to inclusive education ensures that there is a multi-centred knowledge base at the core of the school curricula. Thus the false dichotomy between Eurocentrism and Afrocentrism is replaced by a complex of Euro-American, African, Asian, North American Indigenous centred knowledges, and so on. When knowledge is based in the actual experiences of students, where their respective cultures are validated and accepted, the relevancy, not the origin of that knowledge, becomes the educator's greatest concern.

COMPOSITE CASE STUDIES

Methodological questions and the resulting methodology encompasses much more than practices and techniques of data collection and writing that fall under the rubric of research methods. Both aspects are necessarily complementary. The composite case study approach employed in our study has allowed us to amplify and contextualize the often isolated narratives of the individual informants. Philomena Essed argues, in reference to the researcher/investigator, that "It is important and inevitable that we rely on subjective reality constructions because the complexity, depth, and multitude of experiences cannot simply be observed" by, for example, a participant investigator (1991, p. 59). By employing the composite case study we wish to form a theory and resulting methodology that recognizes and incorporates "difference." Thus, we may balance competing voices without subscribing to a hierarchy of oppression, without privileging formal writings as "received knowledge," while informants voices simply illustrate or contradict scholarly works.

Employing the composite case study allows us to speak personally and specifically without claiming universality, nor an anti-theoretical stance which would privilege experience without critical reflection. The case studies seemed to be the method best able to satisfy both concerns about authenticity, activism, and the rigors of scholarship. Fitting the pieces together meant excising linear/dichotomous views of the world. Theory and practice could not be separated; we could not abrogate the responsibility that being researchers in the school community entails, nor ignore the resulting issues of power. When we leave our own identities unexplored, we leave the research open to the pervasive domination of whiteness which normalizes our own invisibility as marginalized persons committed to our respective communities. By removing our observations or ignoring our own perceptions we are in danger of allowing the dominant group to "make invisible," or "reappropriate" things, people and places it does not want to see or hear and, then, through misnaming, renaming or not naming at all, invents the truth — what we are told is "normal," neutral, universal, simply becomes the way it is (Mirza, 1997, p. 3).

Case Study Composite 1, "Robert," describes a recurring theme in the research of young Black male students who experience particular kinds of systemic and individualized racisms. Robert, a composite of over five narratives, is subjected to an impossible standard that both lowers the expectations of academic achievement, raises expectations in terms of sports, and sets an often impossibly high standard of behaviour that characterizes him as a potential threat and danger within the class and school community. The second Composite, "Maria," represents racialized young women whose intelligences don't quite fit with the norm, or with educators' prejudices. Maria's case reflects the tension between Western individualism (every one is different) and Eurocentric stereotypes (member of a minority group are all the same). The third composite is based primarily on one of the Saturday Schools we visited, with aspects of two others. This study represents the challenges of community organization in an educational setting.

CASE 1: HIGH EXPECTATIONS/EMPOWERMENT/ ACCOMODATION

Robert, a well-behaved Black, male youth, aged 16, is barely passing age-appropriate Advanced level classes, but does very well in English. He is considered by most of his teachers, who are white, to be a success, because they expect that he will graduate from Grade 12, and with some help may be well prepared for community college. He has recently immigrated from the Eastern-Caribbean and has an accent many of his teachers have difficulty understanding. His parents have so far have had little contact with the school, as they both work in the evenings and are unable to attend PTA meetings or Parent-Teacher nights. Robert is respectful to his teachers but does not talk to teachers, administrators or guidance counsellors more than necessary. Recently his phys-ed coach and some teachers encouraged Robert to join the school basketball and track teams, as he shows promise as an athlete. His coaches and teachers mention the prominence of Jamaican track athletes and American runners in order to boost his self-esteem.

Many well-intentioned, yet ignorant assumptions are made by school officials in this case. Robert, simply by passing his courses and displaying acceptable behaviour, has surpassed their expectations. Because he is *not* deemed to be of inferior intelligence and does *not* show an inclination towards violence he is considered a success, irrespective of whether he has surpassed his own expectations or potential. What does Robert want? What are his expectations of himself? Instead of asking him, his teachers are pushing him towards athletics, where they are used to seeing Black males excel. Instead of arranging afternoon, weekend or daytime phone interviews with parents, teachers will wonder why Caribbean parents, don't seem to care about their children's education. A few phone calls could help Robert's parents feel welcome in the school, and possibly inform them that they have a guiding role to play in Robert's plans for the future. Robert may do well in sports, but may have a greater interest in chess. Many studies and reports show that in certain cultures parents have little visible involvement with schools and teachers, out of trust and respect, not disinterest. Furthermore, he may want to go to university to study English, but may not know how to improve his other marks.

Unfortunately cases, such as Robert's are, in reality, all too common in the school system (See Dei, 1996; Dei, Mazzuca, McIsaac and Zine, 1997; Parsonson, 1986; James and Brathwaite, 1996). "Colour-coded" streaming is an issue of racialized, gendered and classed expectations/exclusions within and between the streams. Within the process of streaming, efforts that might ameliorate disadvantaged circumstances for youth are often ignored. For example, increased teacher-student interaction and a change in teacher expectations would provide new opportunities and new possibilities for Robert's educational success. A greater effort at home-school communications would empower his parents to get involved in the process and would help him to strive towards self-determined goal setting rather than those prescribed by his teachers.

Possible Solutions

In an inclusive educational model Robert would have mentors, Afro-Caribbean teachers or other teachers of colour with whom he could talk about what it means to be a "new-Canadian." These teachers could help his other teachers understand the English Caribbean educational system, and give reasons why some Caribbean parents seem to be less involved. In an inclusive model, Robert would access all of his aptitudes, which would encourage him to bring his academic achievement in line with future goals. Athletics would be an important, but secondary consideration. Alternative meetings could be set when his parents could attend. The parents could then tell the teacher about Robert's previous school experiences and achievements. Community members, who are pursuing careers in Robert's areas of interest, could be brought into the school to explain how they achieved their goals. Such a positive role-model could serve the dual purpose of counteracting negative images that come from society, and help all students learn about employment and vocational opportunities.

CASE 2: MULTIPLE INTELLIGENCES/VALIDATION/ SAFETY

Maria, a fourteen-year-old South Asian girl in the public school system, is about to enter high school. English is her third language after Portuguese and Hindi. She has been assessed with ADD, and is slightly dyslexic. Although early assessments indicated that she was a highly intelligent student, her marks remain low. Maria, however is an excellent tutor for her Portuguese classmates and is well liked and co-operative with adults, despite the fact that her teachers consider her to be acutely shy. Maria would like to be chosen for enrichment opportunities usually reserved for A-students. Recently, Maria has excelled in a language arts unit on comparative religion, yet her teachers do not understand why her creativity and insights do not translate to other classes. Every night after school, Maria has to care for her younger sister, and misses after school activities. Because Maria was a new immigrant from India, her teachers and other students repeatedly asked her why she did not wear a sari, or why she ate beef. Lately the taunting has turned to pushing and shoving. Maria has mentioned it to a teacher, but no action was taken. Maria is instead encouraged not to worry, and to try to make more friends.

An involved/invested teacher would seek to balance Maria's learning disabilities with her talents and cultural specificities. Such an inclusive approach would refrain from assuming the pathology of her family and community, as is so often done in the mainstream. Instead, inclusive educators would make use of both individual learning styles and cultural/racial identifications as resources to make Maria's education more relevant to her. From the information above, it is clear that Maria has very well developed "interpersonal" (leading, organizing) and "intrapersonal" (personal goal setting, self-awareness, sensitivity) "intelligences" that are being all but neglected at school (Armstrong, 1994).

High achieving students and their parents often worry about class time being used to "help" students like Maria. Again we see another example of traditional groups having their success needs met at the expense of other groups. Maria and her classmates are missing the potential benefits that could be gained by her full contribution to the classroom. Further, all students will eventually face some kind of adversity. By witnessing how Maria compensates for her disabilities, and offering her support, students are provided with a valuable life lesson about overcoming difficulties and operating within a collective. Just as important, Maria and other students will learn that learning disabilities or other disadvantages do not mitigate her leadership potential, and her ability to help other students in different ways.

The education and attempted assimilation of minority groups into the dominant school system can often be an epistemically and physically "violent" act (see Moreau, 1996; Mirza, 1992, 1997; Essed, 1991; Dardar 1995). Young has identified what she terms "'the five faces of oppression': marginalization, exploitation, cultural invasion, powerlessness, and violence" (Darder, 1995, p. 323). All of these oppressions are acting simultaneously in Maria's classroom. Segregation and the struggle for equity mark the history of education in this country. This struggle is most clearly demonstrated in calls for multicultural curriculum, events such as Black and Asian History months, and the desire to see non-Christian holidays celebrated and embraced within the mainstream system (Mirza, 1992; and Moreau, 1996). For a minoritized student to be a full participant in school requires that educators and other students work to mitigate the effects of this history by removing the barriers to "social and psychological" oppression.

Possible Solutions

As Maria is experiencing various difficulties, some over which the school has little or no control, it is important to concentrate on what can be changed in the short term, with an eye to long-term reforms. First, the very real issue of safety needs be addressed sensitively by Maria's teacher, including racial slurs, and invasive and misinformed assumptions. Immediate intervention must be taken before taunts become increasingly violent. This is an opportunity for the aggressive students to examine their own actions, and for other marginalized students to voice their own concerns. Second, Maria lacks a mentor in school who is familiar with her ethno-racial and cultural background. She sppears to be uncomfortable confiding in her teachers, and when she does take a risk and speaks out, her concerns are often muted or disregarded as "ordinary" issues that she needs to deal with on a personal level. Third, Maria could be given a leadership role in the classroom or school that makes use of her well developed interpersonal and intrapersonal skills. For example, a mediator in a program that matches newcomers to the country and/or school community with more established students, or a student focussed mediation program that is sensitive to issues of race and gender, (i.e., the Ambassador's program and SMILE, mentioned elsewhere in this book). If no such program exists, Maria, her teacher, a few other students, and a community partner could develop a program that could later be adapted for other classrooms.

CASE STUDY 3: A BLACK/AFRICAN FOCUSED SCHOOL FOR YOUTHS AT RISK

The "Program" grew out of a needs assessment conducted by a Community Centre. In this needs assessment, youth articulated a desire for "entrepreneurial training, job preparation training, help with their 'sums', they wanted to go back to school" (Calista). A coalition was established that brought together different agencies that were already working with these youth, and with a mandate to look at issues around employment and job training. Funding was obtained for two outreach workers from the Drug Abuse Program to connect youth to services that were available to them.

The Coalition

Community members constitute the majority of the coalition that originally established and now operate the Program. Also, various social service agencies (literacy, drug prevention, community centre, et cetera) have committed their resources to working with the students concerned. The coalition continues to be open to new membership. They have held introductory meetings in order to encourage school-community agencies to get more involved.

Members of the coalition act as advisors and problem solvers, as referees for the Program, and as resources of organizational expertise to the school. The contribution of expertise, however, has at times been challenged by the change in staff representation in the coalition as well as ambiguity of personal versus organizational commitment. However, the relationships among stakeholders and with the community centre are understood here and among others involved as a strength of the Program. These challenges work to keep community knowledges and interpretations vibrant, and reflective of changing needs. They represent the constituent elements of a community — an educational community that is at times challenged by differences, but always united in their dedication to the youth.

Focus groups with young people were held to identify and highlight issues in school re-entry programs that were reflective of culture and the kind of supports that they required. Work was then begun with the Toronto Board of Education (now Toronto District School Board) to establish an alternative school. The coalition interviewed 140 youth. When these youth saw that they were being listened to, a powerful message of hope was established. It was a commitment that empowered them with the knowledge that they could both influence and bring about change. A coalition member, Merfed, told us:

> ... from the grassroots sense of community development ... it was something that was identified by the community, there was a need, there were these young people hanging out, it was brought to the attention of the staff at the Community Drug Prevention Centre[s] ... they played a role in identifying what the needs of these youth were and how they could better service them and provide them with skill development ...

Providing a relevant education for students, particularly racialized students who, for a variety of reasons, are not functioning within the mainstream educational systems, became the focus of the Program. The definition of such an education is as complex as it is illusive. "Failing" to find such a meta-narrative approach to learning led community educators to a philosophical vision that called for an inclusive and holistic approach to education in this setting.

Struggling for Success

The direction of growth is based on establishing and developing relationships with members of the mainstream education community as well as other related social service agencies. Again, the focus is on establishing partnerships and relationships as constituent elements of an educational community. In terms of the goals set by the coalition and staff for the students, the importance of community was understood as essential and was defined as a dynamic interaction of interests and ideas.

By defining the working relationships of the school in this way, and by establishing a fundamental sense of trust in the community, inclusion became a functioning methodology of community development. An important challenge the school has faced in terms of inclusive governance has been the participation of parents. In many cases, and for a variety of reasons, parents of students at the school were finding it difficult to fulfill their roles as parents:

> One of the things that we're hoping to do is have a parent support group … [W]hat we were finding was that the parents were having so many issues themselves that it was hard for them to cope and deal with the parenting issues, and deal with their kids' stuff … [I]t became mixed up because, of course, a lot of the kids' stuff became their own issues. We found that there was so much going on that it was hard for them to be parents, whether it was because they were unemployed, [or] that parents had lost control in a lot of the situations, and some of them had probably just given up or didn't know how to use new strategies (Calista).

Connection with Community Outreach

Identifying and gaining access to community outreach was a critical practice in the development of the Program. Community resources, comprise services, people and knowledge. The very idea of community contains notions of nationalism and "home" that are becoming increasingly problematic. Our own fantasies of what it would be like to "go home again" are now tempered with the reality of socio-political challenges. Deep considerations have brought our informants to a complex understanding of how and where they plan to live their lives, even if most of them have been unable to completely reconcile "home" and "here." Many of the Black students and parents in our study built their identities around various conceptions of what can be called an "imagined community" of the African Diaspora. In this respect, "members of even the smallest nation will never know most of their fellow-members — yet in the minds of each lives the image of their communion" (Anderson, 1983, p. 15).

To paraphrase Angela Davis, the community "isn't everywhere," meaning that the some class, geography and subject location informs community membership (Davis, 1996). Thus "community practice" should encompass a greater praxis than "donating" time or resources. Doing critical, insurgent work in the community entails the exchange of knowledges and experiences while learning to understand how systems of oppression are interconnected. It means learning from elders, passing on our own knowledge based on "connections, caring, and personal accountability" (Hill Collins, 1990, p. 223). Part of that learning involves using our positions of relative privilege to improve our communities' socio-economic resources and help them negotiate access to services. However, understanding how systems operate is no more important that learning how to develop and practice strategies that will improve and/or resist the systems themselves.

Linkages to different social service agencies are necessary to address the multitude of student concerns. In addressing those matters, the knowledge and expertise provided by community members functions in two ways. First, they deliver the knowledge as content (resume writing skills or trades training courses). Secondly, the knowledge is produced through relationships with individuals, groups and the society in general. This gives meaning to the notion of an "educational community." These community relationships are particularly significant because the knowledge produced has meaning and relevance for the students. At the Program this happened within the context of the outreach worker's Life Management Course [LMC]:

> … we brought role models in, had group discussion around issues
> that were going on in their lives, around problems with the teacher

or problems at home, whatever. [We] took them on field trips, took them to movies, dealt with issues around race, gender and sexuality, and used the LMC as a chance for them to explore the issues that were important to their lives. [We] challenge them on some of their beliefs and how they worked to give them a new perspective, either through the LMC instructor himself, or through other role models who we brought in from the community who could share their experiences and their lives. (Calista)

The point about challenging their beliefs and developing a new perspective is critical. It is one of the reasons why some community based initiatives have been developed in the first place — because community groups are questioning and challenging the status quo of mainstream schools. The notion of community education, especially when it occurs within a marginalized location, contains this political element. Questioning the way things are is a primary basis of many of the community based learning initiatives and it is an essential tool that allows community and students to work together to analyze the world and their role within it. The commitment to this challenge is echoed by another staff member, Natalie, at the Program:

... and my big word with them was *critical thinking*, that was a key word ... to think critically with everything, question everything, things that you've held dear for all your life.

Enhancing Educational Outcomes

Independent learning strategies are an important means of enhancing education outcomes for youth. By independent learning we mean a different way of earning credits. We need to look at different ways in which the classroom can be organized to respond to diverse ways of learning and knowing, and also provide a flexible environment for students. Allowing students, particularly students who have not succeeded within the mainstream system, some autonomy over their educational development provides an element of empowerment as well as a practical means for addressing individual needs:

... the way these kids work you need a Montessori school idea ... you could be doing history or math or English as long as you know that I keep you on track, that you do a bit of each thing so that at the end of the week you accomplish a full amount of credit ... But I guess one of the issues with that is if you've got one teacher trying to manage all that it could be crazy for the teacher ... but maybe a lot of what we're saying in terms of this Program is to be successful, you do need more teachers in the classroom with those few students ... (Natalie)

This comment reveals that it is often difficult to have the most appropriate learning environment and strategies due to endemic funding problems. In other words, such independent learning can be difficult to accomplish with only one teacher. Another staff person, Rachel, posed specific questions around identity, race and the issues this raises in terms of curriculum:

A lot of them are facing issues about who they are, because a lot of them come from mixed families, they don't know if they are white or if they are Black, and they don't know what to do with themselves ... They don't know who they are or what they want to do ... when we get into Black history, or stuff like that, they don't identify with it, although they say this is what they want, but it's not ... whatever the Program is, there must be something that talks about them, their histories and cultures. That is a real issue with them.

Examples of knowledge being socially and collectively created through interactive processes were evident at the Program. Interviews with the "outreach" and LMC counsellors revealed the interconnectedness and importance they place on diverse knowledges. Not only regarding individual, family and communal interactions, but the salience of class, race, gender and sexual orientation. For example, the school has an Afrocentric focus, but as one staff member notes, Afrocentricity could not be presented in isolation from other social identities. Natalie emphasized that within the Program, identity became an important curricular piece:

... [we] looked at issues of identity — "so what did it mean to be Black in Canada, and to be who they were." Some of them as immigrants, some as children of immigrants, some connected to somewhere else along with the Canadian, and looked at issues of sexuality, gender, race, class, education, all that stuff.

Staff at the Program make connections between the experiences of students and those of guest speakers and other community members who volunteer their time.

Students at the Program are encouraged to set their own goals for themselves. Staff members addressed the problems of only presenting class-biased career options to students and highlighted the potential danger in ignoring the larger goal of becoming productive community members:

> ... there was this one vision of what the kids could be, and for me it was part of the notion of recreating a middle class, and I'm not saying that it's a bad thing, but I think we all won't be lawyers or doctors or teachers, and some of us will be other things and be happy with that. Not that we shouldn't encourage our kids to be ambitious and be the best that they can be, but we have to realize that not every kid is at the same level, or has the same capacities .... were we just to produce professionals or produce good human beings who want to give back to the community and take care of themselves and recognize that it is important to have good relationships with your family and friends, the question is how do you find the balance of these things. (Calista)

Recognizing issues of social class and identity must not be dismissed when relating material to youth. Social class constitutes an important part of an individual's social identity and, like race or gender, must be considered in the development of resources for a Program. If material is culturally-centred yet classist, it will not be relevant to all minoritized students. An issue of identity that presented a challenge to the Program community was sexual orientation. The discussion around sexual orientation led to an identification of the need for a real coming together of the Program coalition to discuss and be clear about the policies governing the program. Natalie then questioned:

> ... are we trying to teach them equity or are we trying to teach them, you know, like a value for difference, a value for possibility among themselves?

It became important that members of the Program community (volunteers, board members and staff) were clear on their philosophical understanding of the Program and the politics of difference. At one point, there was a proposal to get Program students together with the students in the Triangle Program for gay, lesbian and bisexual youth. This proposal divided members of the community and raised important tensions regarding respect for difference and how that should be defined. Regarding this tension, Natalie commented on the need to be clear on a working definition for the Program community and the importance of structural support in the form of policy:

> I remember having this one person [volunteer/parent] saying, "Well I don't believe in total inclusiveness." And my thing was, well, what do you mean, and how can you be part of the board ... whose policies talk about inclusiveness? ... I'm concerned because I mean the idea of Program is about that whole idea of inclusiveness and how far you can push those boundaries.

The notion of "pushing boundaries" highlights the dialectical nature of how the politics of difference is becoming defined within this context. Further, it emphasises the importance of integrating a framework that recognizes the complexity of individual and group identities. Natalie noted that the holistic approach to youth and community education can drastically enhance educational outcomes. Within the Program community, this means addressing the social, emotional, academic and physical needs of students.

> ... when the students get identified as students eligible for the Program ... what gets identified is ... their overall needs. They have multiple issues, right? So often they're coming from a referral from another social service agency or even from a home, a parent who's saying, these are the things I'm struggling with ... or the kid is identifying the Program because they have all these other issues. (Natalie)

The Program's community sees themselves as trying to identify strategies and tools that students need in order to succeed. They see themselves identifying the barriers to that success and how they can be overcome. Integral to these goals is a strong communication network among agencies working for each student:

> So the kid that has entered the Program through the justice system, the teacher in the classroom ... is connecting him with some of these other social service agencies that come to bear. So when a

student doesn't show up for two days, you know they're talking to each other …. [I]t's about whoever's in their life working together because I find where there's gaps and where they end up losing out is when people aren't talking to each other … (Natalie)

Also central to this approach is the participation of students in decisions that concern them. In this way, they are a part of the process and are able to determine their future for themselves and take responsibility for that. This is an empowering process.

… it is a whole model where they can self-determine as well, it's not [like] we try to control them, as in we turn them into little clients of the system. They're participants on their own…. Really, I think an innovative model needs to be created that works. I think we have parts of it now, but I think that … that's the missing link … (Natalie)

Part of achieving that model has involved the inclusion of an outreach worker (supported by the Drug Prevention Program) who has various responsibilities with the students: skills development, life skills, and building confidence and self-esteem. The outreach worker has a time period set aside for students in the classroom and also provides time outside of the classroom to help support them with any issues outside of academic ones. The outreach worker speaks to them frankly on a wide variety of issues and provides counselling. In this way, students receive the additional support needed for many of them just to participate on a regular basis:

We found that the kids needed support, even just phone calls to get them to come to school each morning. Some of them were having problems with the criminal justice system and problems at home. School was important, but they were having court days. They came, but it was hard with problems at home. It was hard for them to focus on the education pieces when there was so much going on in their lives. And those problems don't go away if you don't deal with them. They didn't have some of the basic things, such as TTC tickets, or lunch. It was hard for them to focus. That was what we thought the outreach worker would provide, and he did so in the time frame he had. But it was not adequate. With the

Program moving into the school there will be a full time youth worker, and that will be a huge benefit to the program. (Calista)

Lessons for the Mainstream Educational System

... the Program school breaks down, you know, feeling isolated, breaks down the barriers to actually getting an education because there's not that intimidation.

As Merfed noted, an important part of an educational community (and clearly, a characteristic of the Program community) is the welcoming environment that is created for students. When community becomes an extension of family, and trust is an integral part of the relationships, a sense of welcome is the result. Within the mainstream system, a sense of community does not exist for all students. Students who do not feel membership in their school community, feel isolated and, as a result, barriers are created and intimidation sets in.

There is a place for the community centre in the school, and I hope that this could develop some kind of model for how this can take place. I hope we could be a model in how we treat people who are different, and how we make this a welcoming space. (Calista)

As well, the accommodation of difference and the assessment of individual needs are important lessons to be learned from the Program. Merfed identifies these issues as important for the mainstream schools:

I think ... programs that are more accommodating to students, identify cultural backgrounds and pressures that youth are being faced with, whether, if they're "new Canadians," as far as barriers, as far as their English, I think there should be more programs that would focus on identifying their needs and not trying to push them into the mainstream, allowing them to get comfortable first, sort of a specialized program.

This insighful comment draws on the holistic approach to education wherein students are seen by the school as individuals with a whole range of needs, which, if not met, jeopardize the possibility of educational success.

Measuring Success

Program members saw that their definitions of success were changing and evolving as they worked with the students. For example, one type of success was "stabilization in the home"; that is, re-establishing relationships with family:

> [O]ne of the measurements had to be just stabilization at home ... [O]ne of the things that we were able to do with some of the students that we didn't anticipate before would be just to make them ... reconnected to their families, living at home consistently ... being able to attend school regularly ... even if they didn't pass the credit at the end of the term, you couldn't just measure success based on that.... [W]e celebrate the fact that they're back at home, they're in touch with their family, they talk to their mother again, their father's back in the picture, and all those different kinds of things that some of them had issues with, which was definitely impacting on their ability to stay in the classroom every day and learn. (Natalie)

A staff member, Rachel, saw a strong correlation between strong family relationships and success in terms of attendance:

> I think they will be more successful simply because the people they have at home encourage them to come to school, and school is not a choice. You have to go because they have those role models of people in their home who value education. You know, some of them, their parent is going back to school, or their aunt has gone back to school, or they have a cousin who is in the same grade as they are, so they have some kind of role-model to follow. Education is valued.

Again, this makes reference to a broader view of the student as an individual within society who is affected by much more than what occurs within the confines of the school, and that these issues must be taken up in addressing students' needs.

Visions for the Future of the Program

When asked about changes that could benefit the Program, issues included the support of the Board of Education in terms of housing the Program within a school environment. This would increase the facilities available, and make teachers and guidance counsellors within the mainstream system more familiar and able to identify candidates:

> I think, if it's housed in a regular high school, and ... teachers are familiar with it, they can identify students that would be candidates for the program, who would benefit the most from the program. They'd be able to take other courses with the general student population, rather than specifically being isolated all the time. So it would help them blend in a little bit more. Also co-op ... would be something that would really help the students. The ... Program provides students with education during the morning part, five days a week, and then in the afternoons they have co-op placement ... (Merfed)

As the Program develops, it will assume an important role in establishing models of community education and relationships between communities and schools:

> I'm hoping that it could set a model of how communities could be involved in schools ... especially because for African-Canadian kids, the whole notion that only parents can be advocates for their kids. I think in our community that is just not realistic. I think that community centres like ours, who have a mandate, and have an interest in protecting kids, could become sort of surrogate parents and could have a role, in terms of ensuring that kids get the best possible education, and that we can have a role in influencing what that looks like. (Calista)

The need to identify the role of community, in terms of family and advocacy for students, cannot be overstated. Not only do the concerns of individual youth need to be considered, but the dynamics and experiences of the community must be analyzed and taken into consideration in developing strategies. In this case, there is a need to understand "parent" and "family" in a broader and communitarian sense. Flexibility in defining roles allows for more alternatives in trying to solve the issues facing youth within the community. Given the diversity of our society, the future of any educational project intended specifically for any one community will face certain challenges. However, these challenges should be seen at the same time as opportunities to develop creative solutions that draw on the knowledges of such community learning initiatives as those noted herein:

In the Black community we don't always think alike, and have the same vision for the education of our children, but I think there is room for all those visions ... There is no one way of addressing the drop-out rate of our kids. There is no one way of educating and re-engaging them. I think we are better off to try a multi-level or multi-pronged approach. (Calista)

SUMMARY

The necessity of recognizing the way in which community-based practices work to enhance the acheivments of minority youth is reflected in a number of research studies involving parent/family and community participation. Educators may use classroom narratives and practical activities from the community to promote community values, linking academic skills with critical teaching (Bigelow, et al., 1994). Schools benefit from the knowledge that parents bring to the schooling experience regarding their children's prior learning styles, aptitudes, and best learning environments. However, we must remember that parent and community-initiated involvement hinges on a redefinition of teacher roles (see Cummins, 1996; Bigelow, et al., 1994; and James, 1995).

In this context, collaborative relations of power translate into active school-parent partnerships and a feeling of ownership for community learning (Cummins, 1996; Ziegler, 1987, 1989; and Dei, 1993). As already noted, genuine family-school-community partnerships improve academic and social outcomes for youth. Through active parental and community leadership in school programs, many schools have seen dramatic changes that result in significant positive outcomes for youth, as well as for schools, parents, and communities. Teachers feel empowered through collaborative relationships where they learn from youth, families and communities, and the success and self-esteem of youth increase (see also Cummins, 1996; Henry, 1992, 1993; and Ladson-Billings, 1994).

We argue that success must be collectively defined. Since individual teachers cannot fulfill all of the needs of every student, the nature of what we evaluate must change. Educational reform must take a developmental perspective that considers student's learning, interactions and contributions to be basic to the evolution of Canadian culture (Cheng, 1986; 302). The model of the educator who effects a one-way transmission of dominant knowledge needs to be abandoned for the benefit of all students. If educators are made more aware of the learning styles, competencies and multiple intelligences of their students, then each student has a much greater opportunity to access a learning style that will facilitate their success.

We live in a complex society of cross-cultural sharing and blurred cultural lines. Children develop identities that often include the dress, speech patterns and values associated with other races, sexualities and ethnic groups (Steinberg, 1995, p. 139). Evidence demonstrates that dramatic improvement in school achievement, learning outcomes and self-esteem can be gained when Eurocentrism is disrupted, when teachers combine high expectations with a plural curriculum and culturally compatible teaching methods (Gay, 1995, p. 174). Thus a varied teaching style that was originally adopted to suit the "participatory, co-operative [and] collaborative" learning styles found in Afro-Caribbean, Aboriginal communities, would also benefit youth from other backgrounds who struggle in more competitive and individualistic educational settings (Gay, 1995, p. 173).

An expanded notion of "success" could infuse all sites where children learn. If teachers, parents, community members and students demanded to see such school reform, the framers of educational programming and policies would be hard-pressed not to broaden their foci. Thus, student success becomes a multidimensional concept measured in intersecting areas. Every child wants, needs and has a right to be academically successful. However, the realistic fulfillment of these "success needs" will require a co-operative effort between all stakeholders and the students themselves.

CHAPTER 7

REPRESENTATION IN EDUCATION: CENTRING SILENCED VOICES, BODIES AND KNOWLEDGES

INTRODUCTION

> When someone with the authority of a teacher, say, describes the world and you are not in it, there is a moment of psychic disequillibrium as if you looked into a mirror and saw nothing. (Rosaldo, in Rich, 1989, p. ix)

Invisibility, in this perspective, refers to the negation of self and identity which occurs in and through the everyday practices of schooling. These negations erase the social, cultural, historical, and political realities of marginalized groups in society through the exclusive practices of Eurocentrism. Change in educational and social praxis toward a more inclusive paradigm is seen by many as a branch of radical pedagogy rather than as a normative standard for education in a global, post-modern, plural society. The challenge of centring diverse epistemologies within the purview of standard educational practice, requires transcending the notion of multicultural knowledge and "experience" as rituals of song, dance and food. Instead, we must undertake a more substantive approach to knowledge production that situates education within a broad global and epistemological frame of reference. As asserted by Derman-Sparks (1991), extending our educational strategies beyond a "tourist curricula" and towards an integrative anti-racist approach requires a new philosophy of schooling.

This philosophy would acknowledge the multiple identifications that individuals bring to their schooling experience, and it would negotiate that experience respective of their racialized, classed, gendered, ethnic and religious/spiritual bodies. Studies show that marginalized youth use their identities to resist subordination within schools, by exhibiting anti-school behaviours, such as truancy, "acting out," and, in many cases, simply dropping out of school.[1] In other cases, youth cultures within schools have been used in a corporate basis to construct strategies of resistance that are geared towards accommodation and equity for minority issues.[2] Minority students are therefore struggling to find a place within schools that allows their histories and experiences to be part of the curriculum and culture of the school. Student resistance is therefore not a general rejection of education and learning, as it is often perceived. Rather, it is often a rejection of the status quo in education that privileges certain voices and discourses while silencing and marginalizing others.

The link between schooling and the structuring of identity needs to be explored in terms of how students can achieve self esteem, self confidence and self actualization through their schooling experiences. A pedagogy that supports the positive development of student identities must validate the experiences and knowledges they bring with them into the classroom. These diverse epistemologies represent alternative ways of knowing the world and acting within it, and must be accorded a space within educational discourse and praxis. Day to day pedagogical practices need to take into account students "prior learning" and must reflect the diverse histories, values, beliefs, and bodies of the students who enter into today's classrooms as part of a system of learning for all students.

EDUCATION WITHOUT MARGINS: THE CONCEPTUAL CHALLENGE OF INCLUSIVE EDUCATION

The concept of "education without margins" refers to creating a plural centre within educational discourse and praxis that emphasizes diverse epistemologies as core curricular content. It represents an attempt to rethink, re-strategize and reconstruct education as a pluralist project which decentres the canonical texts of Eurocentric traditions as being the primary source of knowledge in schools and society. The production of knowledge from multiple sites and diverse cultural bases must form the fundamental grounds upon which we begin to develop pedagogy in a global, postmodern, and diasporic society.

The hegemonic practices of Eurocentrism represent the imperialism of that knowledge and the simultaneous subversion and erasure of other ways of knowing. There is a need to see Eurocentric knowledge as culturally-situated rather than universal. This calls for a critical, reflexive educational practice which in turn, identifies the role of education in maintaining certain cultural, social, political and economic monopolies. Reproduction theories in education for example, argue that schools produce the ideological, social, and cultural conditions that lead to the reproduction of the social relations of production within a class-based hierarchy. They do this in various ways, according to theories put forward by Althusser, 1971, Bowles and Gintis, 1976, and Bourdieu and Passeron, 1977, through the school's transmission of dominant ideology: practices of differential socialization affecting working and non-working class students; and the cultural domination of the capitalist class. Notions of a "hidden curriculum" are also connected to theories of reproduction in reference to how teacher's attitudes and assumptions affect patterns of differential socialization, evaluation, and treatment. These attitudes and assumptions correspond to the reproduction of social outcomes that are based on racialized, class-based and other hierarchies.

Education, identity and discourses of nationalism also situate education broadly within the sphere of cultural politics. Post-colonial, and anti-racist studies critique the extent to which school curricula embeds notions of dominance and a "nationalist pedagogy" (Bhabha, 1990). Drawing on the work of Homi Bhabha, Depledge (1996), explains the concept of nationalist pedagogy as one which, "encompasses the metanarratives, those particular narrations of the nation which authorize stories that consciously or unconsciously work toward a single voice and, in doing so, repress knowledge of difference" (p. 43). According to Depledge, the nationalist pedagogy of Canada is shaped by multiculturalism and "is a significant feature of the Canadian metanarrative of nation" (p. 43). However, she goes on to argue that it is not the plurality, but rather the binary logic operating within multiculturalism which becomes the salient feature in its narration as nationalist pedagogy (p. 44). By this she refers to the self/other dichotomy of nationality that operates under the guise of multiculturalism. The singularity of the Canadian national narrative is sustained through a superfluous multicultural paradigm that does little to effectively subvert Anglo-Canadian cultural hegemony. Through the study of Language Arts

English policy, curricula and programming, Depledge examines both the role these programs play in "reproducing cultural relations of power in which a narrowly defined we is privileged and protected," and the counter discourses that attempt to rupture these essentialized notions of "Canadianess."

Sajidah Khan, an education consultant involved in the development of anti-racism programs for elementary schools, was a participant in the 1995-96 phase of our research that examined the "best practices" of inclusive education in Ontario schools. Reporting on a unit addressing Canadian national identity, she found that students' perceptions of what characteristics qualified as "Canadian" were very telling:

> Schools and administrators felt that by having students of different colours and backgrounds sitting next to one another was enough, but when we would hold up pictures of different ethnic and racial groups and ask which ones are Canadian, 90 percent of the time they would choose the ones showing people with blonde hair and blue eyes.[3]

The construction of national identity around such essentialized notions maintains the dichotomy of the dominant "self" as it is rooted in the prevailing social norms and the phenotypical characteristics of whiteness, versus the subordinate "other." This is part of a national multicultural metanarrative that gives illusory presence to minorities in schools and society. Educational equity indeed becomes illusory when framed through a dominant cultural lens that fails substantively to capture the realities of students who remain only part of its "peripheral vision." Nurturing feelings of belonging and entitlement among minority students involves pedagogical and curricular strategies that reinforce the notion of Canadian identity as a common, yet plural space, shared by all citizens irrespective of their origins. This must be supported by changes to current educational practices that privilege particular knowledges and histories while silencing others.

For Depledge, inclusive education represents the curricular challenge of constructing alternative programming that opposes the centrality of the "Great Traditions" and canons that infuse education spaces with a singular cultural paradigm. The discussion of inclusivity is therefore situated in this way within broader sociological notions of citizenship and nation-building, where schools provide the ideological backdrop for sustaining dominant interests — at the expense of equity, representation, and power sharing among all of the differentially empowered groups in society.

NEGOTIATING A PRESENCE FOR MINORITIZED STUDENTS

Modes of Representation in Education

As part of a holistic methodology for delivering education to a socially and culturally diverse population, issues of representation are crucial. Representation in education means "describing a world with everyone in it" and reversing the effect of invisibility as related in the opening quote. It begins with rethinking the notion of what curriculum means from a broad multidimensional perspective as is exemplified in the following definition:

> Curriculum is the textbooks and storybooks, the pictures and the seating plan and the group work and the posters and the music, the announcements, the prayers and the readings, the languages spoken in the school, the food in the cafeteria, the visitors to the classrooms, the reception of parents in the office, the races (or race) of the office staff, the custodial staff, the teachers, the administration, the displays of student work, the school teams and the sports played, the clubs, the school logo or emblem, the field trips, the assignments and projects, the facial expressions and body language of everybody, the clothes everybody wears. It is the Whole Environment. (Allingham, 1992)

Understanding curriculum as "the whole environment" and culture within which schooling takes place, means that representation in education is achieved through creating a sense of *presence* for all students in school. It entails that the voices and bodies of all students be central to this holistic understanding of curriculum. Further, it asserts that we see a diversity of knowledges and people within our schools both as knowledge producers and in positions of authority. In short, when we see curriculum as the bodies, cultures, spaces, objects, positions, beliefs, sights, sounds and smells within schools then, an inclusive curriculum, which is positioned through the cultures and experiences of all students, is one that has the broadest range of academic possibilities.

CONCEPTUAL FRAMEWORK

In structuring issues of representation as they are relevant to schooling, three sub-domains can be identified. These are integrative aspects of the process of representation and each must be implemented in order to achieve substantial rather than token forms of inclusion. They are as follows:

1. *Visual representation* or the inclusion of racial and ethnic minorities and their cultures within the visual landscape of the school, including representation in books, posters, art work and other forms of visual representation.

2. *Knowledge representation* or the centring of non-European cultural knowledges and discourses within public education as a means to challenge the centrality of Euro-Canadian/American discourses as the only "valid" forms of knowledge. Alternative books, literature, films and other sources are the central foci of the curriculum. This validates the contributions of non-European peoples to world knowledge (e.g. science, technology, civilization, culture and human development), and brings in a wealth of literary, scientific and cultural resources otherwise absent from the "official knowledge" present in schools.

3. *Staff diversity* or the integration of teachers, administrators and school staff from a variety of racial and ethnic backgrounds. These teachers not only provide role models for minority youth, but bring diverse teaching styles, modes of communication and knowledge into schools for the benefit of all students.

These three sub-domains represent integrative and interactive spheres of knowledge, activity, and pedagogy that re-orient the cultural landscape of schools. They attend to the identity development and self esteem of minority youth while enhancing learning opportunities for all students who must learn to exist within an increasingly globalized local context.

Visual Representation

This sub-domain addresses the need for students to see themselves represented in the physical structures of the school and classroom, what can be called the "visual culture of the school." This involves seeing images in books, posters, artwork, et cetera, that reflect the visual diversity of the student population.

Visual representation is one means through which to validate the experience and cultural knowledge of minority students. It enhances learning opportunities for all students in a world of increasing economic and cultural integration. An understanding of different forms of cultural knowledge must be included in the repertoire of requisite learning for students who must confront globalization as an economic, social and cultural reality. Using the visual medium, issues of identity politics and the representation of marginalized groups in society are centred as a pedagogical strategy of inclusion and are used to re-orient the visual landscape and culture of schools. One of the imperatives of inclusive schools must be to express this multi-racial and multi-ethnic reality in both *cultural form* (i.e., visual representation of racial and ethno-cultural diversity in various forms of art and cultural artifacts) and *content* (i.e., an understanding of the different knowledges , beliefs and experiences that relate to and inform the cultural forms represented). By promoting access to different forms of cultural knowledge through such strategies, the Eurocentric basis for public education is decentred and a global perspective is created.

For primary education, educating differences through the visual medium is particularly appropriate. However, visual representation must be counterbalanced with an understanding of cultural knowledge. This can be acquired through various strategies. We found South and South East Asian heritage and culture visually reflected throughout one of the primary schools researched in this study. The presence of Chinese art and the use of Indian clothes in the dress-up centre were all indicative of a sincere dedication to an inclusive philosophy. Importantly, these visual representations were not displayed as artifacts or as pleasant reminders of a far away and "exotic" culture. Rather, they were incorporated into the visual culture of the school. This was in addition to the use of multicultural and multilingual books that were available to both students and parents. While this begins to integrate both visual representation and knowledge representation, it must be seen as primary step toward a more concerted effort to implement a more "multi-centric focus," where different centres of knowledge are equally represented and not simply "attached" to a dominant centre.

These strategies attempt to link cultural form (i.e., art and cultural artifacts) with content (i.e., knowledge). Also, by utilizing family and community partnerships as part of the educative process, they integrate another important dimension into the process of inclusivity, that of community integration. This approach recognizes that educational reforms must extend beyond the simple placation of minority group concerns. The centring of otherwise marginalized knowledges should be seen as a positive opportunity for all students to gain a broader understanding of the diverse histories and experiences that shaped and continue to shape our world. Cynthia, a kindergarten teacher, reinforces this notion:

> I think it's not only [that] we want their culture to be reflected in the school, but they also have to learn about other children's cultures and to learn a respect for that. And at this age it's so easy, because they don't really come in with a lot of the parents' biases. I think those form later. But, at the beginning of the year we see Chinese kids holding Black kids' hands — there's no boundaries.[4]

Opportunities to cross boundaries and learn through more than one centre of knowledge has specific implications for how cultural relationships are formed from very early childhood. The plurality of cultural forms expressed within the school through visual means, "re-situates" conventional Eurocentric cultural practices as one of many ways of knowing and framing the world. According to an Anti-Racism Education guide prepared by the Ontario Secondary School Teachers Federation:

> Images and events that are affirmed in the school give strong messages about the relative importance of the different racial and cultural groups in the school. These messages are communicated by the absence of equitable inclusion of people of different backgrounds in classroom resources, the visual material posted in the halls and the classrooms and the material in the libraries. (OSSTF, 1995)

A visually inclusive school, therefore, not only affirms difference but affirms the bodies, origins, beliefs and histories of its students. The absence of these images results in the erasures, denials and overall incompleteness of the school culture, and it compromises the self esteem of minority students who remain invisible. Used holistically, visual representation provides a medium for inclusion that can flow through arts, crafts and drama as an integrated pedagogical practice. What we see in school hallways, cafeterias, offices, playgrounds and assemblies is a direct reflection of the culture of the school, and that reflection speaks to who is welcomed, acknowledged, and valued.

The physical surroundings of a school often have much to say about the organization of a school's culture. Much of this can be read by examining what is displayed on the walls. This can inform us of whether the school culture is based on Eurocentric conventions or whether it has an inclusive philosophy. The following example of one school's use of the visual medium represents an example of inclusive representation that is balanced by an attempt to connect cultural meaning to diverse cultural forms.

School A is an inner city elementary school. During the second phase of research on exemplary inclusive practices in 1995, the school became a case study for representation in inclusive schooling practices. The majority of students in the school are from working class immigrant backgrounds, predominantly from East Asia, South Asia and the Caribbean. There were only five white students in the entire school at the time this research was conducted placing them in the ironic circumstance of being a "dominant minority." The majority of parents in the school used English as a second language or had very little or no English language facility. Nonetheless, the students had out-performed students in other areas of the school district and were awarded the Canadian Award for Quality in Education in 1994. Much of the success can be attributed to the principal and school staff's commitment to inclusive schooling practices as being fundamental to the way teaching and learning took place in their school.

Visually, the school presented a very global vantage point for the articulation of student experiences and cultural knowledge. For example, essays in social and cultural transitions, depicting the cultural processes of integration many of the students encountered as immigrants, were created through the use of visual art forms and displayed throughout the school. These were cultural vignettes; a montage of images created through pieces of fabric that were cut into figures and scenery, and sewn onto a large cloth poster with captions such as the following: *"When Vietnam was home...."* *"Now Canada is home ..."* Displayed as murals, they presented student narratives of their homeland and their perceptions of life in Canada. One, for example, contrasted life in Vietnam and in Canada, through images such as: going to the beach in Vietnam and going to the movies in Canada; going to the zoo in Vietnam (picture of pandas), going to the C.N. Tower in Canada. The mural reflected positive images and experiences in both countries.

In other examples of how the visual medium was used to create inclusion, pictures of the students who are predominately non-white and from immigrant families adorned the walls of the school and showed them individually and co-operatively working on various projects, such as painting a large Chinese dragon on a wall. Inside the classrooms there were displays of student art, such as self-portraits, which showed different skin colours. There were books on different countries prominently displayed, and posters that depicted social diversity throughout the school. There was also a display of farm animals featuring animals indigenous to other countries in one of the classrooms. The principal commented on this as part of the simplicity of their approach to inclusive education:

> It's just thinking about things in a different way, saying there are different kinds of farms that have not been mentioned in there and lets find out about them. So, it's really the teachers, once they get to that then it really doesn't matter what the Ministry sends us we just make it inclusive whether it happens to be or not. And I just say to them, just ask the question: "is there something missing here?." Ask the kids, they'll tell you. Maybe somebody grew up on a Yak farm or whatever. (Lata)

Using culture and prior knowledge as the basis for a student-centred pedagogy provides culturally-relevant academic programming that can be implemented using existing curricula. Inclusive education will ultimately be transformative at very localized levels within individual schools. There must be a reconceptualization of how education is to be delivered in a globalized society. In this respect curricular changes will likely entail a re-inventing and adapting of existing materials in ways that interrogate their partiality and inadequacy relative to diverse perspectives and knowledges. The challenge of inclusive education then, is the reorienting of existing materials so that they reflect these multiple vantage points. The visual medium is a particularly salient tool for working against the invisibility experienced by minority students. Nevertheless if it were the only measure of inclusion, it would remain a token gesture. A true remediation of existing standards involves attending to cultural content along with the visual forms through which it may be represented. This involves an interrogation of the kinds of knowledge schools privilege and those which are silenced or absent. The following section examines the issue of knowledge integration as being central to, and contingent upon all other forms of representation in education.

Knowledge Representation

This form of representation takes a critical role in interrogating how knowledges are produced with respect to issues of power. Indigenous, community-based and other forms of marginalized knowledges are seen as part of a multi-centred focus and enter into the sphere of public education as alternative discourses that decentre dominant Eurocentric traditions. The central questions posed with regard to knowledge representation ask: How do educators integrate diverse knowledges, histories, cultures and experiences as part of everyday pedagogy and practice? And, how do we challenge conventional forms of knowledge and create spaces for alternate ways of knowing?

Knowledge representation involves active learning about different cultures, histories, and experiences. Knowledge representation can be implemented in various ways. For example, it may be reflected in the availability of multicultural resources, the active celebration and recognition of different religious holidays, and the use of media literacy programs. These strategies allow students to make linkages between their local realities and broader global issues. While visual representation serves as an outward indicator of a commitment to valuing different cultural experiences, knowledge representation attempts to explore the linkages at an epistemological level. This provides validation for difference through the inclusion of multiple knowledges and ways of knowing.

The role of Indigenous knowledges can be seen as part of an alternate system of education based on experiential forms of learning that have historically been transmitted orally and through song and dance.

> Native education systems handed down folk wisdom on every aspect of village life. Proverbs, riddles, games and songs have all served as educational instruments among illiterate people in small villages. These informal ways, Dewey and others concluded, provided the kinds of dialogue primarily responsible for an individual's intellectual growth. (O'Connor:1995, p. 198)

Under the auspices of Eurocentrism, there has been only one locus for the transmission of knowledge. Education in North American contexts has always proceeded within a perspective that privileges Western "ways of knowing" as neutral and/or legitimate. However, these qualities are not intrinsic to Western knowledge. How we understand "education" and how we determine the validity of a knowledge system is entirely specific to our cultural, political and historical contexts. There are many ways of bringing knowledge into the classroom aside from those accepted in traditional Western frameworks. Indigenous systems employ oral skills, storytelling, drama and song as means to transmit culture and knowledge. Utilized in schools these pedagogical skills can be incorporated as part of a more holistic methodology for learning. This perspective of education asserts that knowledge is not only contained or confined to classrooms. Rather, we would suggest that it involves using the local communities as a classroom and extending the parameters of learning beyond the school walls.

Educational sites are infused with the knowledges of any and all who enter. Parents, students, community members are all bearers of knowledge and should be used as resources by schools. Home and community knowledges must be accessed and the community must be reconceptualized as a site of knowledge production. In School A, parents were invited into classrooms as "cultural informants" to teach the children about their culture through songs and storytelling. It should be taken into account, however, when inviting parents as informants, that they should not be expected to "perform" as part of a multicultural "experience." It cannot be assumed that all parents will have positive life experiences to share, especially those who may have come from situations of crisis within their homelands. Using parents as a source of knowledge is an important aspect of representation, however, it should be seen as one of many strands of inclusion that lead to the centring of experiences from outside of the dominant culture. It is the multiplicity of these experiences that must be taken into account and understood before parents are asked to "share" these experiences.

Adapting these different forms and modes of knowledge into an inclusive pedagogy entails creating a counter-discourse in terms of the prevailing notions of what sort of knowledge and ways of learning are considered valid. Dominant educational paradigms render alternative knowledges as part of an "event-oriented" approach to education, reserved for multicultural festivals. Their efficacy as valid counter-models to current educational methodologies are rarely acknowledged. According to Depledge (1996),

> ... compartmentalization of counter-discourses helps to sustain an epistemology which adheres to a centre versus margin model. Certain knowledges are characterized as curiosities or as special

interest group knowledges which are, by implication, not important or true or disinterested or universal enough to be included in standard courses. The danger is that such courses prop up the notion that some knowledges are ideologically situated while others are not. They may actually protect the homogeneity of mainstream courses by *appearing* to redress their exclusions. (p. 46)

Existing multicultural paradigms are part of a "nationalist" pedagogy that seeks to "manage difference." It is an environment that silences counter-hegemonic discourses and takes them up within spaces allocated to "the exotic" or "the radical."

In creating a multi-voiced counter narrative, a new curriculum of learning must be redesigned to reflect alternate realities and worldviews. Schooling must be reoriented to reflect the contributions of non-European cultures to scientific and academic work. The history of human development in arts, science, culture and the building of civilization is marked by the absenses, erasures and denials of non-European contributions and historical developments. Historical reclamations by marginalized people have retrieved accounts that tell of African and Arab explorers in North America and the Caribbean prior to Columbus (see Austin, 1984; Van Sertima, 1987; and Quick, 1996). According to Hamdani (1990) studies suggest that early Muslim traders from West Africa explored America prior to Columbus's "discovery" of the "New World." These studies show that the Mandingoes of West Africa had established trade with Native Americans along the Mississippi river all the way to Canada. Although well documented and researched, these historical facts and developments have failed to enter into school curricula or North American historical discourses. An understanding and representation of diverse histories and how they collectively have come to constitute and contribute toward North American society and civilization are crucial to developing inclusive education.

Representation of diverse knowledges must cross-cut all disciplinary foci (i.e., arts, sciences, economics, history, politics, et cetera). Contributions of non-European societies within these disciplines must be central to the discursive representation of knowledge. The partial readings of human development, which have denied the accomplishments and achievements of these groups, must be addressed. Understanding the totality of social and intellectual forces that have propelled human development over the centuries and into the present millennium, is not simply the recounting of "folk histories." A reading of this nature represents a context for all humanity, including those who have shared in the benefits, struggles and discontinuities that have occurred as a result of partial historical truths.

Knowledge representation also involves understanding the link between knowledge production and identity. It represents the curricular challenge of understanding curriculum as a form of representation that embodies a politics of identity. Seeing knowledge as it is embodied within the social actors who are part of the educative process (students, teachers, parents, administrative staff, community members) means creating a broader purview for knowledge production and the development of new discursive sites. A holistic understanding of curriculum places these bodies as "mico-centres" of knowledge, which collectively comprise the overall culture of learning within the school.

According to Pinar (1993), there is a need to understand curriculum as a "racial text." Although Pinar refers to the American context, his observations hold relevance to the plural nature of North American society in general. Using a psychoanalytical approach, he states: "Curriculum is one highly significant form of representation, and arguments over the curriculum are also arguments over who we are as Americans and how we wish to represent ourselves to our children" (p. 60). He describes curriculum as "a discursive formation of identity and difference," that selectively represents and supports particular formations of identities at the expense of others which result in "splitting off the excess as 'difference'" (p. 61). He speaks of the American "self" and "identity" as multivocal concepts that are expressed only through binary realities and oppositional discourses. Understanding curriculum as racial text, he argues, means understanding ourselves as racial texts (p. 63). This means acknowledging the racialization of society as being all pervasive and representative of the North American social condition and psyche. He argues that the splitting off of self/other through the denial and unrecognized histories of Africans, Asians and Latinos, disallows the white American psyche to know itself as it is intrinsically connected to these other histories and subjective realities. Denying issues of race within the curriculum does not make it less of a racialized text. Rather, according to Pinar, it only denies whites the opportunity to also conceive of themselves as racialized: "All Americans are racialized beings; knowledge of who we have been, who we are and who we will become is a text; curriculum — our construction and reconstruction of this knowledge — is indeed a racial text (p. 63)."

To deny the racialized basis of curriculum is a form of psychic repression according to Pinar. Venturing through a denied past, is in his estimation, a social-psychological remedy for coming to understand the plurality of identifications that are part of the American national identity and North American experience. Correspondingly these identifications must be acknowledged through the curriculum as contributing to a racialized text. Understanding this means recognizing that knowledge, like the identities through which it becomes produced, is racialized and therefore discursively situated within specific relations of power.

Examining issues of knowledge representation lead to a singular conclusion regarding pedagogy and the cultural politics that pedagogical practices often seek to avoid. Educational practices must apply techniques of critical self-reflexive thinking and explore new centres of knowledge and ways of knowing in order to be relevant and necessary in a changing global atmosphere. This represents an integrative approach to addressing issues of race and social difference within the politics of social justice and educational reform. The starting point toward this end will proceed from different vantage points. The following section will explore the politics of representation as it is situated in the bodies of those who represent positions of authority within schools.

Staff Diversity

The sub-domain of staff equity includes those practices that actively pursue the recruitment of teachers and support staff from various racial and ethnic backgrounds. Employment equity and diversity in schooling is critical to inclusive education and the corresponding issue of power sharing. A representative staff can, provide role models for students, contribute a diversity of worldviews to the school culture, and validate difference for students.

School principals interviewed during the 1995-96 phase of our research pointed out that most teachers are transfers from other schools. However, one principal mentioned some consulting that she had done as a senior member of the Principal's Association. She said there are two important questions that a Board of Education must ask. First, how can we attract racial minority educators? Second, how can we remove barriers to equitable hiring practices? In her work with the Principal's Association, she noted numerous problematics in the hiring process:

There were some assumptions being made about … how people were responding. You know, eye contact … kinesthics, all that stuff that [is] culturally bound. (Ann)

She tried to develop sensitivity among the interviewers, in order to ensure that they were listening to the content of the responses. In addition, the interview questions are screened for culturally laden language:

previously when you say … "tell us what you did," you would be looking for someone to really brag about themselves … it would come across in some cultures as bragging about themselves which would be culturally inappropriate. So now we say things like "describe what you would do if." (Ann)

When grade eight students at one school were asked who their favourite teacher was, they referred to their grade seven teacher. One Black student reported a significant increase in his marks from grade six to the end of grade seven. He attributed this to his grade seven teacher, a Grenadian-Canadian who has since retired from teaching. The student stated that his teacher pushed him to do well, and from a 72 percent in grade six, he jumped to an overall average of 84 percent at the end of grade seven and was on the honour roll.

He would tell me that I should do better … made sure I was organized, he was pretty strict. (Alex)

This teacher stressed excellence and had high expectations for all of his students. When he returned to the school for an assembly, the students flocked to him; he was very much admired by all of the students. It was evident, seeing so many students of African descent (of African and Caribbean origin) all around him, that he had a great impact on them. This response by students speaks clearly to the need for a greater representation of African and racial minority teachers.

The benefits of a culturally diverse staff reflect in areas of knowledge representation as well as linguistic diversity. Teachers and teaching assistants from different racial and ethnic backgrounds can impart their cultural knowledge to students as well as share their particular language skills. The following section provides a brief case study from the 1995-96 phase of this research that examined innovative shifts in hiring policies that enabled teachers from Somalia to teach in local schools with school and community-based support.

CASE 1: TEACHER TRAINING PILOT PROJECT FOR TEACHERS TRAINED IN SOMALIA

The Somali-Canadian Association (Metro Toronto Chapter) received approval for a program from the MET for certification of teachers who were qualified to teach in Somalia. This was a community-initiated project in partnership with the local Board of Education. The teachers worked with the host teachers from the local schools. Workshops and staff development (for both Somali-trained teachers and host teachers) were included in the program. At the end of the year long certification course, Somali-trained teachers received their Letter of Permission to teach in Ontario. The Supervisory Committee for the project consisted of two Somali-Canadian community representatives, one anti-racism educator, one ESL coordinator, two principals and one superintendent. At one meeting, the two Somali-Canadian members of the Supervisory Committee indicated that their community outreach had resulted in twenty candidates (the number they had proposed to the MET). Seventeen of the candidates had documentation. For those who were not able to present documentation, affidavits were made on their behalf.

The program consisted of 30 percent community service and 70 percent practice teaching in elementary and secondary schools. The community service would include liaison work and translation, but emphasis was on a tutoring club for Somali-Canadian students, which has since begun. The tutoring was identified as a need by parents to the principal on the elementary school report card.

MAKING CONNECTIONS TO RACE, CLASS, GENDER, SEXUALITY AND RELIGION

Issues of representation in education are basic to issues of equity in education. In most schools, visual, knowledge and staff diversity, are areas where various social differences such as race, class, gender, sexuality and religion, are either absent or marginally represented. These categories represent multiple layers of identity, as well as multiple sites of political engagement and contestation within education. Claiming voice and representation in education is a political act that currently involves many historically disadvantaged groups in society vying for spaces of inclusion. The challenge in negotiating these spaces involves operationalizing the notion that all systems of oppression are connected and "interlocking" and therefore addressing only one oppression ignores the interelationships with other oppressions; a strategy that ultimately fails to dismantle the overall structure of domination. Schools must become a primary arena for anti-discrimination and human rights education that confront issues of access and equity in society. Programming that targets various forms of discrimination and unravels the relationships of power that sustain them are necessary to contribute to the goal of "safe schools" as sites where all students are free from harassment.

Many traditionally disadvantaged groups in society are also connected to bases of knowledge that come from racial, ethnic, religious/spiritual roots. These knowledges have historic value as part of a silenced legacy that has contributed to social and cultural development globally. It is necessary to begin to centre these knowledges as part of a more holistic reading of history and the events that shape and continue to shape our world. The role of women has also been a silent factor, traditionally absent from the versions of history taught in schools. According to Thomas (1997) "...school curriculum has traditionally mirrored the experiences of middle class, heterosexual, able males of European heritage" (p. 56). Moving beyond this limited epistemological framework toward a multicentric focus, means that education must be envisioned and delivered in a way that challenges multiple oppressions. The various ways that issues of race, class, gender, sexuality, religion and ability have been excluded from schools must be addressed within an inclusive framework.

Social differences are ontological categories that represent positions of individual and collective identification. These are multiple/overlapping layers of identity that simultaneously inhabit and situate us in society. Even among minoritized groups there are differential positions of power and subordination. Strands of privilege and subordination cross-cut boundaries of difference that complicate simple equations between these categories. This also problematizes the notion of there being such thing as a "unity of oppressions." In fact, there are often competing and conflicting interests among various marginalized groups in society. Moving beyond these paralyzing differences means finding common ground with regard to how we envision schools as safe learning environments for all. For example, gay and lesbian students often experience physical and verbal harassment, not just from other students but also teachers and other staff (see Campey, McCaskell, Miller and Russell, 1994; Smith, McCoy and Bourne, 1995; Lenskyj, 1997). Making sure schools engage in human rights education to protect and preserve the ability of all students to be free from discrimination and harassment in schools is necessary to the reality of living within a plural society and respecting the human rights of others.

Along with issues of discrimination, there are concerns regarding the production and dissemination of knowledge related to women, and racial, ethnic, and religious minorities. The erasures of women's realities from the school textbooks and the modes of representation that subordinate the role of women vis-à-vis men in society, have been documented in the narratives female students presented in a study by Smith, McCoy and Bourne (1995). One student commented on the marginalization of women within the school curricula and how this rendered her identity as "insignificant":

The art history books don't emphasize women as being the masters of art — any of the areas where women could be role models or inspiration for other women. Along the top of the art studios there's a time chart from the beginning of art to now — there isn't one woman on that time chart. I went to the head of art — he's a man…he didn't really understand why I was upset with it ; that I could look at that and then feel insignificant as a woman artist (p. 23).

It is not only the lack of representation, but the portrayal of women that can be problematic. For example the role of women as "damsels in distress" in children's fairy tales presents women through a victim-centred stereotype and situates men as the "rescuers." Stereotypical representations such as this are commonplace and need to be interrogated as biased and uni-dimensional portrayals of womens' realities. The politics of social positioning as it relates to the maintenance of patriarchal or Eurocentric dominance is important to unravel through the use of biased texts as part of a critical pedagogical approach to rupturing stereotypes. Using biased textbooks and storybooks to help students identify the images and tropes of power and subordination can be a powerful pedagogical strategy for critical reflection on the representation of difference.

In examining the concerns of female Somali students in Toronto, Rezai-Rashti (1997) also looks at stereotypes through the contexts of race, class, gender and religion in the schooling experiences of these students. She critiques the way in which schools have taken up "women's issues in other cultures" through essentialized treatment and "old colonial attitudes toward women." She argues that:

It is very important to discuss issues specific to gender treatment in different cultures as long as it is understood that not everybody in those cultures fits the stereotypical descriptions and that a woman's situation varies depending on her social class, rural/urban setting and many other variables (p. 24).

In her work as a school community liaison counsellor, Rezai -Rashti confronted issues of discrimination encountered by female Somali students that have in some instances, erupted into physical aggression. These students were harassed as the result of a television documentary on female circumcision, which they felt had generated racism against them at school. Rezai-Rashti reports that they were persistently asked "why they could not abandon a culture that was so obviously backward when compared to 'Canadian culture'" (p. 25). The essentialized representations of their identity and perceived reality through practice of female circumcision, was used as a means to further "otherize" these students on the grounds of the multiple social differences they represented and embodied. Rezai-Rashti writes that:

These students felt that because of their socio-economic status, race, culture, religion, and last but not least, their gender, they were perceived by other students, and sometimes by their teachers, as inherently inferior in terms of a pseudo-hierarchical order with other cultural and religious groups in their school. Because of their religion (Islam) and gender, they came to believe that other students thought of them as, submissive, obedient, oppressed and even mutilated individuals incapable of experiencing any sort of sexual pleasure (p. 26).

The notions of difference that are embodied within identities and their representation within both schools and society need to be understood through these multiple intersections of race, ethnicity, class, gender, sexuality and religion. Moving beyond the colonial and victimized representations of women that paint a unidimensional portrait of their identities vis-à-vis men, or as racialized others, we begin to rupture the static representations that marginalize and limit the potential of all young women growing up in today's schools.

Religious discrimination is also prevalent in schools in various ways. For example, the recent debate in Saskatoon over the Lord's Prayer being recited in schools reinforced the dominance of Christian traditions in a religiously plural society. According to a newspaper report,the province of Saskatchewan was given the power to allow the Lord's Prayer and Bible readings in public schools under the law that brought the province into Confederation (*Toronto Star,* 07/14/99). However a lawyer for the Saskatchewan government denied that the law prevents Saskatoon's public board of education from "making spiritual education more inclusive" (*Toronto Star*, 07/16/99). Nine parents from non-Christian backgrounds have accused the school board of discrimination on the basis of religion. Other school boards in Ontario and Manitoba and British Columbia have ruled that reciting the Lord's Prayer interferes with freedom of religion provisions in provincial human rights codes as well as in the Canadian Charter of Rights and Freedoms.

While these rulings disallow the privileging of Christian prayer in schools, other Christian-based holidays and traditions such as Christmas and Easter still comprise a large part of elementary curriculum as dominant pedagogical themes. The issue here is not to take away from dominant cultural practices, but to decentre them and make room for other cultural realities. Otherwise, the attempt to keep schools "secular spaces" ignores the fact that while schools may attempt to be secular — many students are not. Attending to the emotional and spiritual aspects of students' identity as we have discussed previously, is an important aspect of their sense of self and how they create meaning in their lives. The failure to provide space for students' religious and spiritual identities to be an instrument in their learning experiences negates an important aspect of their being. While avoiding prostelytizing any faith, schools can still be open to the idea of various religions and spiritual traditions. To do so would allow students access to ways of knowing and reading the world that have had a profound impact on human history.

Social class is another factor in schools that becomes racialized through the differential value and treatment accorded to white middle-class standards. Delpit (1988), refers to these standards as the "culture of power" (p. 283). The social rules within the "culture of power" specifically govern "linguistic forms, communicative strategies, and presentations of self; that is ways of talking, ways of writing, ways of dressing and ways of interacting" (p. 283). By privileging only dominant middle-class standards as the marker of appropriate forms of communication, dress and interaction, schools effectively mute and marginalize students who do not conform to these racialized or class-based standards.

Attitudes toward success, as we have seen, are also classed. Schools that encompass only white middle-class norms and values do not adequately represent the realities of working-class families. Poverty and low economic status are seen as individual failures rather than the product of social constraints. Promoting visions of meritocracy, where individual success and failure does not consider the effect of structural barriers as they affect the progress of minority groups in society, fails to allow students to develop a more complex understanding of social organization. Examining issues of class historically for example, through lessons relating to different kinds of social structures that have characterized previous societies (feudalism for example) can help students make connections to the current relationship between class and other forms of social difference. According to Thomas:

> Understanding that all human experiences (including our own) are grounded in one's ethnic, racial, sexual, class, and gender identities creates a new lens for viewing both the content and processes of the school curriculum, and gradually, our curricular thinking may become more inclusive (1997, p. 55).

Gazing both through and past our own lenses in order to understand the complex arrangement of social differences in society is a necessary challenge for educators in a plural society. Transcending our own subjectivities to understand the constructedness of all subject locations is an important first step toward using knowledge to engender social change.

SUMMARY

Drawing from the preceding sub-domains and case studies it is possible to see how visual representation, knowledge representation and staff diversity can provide the optimum conditions for learning within an inclusive environment. Individually they address the issue of antiracism and equity in various forms. First, equity is promoted through the visual culture of the school. Second, the content of the curriculum and the need to make it more consonant with the gender, racial, ethnic and religious diversity found in society and the global realities and histories that inform the lives of all students is achieved through representing these various knowledge bases. Finally, employment equity is achieved through the recruitment of teachers from various backgrounds who serve as role models for minority students and provide an important cultural resource for the school. When these strategies of inclusion are combined, they address the inequities of both representation and power by according legitimacy and voice to minority cultures and by actively implementing employment equity as a means to encourage a racially and ethnically diverse school staff and administration.

While these case studies have identified certain forms of representation, they must be viewed as part of an ongoing process. Furthermore, they must be grounded in a sincere attempt to achieve equity; otherwise, they can be negatively constructed as token gestures that amount to little more than a "tourist curriculum." For example, social studies classes are frequently the context for learning about different cultures and histories. In a grade six class during our research, students commented that they were learning about Mayan culture and were working on a project. When asked what the project entailed, two students indicated that everyone had to present an article about Mayan history or mythology; they also added, however, that they had to do an advertisement "... since [Mexico] is like really hot, so we're talking about ... hat and sunglasses" (Matt). Although students revealed some knowledge of Mayan history and mythology, there is a concern that the culture is being reduced to what could amount to a travel brochure. One grade eight student whose family was from Jamaica commented on the contradictions between what she had learned at school and what she learned from a visit to Jamaica:

> The tourist parts, they make it look so pretty like the sand is all one colour and the beach and there's no garbage, no this, no that. But where I come from, it's a totally different story.[5]

Decontextualizing culture and historical realities runs the risk of producing "otherizing" notions of culture. It does little to produce genuine inclusion, or cross-cultural knowledge of the realities in other countries.

Styles (1988) developed a metaphor for curriculum as being both a "window" and a "mirror." Curriculum as a "window" allows students to see the realities of others, while curriculum as a "mirror" allows for the representation of their own realities (cited in Thomas, 1997, p. 55). This provides an interesting conceptualization of curriculum as a medium for knowing oneself and others. However, the same caution needs to be applied in terms of the nature of this representation being truly connected to students self conceptions and not stereotypes. As Pinar (1993) has reminded us, "understanding the curriculum as a racial text, means understanding ourselves as racial texts." This is an important aspect of reading diverse bodies within the curriculum and still being attentive to the issues of power that govern such possibilities. Issues of racialized, classed and gendered power and privilege are embedded within the curriculum and texts within schools. Understanding how this limits the choices and possibilities of minority students is the first step toward curricular reform based on an integrative and inclusive framework.

It is important for the school's promotion of multicultural representation not to hinge/rest on the mere or bland recognition of cultural pluralism. The question of race and difference is central to the promotion of inclusive representation in schools. This means education, for example, must see the centrality of race and difference in all facets of the schooling experience for youth. Schooling in North America is a racially mediated experience. This racialization of experience demands that questions of representation be dealt with in ways that recognizes both the primacy and saliency of race and difference. Schools should openly promote knowledge about race and social difference through a variety of educational practices. Similarly, the importance of schools having diverse staff representation rests on the theoretical idea that knowledge production is linked with questions of identity and history. Our individual histories, personal identities and identifications influence how we read the world and how we construct social meanings. Questions of representation are read as dealing with power and structural equities in the school system. The presence of diverse bodies in schools should be seen as an effective means of dealing with structural hegemony and as an attempt at rupturing Eurocentred dominance and normativity.

NOTES

1   See Willis, 1979 and Davies, 1994 , for discussions on class-based student resistance, and Solomon, 1992 and Dei, Mazzuca, McIsaac and Zine, 1997, for discussions on race and resistance .

2   See Zine, (forthcoming), regarding how students develop corporate modes of "formalized resistance" based on religious identification.

3   Dei et al. 1996. *Unpacking What Works: A Critical Examination of "Best Practices" of Inclusive Schooling In Ontario.* Ontario Institute For Studies in Education/ University of Toronto.

4   1996. Dei et al. "Best Practices."

5   1996. Dei et al. "Best Practices."

CHAPTER 8

INTEGRATIVE AND INCLUSIVE APPROACHES: COMMUNITY SCHOOLING

INTRODUCTION

The notion of "community schooling" is often complicated by scholars who debate the problem of finding an accurate definition of what the term means in theory and in practice (Fletcher, 1987; Mitchell, 1987; Martin, 1987). As suggested by Martin (1987), "community" has become an ubiquitous label that in some sense has lost its political flavour. The term, in its common and often haphazard use, has come to have a sort of "functional ambiguity." So much so, that "community" as a term, has often been co-opted in political dialogues and discourse. The sense of malleability that accompanies the term has allowed its meanings to become site and temporally specific. In fact, by 1955, ninety-four specific definitions of "community" could be found in the literature (Fletcher, 1987, p. 34)

In Martin's view, how we define community is crucial because it implies a critical and informed choice between an intrinsically hierarchical, regressive, static model of social relations and one that is emancipatory and dynamic. Yet, he argues, community educators often explore meaning at the expense of "espousing a cause" (p. 12). Seeing communities as progressive social and cultural bodies has important implications for their role vis-à-vis schools. This provides a vantage point for linking the changing conceptions of community to locally based causes for social change.

Two central questions necessary to unpack the meaning of community education must be: How can we define community in ways that best capture the social relations embedded within it, and, what should the role of community be when we speak of "community education"? According to Fletcher (1987), "community is defined by one's relationship with people," and is not necessarily geographically fixed or even based on amicable relations, arguing that social bonds of enmity can also be constituted as "community" (p. 34). Indeed, the boundaries of definition can be greatly reductive or conflated depending upon the urgency and need for meaning to be derived. As is the case with many other social categories such as race, gender, class, and sexuality, postmodern orientations against essentialized meanings often result in contestations over the elusive nature of social reality and, therefore, the fundamental difficulty in naming anything. There is, however, a need to get beyond the perpetual instability of postmodern visions of society, which can be ultimately paralyzing to attempts at theorizing transformative possibilities, in order to examine the relationship between communities and schools in an albeit changing society.

CONCEPTUAL FRAMEWORK

The domain of community schooling recognizes schools as "situated sites" located geographically, culturally and historically in local sites and settings. The "local community," within which schools are constituted, is represented by parents/caregivers and extended families, neighborhoods, and racial/ ethnic/cultural/religious groups. Therefore, a school's policies, practices and curriculum should integrate and reflect the knowledge, experiences and histories of the local community. In a plural and increasingly globalized society in North America, the notion of community schooling provides points of access from local sites of learning, such as the "pedagogy of the home," or community learning centres, and connects them into broader systems of knowledge. Education within a diasporic context represents a dialectical relationship between the local sites and discourses, and global realities.

According to Stuart Hall (1991b), the "local" represents, in part, a retreat from the "global." He argues that the local is often a response to globalization (p. 33). The grand scope and all-inclusiveness of globalization, he argues, causes some to "opt out" of a system to which they have little access.

According to Hall, the familiarity of the "local" develops in that the neighborhood, village and community, are knowable terrains against the "anonymous impersonal world of global forces" (p. 35). Increasingly, however, with the post-colonial world of diasporas, supra-territorial flows of culture and mass migrations of people throughout the hemispheres make it impossible to link culture to discrete spaces. This, in many contexts in North America, makes it difficult to define the local in homogenous terms. Instead of a retreat from the global, what results is, the "globalization of the local."

De-spacializing notions of cultural differences problematizes the formerly clear distinctions between home and abroad. The plurality of migrant/displaced races and ethnics has infused centres across the globe. The result has been a mass importing of cultures and habits... eventually leading to the development of hybrid cultural forms. This makes it clear that "the erosion of such supposedly natural connections between people and places has not led to the modernist specter of global cultural homogenization" (Clifford, cited in Gupta, 1992, p. 10).

In theorizing community education from this understanding of the local-as-global, we can develop a basis for an integrative and inclusive model for community schooling. Yet, according to Allen et al. (1987):

> Community education recognizes that people have needs, that these should be identified or diagnosed and that these needs are diverse. Needs-oriented education starts from a vision of humanity rather than a structure of knowledge (Allen, G. et al. (eds.) 1987, p. 273).

The contention that separates education as a "vision of humanity" from "structures of knowledge" fails to recognize the social constructedness of knowledge and how "visions of humanity" are inscribed (often singularly) within the bases of knowledge promoted within schools. Analytically separating notions of humanity and structures of knowledge may not be the ideal way in which to conceive of a needs-oriented approach to education, which would surely benefit from a reconstructed understanding of how they inform and are implicated within one another. Also acknowledging the diversity of needs and voices through which communities must come to be represented in schooling, O'Connor (1995) states that "The public must be defined as a polyvocal conversation rather than a single culture" (p. 200). Poly-vocality in education is actualized through the plurality of actors involved in its delivery.

Homes and communities are sites where education and learning take place and this informal schooling frames students' learning styles and ways of knowing when they enter formal schooling. According to O'Connor, the artificial separation of homes and communities from the system of schooling reproduces the early colonial nature of schooling in North America:

> The disruption caused by the colonial nature of American schooling has made public education a crippling force in our communities. The separation of education from real involvement in personal and social life undermines cultural voice, contributing to the oppression of whole communities and the reproduction of inequities throughout the country. It has become difficult to imagine the proper role of public schools within local communities (O'Connor, 1995, p. 197).

The "proper role" of public schools, as O'Connor states, is indeed difficult to imagine when they are systematically and philosophically removed from the local sociological context in which they ultimately operate. While O'Connor refers to the context of the United States, this observation can also be extended to the Canadian context. The role of community schooling becomes increasingly salient when examining the transformative possibilities and potential of educational reform in North American contexts. A re-imagining of the role of public schools and communities, as they are intrinsic to one another, involves a new perspective on the role of teachers. Focus group sessions with educators conducted during this research explored new ways to conceive of community schooling. Central to the visions of community partnership in development and knowledge production was a redefinition of the role of teachers as "community development workers." Ibrahim, one of the educators consulted, felt strongly that teachers were part and parcel of the local community and therefore had to be able to contend with issues and concerns that were relevant to local social, cultural and economic conditions:

> You cannot say on the one hand , "well look I am going to work in your community but please don't bring any problems to do with your child, don't bring any problems to do with your marital situation, don't bring any problems to do with hunger and poverty." How can you say that?! You see the teachers are community development workers, whether you like it or not and this is the sad reality.

Envisioning the role of teachers as adaptive to local sociological conditions is fundamental to the needs-oriented approach as well as, on a broader level, making education a more relevant experience for a variety of learners. Participants in the focus group also proposed that pre-service teachers should spend part of their practicum teaching in community-based learning programs as well as working within various community organizations. This, it was argued, would allow them a greater connection within the community they would be working within, as well as allow them to learn culturally-based pedagogies from community educators and gain experience teaching toward a variety of learning styles. With regard to the requisite skills required for teaching in a community-based model, Mitchell (1987) also writes:

> There are other skills essential to teachers as potential support systems for community education and they involve the development and experience of social skills as well as intellectual ones: a commitment to practice, stamina in the face of difficulties, and an ability to think around contentious issues (p. 97).

This relates also to Martin's (1987) conception of community education as a "sustained educational engagement with the social reality of people's lives in the community" (p. 17).

In other societies, there are more seamless connections between schools and communities. Education is viewed as a communal responsibility in which all members participate and teachers in formal schools occupy a variety roles. Ibrahim commented on the role of teachers "back home" in Sierra Leone where he was born and raised:

> [W]hen I go back home the role of the teacher is so important, because the teacher is so important … the teacher is a father, the teacher is a mentor, a psychologist, a mediator, and everything you see. So the community looks up to the teacher — and I think for us it also becomes linking the teacher as also a spiritual leader — in other words. Because the role of the teacher in terms of the imparting of knowledge and how important that knowledge is, is so precious to the development of the human being. It gives that status the teacher will always have, and I tell you, even as I sit here when I go back and see my old teacher, I never call him by his first name.

The surrogate role of the teacher as a father (or mother), mentor, psychologist, and mediator in Sierra Leone serves as an important model for re-envisioning teaching in local North American contexts in a more complex and multi-faceted way.

This is not to overburden teachers with inordinate responsibilities, or to take responsibilities away from families in this regard; rather, it is to envision a role for teachers beyond the didactic structures of conventional schooling. It situates their work as being broadly linked to social and environmental needs. It is not to suggest that we should encourage teachers to do more, but rather to suggest ways to do it differently (O'Connor, 1995, p. 200). According to O'Connor:

> Local communities have always maintained patterns of teaching and learning suited to these relationships. Before modern society, the local community had the primary role in the production and transmission of knowledge. Intellectuals had vital positions in traditional cultures and small communities.

Looking at local, Indigenous models of educational delivery, O'Connor sees a deficit in the way current approaches toward education fail to achieve positive results and often are at the core of struggles for social justice and equity:

> Curricular and pedagogical reforms have failed to create authentic learning connected to the themes and concerns of the neighborhood. Even many radicals have described the schools as sites of struggle for a just, equitable, but common modern social institution. Resolving the conflict between local community and the great society is the core problem for constructing non-alienating, truly multi-voiced education. (p. 200)

O'Connor differentiates between what he calls "education for the great society," and "authentic learning," which is community-based. In moving beyond the false image of a "common culture" as represented in the "great society" perspective, community-based education is a transformative project that attempts to infuse the sphere of public education with multiple knowledges. The inclusion of different worldviews and experiences into the mainstream, would work to decentre Eurocentric ways of knowing the world.

Furthermore, he is specific in his assertions that students themselves must play a key role in bringing their heritage and culture to "democratic" and plural spaces (p. 200). Bearing these issues in mind, what do we do when the local community lacks the ethno-cultural diversity necessary to inform the building of a truly inclusive school?

O'Connor begins his essay with a description of small town America and also raises the question: "How would we make learners ready for the global marketplace by focusing on the lifestyles in the mountain hollows?" (p. 195). The same question could be asked in the Canadian context. Can a system be an inclusive model if it represents the local in terms of a only a particular representation of society — even though that may be the reality?

The evolving cosmopolitan aspects of urban centres in North America are counterbalanced with the monocultural nature of other, particularly rural areas. The question then becomes if we use the community as the basis of an inclusive model of schooling, how can we achieve equitable results when the local model lacks diversity? The answer to this problematic may lie once again in our conception of the local and how it is situated among other local and global sites. Even if local sites are relatively homogeneous, the overarching effect of globalization on the "marketplace" and society at large should be sufficient to encourage communities to look beyond their immediate circumstances and focus on broader possibilities and contexts. The metaphor of the global village is particularly appropriate to this sort of revisioning of local education in sites that are otherwise fairly culturally segregated. Therefore, community-based education, while maintaining ties to the local community, becomes inclusive in that it embodies a global outlook as part of its philosophical and practical purview, if not part of its geographic and social reality.

UNPACKING COMMUNITY SCHOOLING

A decentred/multi-centric pedagogy reflects the situated character of schools in local communities through reflecting and engaging with actors within these discursive sites. Also the envisioning of community models of education must explore possibilities for schools to act as sites for social activism and community engagement with social, economic and political issues. These must be addressed and understood with respect to how these issues are linked to social justice and equity as well as education and achievement. Keeping this broader connection in mind, the domain of community schooling can be organized into three integrated spheres:

1. Local community-based forms of knowledges;
2. Homes as local sites of learning/ parents and community members as knowledge producers;
3. Governance in a community school model/ collective ownership and power sharing.

The following sections provide a more in depth analysis of these spheres using data from the 1997 phase of our research on Home, Family and Community-Based Learning[1] They will also explore the implications for policies, practices and pedagogy within public schools.

LOCAL AND COMMUNITY BASED EDUCATION

Local community based knowledges refer to the alternative educational programmes and strategies that are based in cultural and/or linguistic communities that supplement the education in the mainstream school system. Parents, community organizations and students turn to community educational initiatives for many opportunities they feel are lacking in mainstream schools:

1. Attention to the individual learner;
2. Integration of language, culture and spirituality (discussed in other chapters);
3. Inclusive governance and empowerment opportunities;
4. Representative teachers;
5. Inclusive curriculum;
6. A sense of discipline.

The following quote effectively illustrates just how much thought and practical skills parents and community organizers are putting towards the development of their own community schools, and the examination of the deficits of the mainstream schools that spurred them to create alternative educational strategies. Ron, a teacher in the Saturday School said:

When I look at a student's record, for example, and I see that this student has been to ten schools, I don't need to do much to know what the problem is; ten schools in eight years, or six schools in eight years, I know there is a problem. This is because security and stability is not there.

ATTENTION TO THE INDIVIDUAL LEARNER

For learning to be truly effective, it must be personalized to suit the needs of the individual learner. Of the seven kinds of learning styles outlined by Gardner (1964) (Linguistic, Logical-Mathematical, Spatial, Bodily-Kinesthetic, Musical, Interpersonal, Intrapersonal) often, only a few are regularly employed in the mainstream classroom, with the variety greatly diminishing as a student reaches high school (Armstrong, 1994). Community educational sites are structured to allow teachers and educators to work with smaller classes or groups of students. This provides individualized attention to the learner and thus develop her/his learning styles. Individual attention permits the educator and the learner to begin with the self and then to project onto the group. In this way, individualized attention goes beyond child-centred learning. In these community educational sites, learners are grouped into classes that are sometimes mixed in terms of age, grade and ability, which allows for a free flow of knowledge and resources among the community of learners. In a class of 30 or more students learning styles that involve the teacher to student transmittal of knowledge are the norm. For example, the linguistic learning style can include debates, storytelling and discussions, which are interactive, but time consuming and not easily measured by conventional means. Instead teachers often resort to reading, writing and lecturing, which also strengthen language skills, but can fail to engage many children in the present topic. One parent from a community Saturday School program remarked:

> The [regular school], in the classroom, it's large. She don't get that attention from the teacher in a classroom at school. But she do get the attention in this program because it's a smaller group. And they attend to her and they listen to her. So that way, it's kind of different. (Sonia)

When teachers really listen to a student, they will be able to better assess her individual learning strengths and weaknesses. Nonetheless, this discussion of individual learning should not lead to the isolation of the learner outside of a broader community setting. That this parent believes in the effective difference of the Saturday program is an important principle of community education: communication, trust and collectivity. Community education has a philosophical understanding that all knowledge is socially and collectively created through the interactive processes between individuals, groups and the surrounding world.

EMPOWERMENT DEVELOPMENT OPPORTUNITIES

The philosophy of community education is anchored in a broader definition of education that encompasses emotional and spiritual dimensions, parental and community advocacy and youth empowerment. Many parents from Saturday Schools related their experiences of the disempowerment that took place in their children's mainstream schooling experiences. In encouraging student enthusiasm for learning, these programs not only allow students to explore their full potential, but also provide support and development opportunities for parents. The significance of student/parent empowerment cannot be overrated. Students commented that the community programs helped them to build confidence in themselves and found that this was transferable to the mainstream school experience. Parents are learning the skills needed to ask informed questions about their child's education in the mainstream school. Some strategies include high profile community role-models as teachers and organizers, career seminars, job and life skill training and cultural enrichment opportunities. Beyond all of this, the programs help students to imagine their own futures away from negative societal portrayals, and the low-expectations of the mainstream school system. The programs give them the tools to achieve their goals:

> What we are doing in this program is to pass the culture and the language that accompany the act of teaching and learning. So, by doing this, students will have the language, they can discuss the issue, and so they will have a sense of what is required from them. It is important to pass that knowledge. You are not answering questions for them, but they are getting a sense of what to expect. This is what I call stretching the horizon.

Community-based education programs recognize the important roles of parents and adult community workers as sounding boards for the young learners. Parents are accorded a special place in education as knowledge creators and disseminators. But more importantly, parents, guardians, caregivers, and adult community workers are seen as "initiating, creating and resisting subjects" as discussed earlier. They are not simply inserted into the existing structures of community education. For parents and community members to claim an important degree of collective ownership of community schooling and education, how they aquire power is as important as the delivery of education. Parents, guardians, caregivers, elders and other community members participate in the running of schools, including the production and dissemination of knowledge (e.g., act as tutors of community knowledge and history, run periodic workshops and be partners in the learning and educational process).

Parents are educators in their own right and are recognized by learners and teachers as significant partners in the learning and educational process. Parental involvement is defined broadly to include the myriad ways and spaces in which parents and adults contribute to facilitate youth learning and education. These include activism and educational advocacy for youth, attendance at community and official school meetings, assistance with homework, attendance at community meetings to discuss social and educational issues and offering mutual support to peers in dealing with the conventional school system.

REPRESENTATIVE TEACHERS, CURRICULUM AND DISCIPLINE

Community educational practices address issues of representation in three areas as discussed previously. First is *visual representation* or the inclusion of racial and ethnic minorities and their culture within the visual/physical landscape of the school and the classroom. Second is *knowledge representation* or the centring of non-European cultural knowledges and discourse. Educational practices must promote active learning about different cultures, histories and experiences. Finally, *staff representation* or the integration of teachers and educators from a variety of racial, ethnic and gender backgrounds is critical. Representation was a major theme evident throughout the interviews.

One mother of Jamaican background from the Milliken African Caribbean Canadian Uplift Program (MACCUP) identified the issue of role models with regard to minority representation:

[I]t's good for the kids to see ... when they come here, they see a lot of role models being in an ethnic background, like from an ethnic point of view. They see more of themselves. They see the helpers, the teachers, other kids are going off to university or are in university.
    Q — Is that not seen at a school setting?
    No, I don't think so, not as much. Like in the school setting, there's not a lot of schools that have minorities as teachers. Most of the school, they're white. The teachers, they're all white. Whereas here, when they come here, they can see minority people up there, too. It's like a role model. They're there, you be up there, too.

A female teacher involved with Muslim Education Network, Training and OutReach Service (MENTORS) after school tutorial program, indicates the pride and comfort that students feel when they see that there is someone in authority who shares a similar background and experience with them. There is the sentiment of "this is someone who knows me and understands":

I think just seeing someone there that you can identify with really makes a big difference. The response I get when I go to the school is really good. I find the kids are very positive and they come to me quietly and ask me, "Oh, you are Muslim too?" And then I'll say, "Yes," and then they're really excited. And I've always found the teachers that I've worked with very appreciative of the fact that I was there and providing them with some information to help them deal with issues or deal with some students or dealing even with parents ... (Aneesa)

Issues of representation, voice and inclusion in education were of primary importance to the members of this community-based organization. According to Ibrahim, another member of MENTORS, being visible in schools and the community was seen as a means to create a higher profile for the Muslim community in education. In doing so, we counteract many of the negative misconceptions people may have of Muslims; misconceptions that are most commonly formed through biased stereotypes in the media. The MENTORS community-based program became integrated with the public school system when they initiated a series of seminars for mainstream teachers and guidance counsellors. In focusing on how schools might accommodate Islamic beliefs and practices, MENTORS has advocated for the integration of Islamic experience and knowledges as part of a multi-centred educational system.

The community-based practices examined during this study were committed to an inclusive, integrative anti-racist approach to education. The idea of "equity pedagogy" was central to community educational praxis for many groups. This form of pedagogy highlights educational strategies and practices that deal directly with issues of race, gender and class equity in the school and society, and actively work toward the elimination of structural barriers to equality of opportunity and outcomes for all learners. For the community pedagogue, the categories of race, gender and class are regarded as starting points for understanding discrimination and social oppression.

Community educators allow learners to participate fully in school life and culture while continuing to develop and practise their home cultures and personal and collective identities. The "educational curriculum" includes a recognition of the importance of local, family, cultural histories, religion/ spirituality, and individual epiphanies. Community and home-based educational pedagogies often highlight the specific cultural, historical and political achievements of local people. In these educational sites it is not uncommon to find such local knowledges and experiences being incorporated into the process of schooling within a holistic framework. In contrast, mainstream schools tend to compartmentalize these knowledges from the "regular" curriculum (e.g. Black History Month, Asian Heritage Month).

Pedagogy and practice in community-based educational sites draw on existing cultural and community knowledge to select and engaging their visual and textual resources. Teaching and instructional methods are therefore responsive to students and their varied identities. These learning styles employ diverse strategies and are anchored within the student's cultural knowledge base. In this way, the learner is centred in her/his educational experience.

Community educational pedagogies also stress the need for strict discipline. In some cases, discipline was understood as part of a religious and spiritual dimension of education that encouraged learners to be attentive to the traditional norms of their faith and spirituality. This was understood to help them make sense of the world, as well as their rights and responsibilities within it. In other cases, discipline was understood to mean respect for difference and diversity. Generally, for teachers and parents, respect was defined as something which is given to others and expected from students. In community-based schools, pedagogical strategies also aim to facilitate easy access to educators and teachers. This is considered vital in developing emotional and social bonding with learners. Community schools view the idea of representation and teachers as role models as crucial for the learner to develop a sense of identification with, and connectedness to, the learning process.

The community based learning programs observed may be described as having two roles. First, there was a definite perspective among all the communities that, as racial, cultural, ethnic, and/or religious minorities in Canada, they are treated unfairly by the dominant culture, in representation and imagery. That is to say, their history is being ignored or marginalized by the school curriculum, and as a result, their children are not doing as well as they should. Community-based learning programs were initiated to remedy these experiences within the mainstream school system and the broader society.

Four features are common to all of the community programs. First, there is a sense of community whereby the teacher is a mentor and "a friend" and parents are there to help. Second, students get immediate help without being looked down upon. Third, there are fewer students, so there is a greater chance of one-on-one help from teachers. Finally, these schools are viewed as safe spaces where an emphasis is put on feeling comfortable and "at home."

This understanding of the role and function of community schools helps to make the link between individual learning and the need for holistic approaches to meeting the needs of students. Addressing only academic needs does not help many students whose everyday realities prevent them from focusing on academic concerns. All of the community based programs examined recognized the importance of approaching students and learning in a holistic way by attending to the social, emotional and spiritual aspects of their lives and beings. This approach allows for the academic needs of students to be fulfilled through remedial support, but at the same time helps students to recognize other factors in their lives that may be inhibiting their learning in a school setting.

LINKING HOMES, SCHOOLS AND COMMUNITIES: COMMUNITY LIAISON COUNSELLORS

Bridging the gap between homes, school and communities epitomizes the role of community liaison counsellors working for the various Boards of Education in the Greater Toronto area, which amalgamated in 1998. Creating inclusive schools involves the integration of families and communities into the social and cultural fabric of school life (see, Dei et al., 1996). According to O'Connor (1995):

> When we understand children as cultural beings growing within local communities, it is evident that multicultural educators must break schools away from the denatured, pseudo-universalized framework of standardized education. To counter the hegemony that has marginalized and debilitated local communities, public education must be reconnected to local communities (p. 200).

Reconnecting public education with local communities will involve a re-forging of partnerships between home and school. Creating such an environment, however, can be a difficult process because it calls for a fundamental acceptance of, and dedication to a philosophy of power-sharing. Many barriers exist which prevent immigrant and minority parents, in particular, from engaging with the school system. There are often disjunctures between the cultural expectations of parents and the demands of mainstream schooling. Issues such as rights and responsibilities in education are referenced by culturally mediated views on education. Community liaison counsellors in the school board we examined are normally hired ethno-specifically so that they can help mediate the incongruencies between home and school life for students outside of the dominant culture. They also provide an avenue through which community knowledges can become articulated as a relevant frame of reference for public schooling in a plural society.

Community liaison counsellors advocate and provide support for the social, cultural, economic and academic needs of students. Advocacy for students, being their primary concern, often puts counsellors at odds with either parents or the Board. Balancing student, parent and community needs with Board requirements makes their role politically challenging and often contentious. The following section will explore the role of community liaison counsellors and some of the concerns that they address in attempting to enact inclusive practices through grassroots community engagement.

Roles of Community Liaison Counsellors

The roles of community liaison counsellors are as diverse as the needs of the communities they service. Within the local school board we examined, their activities are centred in six main areas:

1. Linguistic support for non-English speaking students and parents;
2. Assistance in academic placement based on first language screening;
3. Addressing racial, cultural, religious concerns within school policies and practices;
4. Helping parents understand and adapt to the Canadian educational system;
5. In-servicing teachers, guidance counsellors and school administrators by providing information on the specialized needs of their particular communities;
6. Community counselling in order to mediate conflicts or concerns among families, schools and communities.

Within this broad framework, community liaison counsellors balance themselves between the dual and yet often conflicting roles of community advocate and school board employee. Involvement in community counselling for many of the counsellors often led to a greater personal involvement with the social welfare of particular students and their communities as a whole.

Being sensitive to the socioeconomic and family needs of the community becomes essential to providing students with the life skills they need to negotiate their schooling. Gail, a liaison counsellor in the Caribbean-Canadian community, promotes motivational workshops for Black youth. The workshops are lead by Black community members, and function to teach life skills to Black youth that often feel marginalized within the mainstream. Gail explained the kind of social and emotional skills she works with other community members to instill in Black youth:

> It's guidance on how to deal with the world. It's everywhere, its how to conduct yourself in a way that people won't blame you for things, people will respect you. Respect for others and also deal with people in authority in a positive way and not show anger and distrust and abuse and all the things that they normally do because they usually imitate what they see at home or on the streets or on television and that is not the way to do it.

For Gail, focusing on student needs must be a holistic undertaking, which attends to the ways social, cultural, and economic issues impact on schooling for Black youth. Providing students with the necessary "cultural capital" or mainstream social skills they will require to negotiate their schooling experiences is part of the life skills training that she hopes will help them mediate their relationships with teachers in a positive way. While this can be read as simply making students conform to the existing hegemonic structures within schools, the goal was to help these youth develop the skills they need to negotiate the barriers they encounter, rather than to simply accept and make do within the status quo.

Parents and the School System

Lessons on how to "deal with the system" were also extended informally to parents in the Portuguese community by Isabelle, a community liaison counsellor. In her seventeen years working with the Toronto school board, Isabelle spoke of the frustration many Portuguese parents felt in attempting to bring their educational concerns to the school system. She remarked that, due to the "frustration and enormous pain that they felt, they've given up negotiating or conversing with the system." Isabelle recalls how she has, on many occasions, become the sounding board for parents' concerns and complaints. She reported that successful dialogue with schools often meant that parents had to become schooled in the language skills which would enable them to express their views without anger. She went on to say:

> ... those who immigrated many years ago and they didn't have the skills, you know university degree or whatever, they don't have the skills to talk politely with these teachers and the principal.

Relying on what Isabelle referred to as "working-class skills" many parents felt that their concerns were disregarded by the school system. Those who were successful, according to Isabelle, "... have learned how to talk with the principal. By being confrontational they won't get anything, but by using different ways of talking, some of them have learned that's the best way to get things their own way." This form of empowerment requires tapping into the institutional language of schools and presenting concerns according to the established protocol. For many community groups, such as the Portuguese, where language is already a barrier, being able to communicate effectively with schools is a difficult process.

Isabelle reported how many parents felt powerless in dealing with the school system and trying to affect change. Many parents felt disempowered by the lack of input they had with regard to curriculum issues or the hiring of teachers. Confronted with a pedagogy that is unlike what they were accustomed to "back home," many immigrant parents feel that the current school curriculum is not stringent enough in providing students with "the basics," and they find early childhood education concepts such as "learning through play" to be superfluous.

Cultural disjunctures in modes of learning were evident also in talking to Grace, a community liaison counsellor for the Chinese community. Part of her role was helping parents understand schooling in the Canadian context. Grace found particular difficulties with parents understanding the report card system since Chinese parents are used to seeing a grade on paper and find the system of reporting student's progress in Canada as being too vague. She explained how she helps parents to communicate with teachers to get the information they need to help make sense of their children's progress:

Yeah, you know like "Johnnie's making progress" — how much? You know so I often have to coach the parents, talk to the teacher and say OK, making "progress" are you saying that my kid is now almost at grade three level, or what? You want to know more than that. What does "making progress" mean?

Grace found that most Chinese parents do not find the system to be challenging enough, and feel their children are regressing rather than progressing. Canadian teachers, she explained, are not demanding a high enough standard to meet with the expectations of Chinese parents:

The big difference is that our teachers are praising the kids saying "You're doing well" and the Chinese parents are saying you don't have to do that, because the Chinese parents way of encouraging the kid is saying "Good you got 80 percent this test, so why can't you get 85? Next time get me 85." The parent never says that "Oh wonderful you got 80 percent" never from a Chinese parent. They will say that's good, but I expect more. To our parents that is the only way to push the kids because they always want the kids one step ahead.

According to Grace, conflicting cultural values cause teachers to complain that Chinese parents are not attending to the emotional side of their children, but as she counters: "Chinese parents say 'What are you talking about? It's the kid's responsibility to do well in school.'" These conflicting values represent how educational expectations are culturally mediated according to differing standards. The challenge in a plural society is to address and accommodate the differences not by measuring them against a dominant standard, but by beginning to explore the possibilities for change based on different cultural ways of knowing.

RIGHTS AND RESPONSIBILITIES IN EDUCATION

The disjuncture in the notion of educational rights and responsibilities can be found between various groups. The greater emphasis on individual responsibility in the Chinese context is in contrast with a more communal sense of educational responsibility in the Caribbean community. Gail explained how, in the Caribbean context, the notion of educational responsibility was regulated by the community at large and, with extended family, there was greater social control on students' behaviour and performance in school: "It's a community and the child will be reprimanded by anyone in the community." She also commented on the more informal channels of communication that exist between schools and families for addressing concerns in the Caribbean context, versus the more formal structures in Canada: "... the news gets around, but in a different way, it's not this official way and they're not used to it and they feel very intimidated at times going into a school for a meeting or a board office for a meeting. This is why we many of the times we try to do it in a church or some place where they are comfortable."

Finding ways to reach out to parents is often difficult, but when dealing with newly immigrated parents or those with limited English language skills, the task becomes even more daunting. In these circumstances, or in those cases where economics begins to play a factor, we must consider the need to accommodate schedules as well as cultures. Many of these are duel income families where both parents work multiple jobs just to make ends meet. This often means arranging meetings outside of the school itself, as Gail explained, "… Caribbean parents just don't feel that their place is part of the school. They send their children to the school, they expect the teacher to teach, the headmaster to teach and discipline." Therefore, learning to engage with teachers and schools in completely new ways, according to the structures for participation in Canada, can prove to be an alienating and intimidating experience for minority parents. According to Grace, parents in the Chinese community are well organized and have formal parent organizations. Yet her strategies for parent outreach also extend into the community rather than within the confines of the school. It is through the avenue of outreach within community-based sites that counsellors are able to determine and help negotiate the concerns of parents.

Student Placement

The issue of student placement often involves the intervention of community liaison counsellors, particularly when first language screening is involved. Many of the counsellors were highly critical of the process of "age appropriate placement" for immigrant students and ESL students. Many of these students, due to war or political circumstances in their countries, have gaps in their education. Further, students coming from village schools abroad, cannot have their education measured according to the same standard as those who come from urban areas. Placing students from these contexts in classrooms according to their age without the necessary academic foundation or English language facility is highly problematic and does not adequately address their academic or social needs. The counsellors all argue that knowledge of students' prior learning is essential in placement. Schooling must take into account students' social, cultural and economic situations, as well as the conditions from which they arrived in Canada, in order to make informed decisions regarding their academic placement.

Community Health, Nutrition and Education Issues

Other community liaison counsellors also saw the integral links between socioeconomic and cultural needs and student achievement and success.

Sureya is originally from East Africa, where she worked as an ECE (Early Childhood Educator) for eight years. She taught at an elementary school for one year in Canada and has worked as a community liaison counsellor for the South Asian and Muslim community for eight years. Sureya also works part-time co-ordinating the re-structuring of breakfast club programs into snack programs. She sees the issues of health and nutrition as being intrinsically tied to educational achievement, particularly for immigrant, refugee and working-class students.

Some of the more immediate concerns for the families she deals with are related to poverty and hunger. Her work with community-based nutrition programs is in response to the need she saw within the South Asian and other communities for the provision of basic needs. "In some families they actually take turns having breakfast," Sureya reported. Yet she recognizes the limitations of school breakfast programs for having a lasting impact on poverty and hunger unless, she argues, they are structured with a holistic perspective that responds to all components of the cycle of poverty. She advocates a process of strengthening local school communities as a whole. This would see the inclusion of seniors, parents, local business people and politicians, whom she feels all have a stake in community-based education and need to be integrated within the school.

Looking at student success, according to Sureya, involves taking into account the socioeconomic as well as cultural factors that structure students' lives and mediate their schooling experiences. Difficulties resulting from lower socioeconomic status in homes where often both parents are working, or where there is despondency over the loss of a parents' job and the corresponding economic changes which take place within the home can lead to difficulties at school. Suspensions were specified as being the result of students' behaviour and attitude when they come to school and "act out" — the result of having to deal with outside pressures. For many South Asian students, these are compounded by pressures within the school related to their position as racialized and religious minorities.

A local board of education had adopted the African proverb that says "It takes an entire village to raise a child." However, cities are too large to serve the communal function of the village, which, Sureya stresses, must be locally characterized according to smaller wards. She suggested the development of a steering committee to look at issues such as hunger in the local community, which would be a networking of schools, community groups, religious groups, doctors, police, parents and trustees. This would provide a multi-focused vantage point for seeing how issues such as poverty and hunger become implicated in issues of health, schooling, and crime and social inequality.

SCHOOL-COMMUNITY PARTNERSHIPS IN EDUCATION

Compartmentalized interests, according to Sureya, preclude community development as a holistic, emancipatory project in which schools have a central role to play. Sureya does not believe in working in isolation to find the solution to problems that are connected to broader systems of oppression. She felt that networking and brainstorming were essential to developing a community-based investment in issues of race, class and schooling. Sureya suggests that school policies and guidelines be adapted to these social conditions so as to keep in touch with and reflect local perspectives. Policies must be set with regards to the racialized and classed dynamics of the local school community, what she calls a "grassroots connection" with the local area, including businesses, community, religious groups, and police. She sees this as the most effective way to achieve true community partnerships in education, which are reflective of the needs and interests of the local community. Community-based education, from this perspective, is a concerted effort among community groups and incorporates an inter-generational dialogue. Negotiating strategies for change, therefore, cannot be strictly localized within the school, but requires a broad based and integrative approach.

HOME-BASED LEARNING STRATEGIES: HOMES AS LOCAL SITES OF LEARNING

In this section, homes are explored as sites of knowledge production and learning that are vital to human growth and development. Interviews with parents emphasized that a healthy interaction between children and parents is necessary to meet the social and emotional needs of children, and that this provides the basis for promoting learning in the home environment. Understanding the "pedagogy of the home" provides important insights into how learning takes place within the context of homes and family life, and how this varies according to the social and cultural backgrounds of families and the specialized needs of the children. It also provides an understanding of parents as producers of knowledge.

Formal and Informal Strategies

Home-based learning incorporates both formal and informal elements. Formal aspects of learning are structured around students' classroom work and include: helping children in their homework/project work, getting information from libraries or other sources, and supplying the child with age appropriate educational materials such as books, magazines, newspapers, encyclopedias, computers and related resources. While formal strategies are geared specifically to support school work, informal strategies indirectly augment school-based learning by providing emotional and academic support to students in ways intrinsic to the social and cultural lives of their families. For example, discussing and showing an interest in the daily activities of children in their school, as well as telling children parents' own schooling experiences, particularly in their country of origin, were identified as informal ways parents provide support and pass on knowledge.

Storytelling was identified by many parents as an important means of imparting cultural knowledge and experience. Telling stories of positive role models was identified as an important strategy for promoting learning in the home environment. Lynette, a sixteen-year-old student of Guyanese background, discussed how hearing stories from her parents about how they were brought up instilled a sense of pride in her culture. Lemlem, an Ethiopian parent, discussed how she helps her daughter concentrate and stay focused on her studies by telling her about other successful relatives, like a cousin who is a graduate of Harvard University. According to Lemlem, telling children stories of good role models can encourage them to go farther with their own academic aspirations or other activities in life.

Having positive role models in education is particularly salient for the Black community, where negative stereotypes have characterized Blacks in subordinate roles in both schools and society. This has had negative effects on Black students' achievement and has contributed to their disengagement from school (see Dei, Mazzucca, McIsaac and Zine, 1997). Home as well as community-based learning initiatives are often geared to provide positive emotional as well as academic support in order to offset the negative images of the Black community as constructed in the media and promoted in society at large.

As a Black student, Truwork spoke of the pressures she felt from her community to succeed and become a role model herself. Coming from a well-educated family background, she expressed a desire to give back to the community, and to show that, in the Black community, "the number of role models shouldn't be limited," adding that: " If I don't succeed, the number of role models would be fewer." The notion of individual success for Truwork, then, is tied to the success of her community at large. She sees herself as having a social responsibility to provide a model of success for her community. Truwork wants to see Blacks having greater visibility in the broader community and felt community activities and events on a national scale, such as the "Million Man March," were a way to promote advocacy for Black youth and provide community support and encouragement. This, she felt, leads to the development of positive self-esteem for Black students. Truwork related feeling alone as a Black student in pursuit of higher academic goals. She wants to see Black students strive for "the maximum pick— not just leftovers," and she sees community support as essential for that success:

> Students need guidance, especially minorities and we need the community to become more active in that sense, to share ideas, to teach the new generations that ... there are people to support you in what you do.

Truwork's comments show how the notions of "community," "home" and "self" are linked within the cultural conceptions of certain minority groups. When positively correlated, these concepts can provide the formula for student achievement. Truwork's quote shows a respect for the knowledge gained by elders in the community and a desire of the younger generations to share in that collective cultural knowledge and expertise as part of their own process of learning.

According to Lemlem, who studied nursing and office administration, parents are the primary role models for their children: " the most important thing is that they [parents] should love their children and respect each other ... be a very good role model for their children and also children should be provided with ... basic needs." In a new cultural milieu however, many minority parents see disjunctures between the way they are accustomed to seeing children being reared and educated, and the norms that exist within Canadian society. Discipline standards and dominant pedagogical practices, which are both regarded as being too "lax," are two points of contention for many of the minority parents interviewed.

Discipline

Menbere, an Ethiopian parent, felt that children in Canada to be too wild and undisciplined. She felt that, compared to her own experiences in Africa, there is a lack of respect for teachers and elders among youth in Canada. Truwork felt that African parents are stricter with regard to their children's education due to discrimination in society:

> I noticed in a sense that more Canadian families are not as strict or are very lenient on their children when it comes to education, whereas African [families] are more serious and dedicated and they want their children to succeed a lot higher because of the fact they know their children are going to be discriminated [against] to a point. So if you have the education and you have the knowledge no one can discriminate [against] you, right?

Lemlem felt that parents, teachers and the whole community should be involved in promoting discipline in children: "… students who are intoxicated and students who are taking drugs are dangerous for each other. The community as well as the parents should be involved in this matter and also the teachers." As Abate, another Ethiopian parent, explained, in Ethiopia, discipline involves respect for elders and respect for religious education, manners and behaviour, and that these are not only learned from parents and schools, but also from the entire community. As Menbere also put it, "in my country [Ethiopia] … a child is a child for everybody." This is a social philosophy that makes the community as a whole responsible for maintaining values and standards and promoting discipline among children.

Life Skills

According to Abate, who holds a post-graduate degree, promoting self-discipline for children is a strategy that can help them to be effective in their education. He encourages his children to develop effective time management skills, which allows them to balance their academic responsibilities with recreational and leisure activities. Helping his children acquire self-discipline also involved maintaining consistency in study habits and developing independent learning skills, which sometimes entailed helping them with their homework. He saw the informal education children receive at home as being geared toward life skills, something he felt was lacking in the current educational system. He felt that students were not being adequately prepared for the demands of career and life in general. He felt that Canada has "an outdated education system for a very advanced society." He went to explain his more holistic view of education:

> More homework is not necessarily more education and as opposed to pure academic education, there must be a life skill training as well, on how to adapt to life as it is coming in the future.

Creating awareness among children in terms of race relations and advising children how to overcome problems related to race were also discussed by parents as part of a methodology of preparing their children for life. Abate believed that interaction versus isolation is important in overcoming racial bias. He advises his children to participate in every task that is presented to them and to mix and mingle with the students in the school. He believed that, in order for Black children to negotiate the problems they encounter in schools, they must not become ghettoized. He also advocated a more positive and proactive approach for Black youth as opposed to the aggressive stance he felt many adopt in response to their subordination within schools.

Therefore, methods for dealing with issues of racism are part of the life skills that many Black children learn at home. Owen, a Black parent originally from Barbados, had children, ages nine and nineteen, attend a community-based learning program outside of their regular schooling. He pointed out that it is important for Black parents to teach their children to deal positively with the problem of racism. He felt that parents should encourage their children not to give up their effort toward success in spite of the tremendous hurdles they may face. Learning to cope with the barriers of race and social difference are important life skills that students learn by drawing on the resources and experiences of their families and community.

Natalie also communicated an understanding of education that is more experiential and not restricted to text:

> I want them to receive the best education they can in Canada. That's why I very much encourage them to get a lot of different

learning through community participation, through going to the library and many other activities.

Natalie also emphasized how parents' own knowledge serves as a primary resource for their children's learning. Before exploring other avenues, she and her husband would make sure that they had helped their children on their own as much as they could. Instead of seeking outside help, they found that teaching their children themselves was an excellent form of encouragement.

Creating a Home Learning Environment

According to Attiya, a Muslim parent from India, learning and play are integrated components that can provide the opportunity for more experiential forms of learning in the home environment. She, for example, used even mundane chores around the house as a means to teach her two elementary school age daughters concepts such as fractions (when cutting vegetables) or measurement (when cooking). She felt that children can learn a great deal from these experiences when guided by their parents or caregivers. Attiya remembers this form of learning being part of her own experience growing up in India. Many other immigrant parents, however, report having a more formal and didactically-oriented education back home. Therefore, unlike Attiya, these parents had difficulty accepting the more play-oriented and experiential pedagogical styles found in Canadian classrooms. Discussing other issues that centred within the realm of the family, many parents indicated that stability and togetherness in the family are important factors in promoting children's educational activities in the home environment. Parents found spending quality time with their children, whether in formal or informal learning activities, had a positive affect on educational success. Being able to afford this necessary time, however, is a factor mediated by social class and the work situations of the parents. Families where parents work shifts or are unavailable for support on a regular basis often cannot meet the ideal conditions for providing consistent academic support at home.

Creating an atmosphere conducive to study was also cited by parents as an important element in promoting children's concentration. Quiet and comfortable rooms with no distraction were considered important in creating a good working environment at home. Terrence, a Black parent, explains his philosophy of home-based learning:

[F]irst of all … you have to have family togetherness for the kids to learn. You have to have dinners together, you got to make sure that you sit at the table as parents and as family. I have an area where my daughter studies, where there is no distraction of TV. All she has is a computer and her books. There is no picture on the wall to distract her.

Providing children with the educational resources they require was also seen as important in promoting their success. Educational materials such as computers, encyclopedia, calculators and other related materials were seen as important tools for promoting learning at home. Again, however, parents' ability to provide many of these items is dependent upon their economic situation. Therefore, as a result, class-based disparities exist in terms of having access to the various tools required for educational success.

Almost all the parents indicated the presence of TV in the home posed a serious problem as far as children's study habits were concerned. They expressed strong views that television and telephones distract children's concentration from learning. Lemlem noticed the disjuncture between her own experiences in Ethiopia, and what she saw as an over-use of television and telephone among Canadian youth. Marcus, another Black parent, found that by not having cable TV his children's grades went from Cs to As and Bs. According to Marcus: " The TV is a great inhibitor of learning." While the battle over the television set has created a struggle between parents and children in many homes, the parents interviewed felt the need to impose certain boundaries on the time their children spent watching television so that it did not interfere with concentration on their school work.

Parent Perspectives on the Educational System

Many of the parents indicated that the involvement of parents in educational policy decisions and curriculum is minimal. They argued that there is a need for more parental involvement in educational policy decisions particularly in terms of hiring teachers, determining curriculum content, and in the running of schools. Marcus emphasized that the school council meetings he attended were dominated by a clique, which limited an individual say in policy decision making. On the other hand, many participants indicated that parents are not exercising enough effort to involve themselves in the education of their children and need to be more proactive so that their voices are heard. For example, Terrence advocated a more community-centred involvement within schools where all members of the community would become involved and share a collective interest in youth education.

Explaining her notion of the goal of education, Lemlem explained: "… education is very broad for me. It's not only going to school, finish high school or University and earn money … it means … to follow the right path … to use money wisely … to live a better life." Khadija perceived the goal of education as preparing people to be productive in their lives, or as in Marcus' estimation it is one of enabling people to challenge the odds in life, particularly in the case of racial and ethnic minorities. For Abate, education is the cumulative process of acquiring life skills that prepare individuals not only for higher education, but also for the social, cultural, and economic challenges they may confront in their lives. For all of these parents, education is broadly construed as a holistic methodology for life. It is perceived as being the medium for acquiring life skills, both formally at school and informally through the pedagogy of the home and community.

Being educated for success, then, involves the opportunity to engage in a variety of learning experiences that often take place outside of the traditional classroom. Education in such a broad context is rooted in a sense of one's community and home, and their relationship to schools and societies. There is a need to articulate the experiences and knowledge acquired within these various educational sites into an integrated broad-based approach to learning that includes the cultural knowledge of traditionally marginalized groups in society. This approach to inclusive education ensures that there is a multi-centred knowledge base at the core of school curricula that privileges a variety of life experiences and knowledges. This provides an opportunity for parents, schools and communities to pool resources, knowledge and expertise for the benefit of all students in the school system.

GOVERNANCE, COLLECTIVE OWNERSHIP AND POWER SHARING: TAKING A LOOK AT SCHOOL COUNCILS

Some of the current entry points for greater parent involvement in school governance are the school councils mandated by the Ontario government. Following a report by the Royal Commission on Learning (RCOL, 1994) that detailed plans for encouraging parent and community involvement in the form of school-community councils, the Ontario Parent Council (OPC) outlined a plan for the development of new school councils. This plan called into question the traditional power structures within schools and suggested that a new model of school governance should include a greater role for parents. In the second phase of our research, which explored the links between homes, schools and families (Dei et al., 1997), our examination of the role of parents within the new school councils revealed many doubtful accounts of their inclusivity and efficacy in providing genuine parent and community input.

When parents, community organizers and students were asked about the "New School Councils" the great majority had never even heard of them. Under the new Ministry of Education mandate, the School Council Handbook details the ways in which schools should attempt to be inclusive: racially, ethno-culturally, linguistically, and socioeconomically (1996:19). However, based on the interviews conducted in our research, the practice has not corresponded to the theory. Most parents, students and other educational stakeholders had little or no knowledge of school councils or their intended purposes.

A Ministry of Education and Training memorandum regarding school councils reads that, "Members of a school's council shall include, but not be limited to a community representative, and non-teaching staff member" (1995:2), yet the parents and community members we interviewed felt frustrated that councils were not fulfilling their outreach potential. Marjorie, a member of her school advisory council and chair of her son's elementary school fundraising organization, spoke about the importance of using her own experience with the school system to help other parents advocate for themselves. Her remarks are particularly relevant given the degree to which socioeconomic disparities can discourage some parents from becoming more directly involved in their children's education:

> Economic disadvantage ... the schools continually have their meetings in the evenings, when some parents work, when all they would have to do is schedule some meetings in the afternoons. To me, if you really mean to be good to people you accommodate [them].

Parents who were school council members also complained of the often-overwhelming role of the principal. The School Council Handbook also states that the role of the principal is to facilitate the operation of the council and offer resource and administrative support of the council and open communication and participation for council members and the larger school community. Yet some parents reported that their councils were dominated by the principal, vice-principal and established teachers, and felt that their own role was too superficial to effect any real change. Doris, an African-Canadian mother and community organizer, noted:

> In my school, the principal is so dominant that the other poor parents are afraid to speak up. When they do, he speaks in jargon so we can't understand, or ignores us. Because I speak up a lot, they [the principal, vice-principal and one teacher] gang up on me, or "forget" to tell me when the next meeting is to occur. I find that I have to look on the bulletin boards and call other parents to find out where the meeting is. And I was elected to be part of the council; the other parents don't have much of a voice at all.

Yet, despite some of the concerns parents had about the school councils, many still remained optimistic that their continued participation would result in providing greater advocacy for other parents, and better outcomes for their children. As Marjorie told us, her council was both effective and inclusive. As a Council member and parent, she saw her role as one of teaching other parents how to negotiate the system. In the interview she expressed general satisfaction with the work that she and other parents were doing to be involved with their children's education. Marjorie wanted to leave a legacy that would show parents and students could have a sophisticated knowledge of the school system, and can help to influence and even create school policy:

> Most of the people are "real people"... in the sense that they believe in inclusion ... People should have a voice, and [I] don't believe it should be an elite club. So we have enough people that we set up five or six committees on literacy, curriculum, extra-curricular activities, grade one transition year, computers and others. We want the emphasis on result-oriented solutions. We are working on doing a workshop on teaching parents how to advocate ... your mouth just drops because you can't believe that parents could be so ignorant of their rights. They talk to the teacher and can't get satisfaction. What do you think the principal is there for? We are going to teach them how powerful they are!

The School Council Handbook reports that the school council actively seeks and represents the views of its school community and should therefore ensure that the school community is informed of its roles and functions. It further states that the mandate of the school council "focuses on the best interests of all students," and "involves its diverse school community." And yet it also states that it "works within the policies of the school board." Yet these sets of goals are at times contradictory, particularly when parents feel they have no real input into developing board policies. Despite the stated claims of inclusion, marginalized parents felt at odds with a school system they saw as inaccessible and unable to meet their needs. In fact, many parents reported feeling isolated and disempowered by school officials. The involvement of racial and ethnic minority parents was often tantamount to token representation since genuine power sharing and collective governance does not occur. All too often parents were forced to take on reactive roles addressing problems within the school, but were unable to play proactive roles in creating possible solutions through avenues such as the development of policies.

Community Liaison Counsellors often felt so over-burdened with the need to explain school procedures or other linguistic or cultural translation to parents that the task of improving learning outcomes for children is not given the attention all stakeholders would like. As Gail, an African-Canadian counsellor noted, a lot of work needed to be done around certain key areas:

We have access to a lot of information that puts me in a privileged position, but [also gives me] an enormous responsibility to inform the parents what is going on in their schools. I [facilitate so] that parents who ask insightful questions and have constructive comments [get] access to the boards. I work with them and guide them about getting things done. They often feel powerless about hiring and firing teachers or principals who they feel are not responding to the needs of their children. I feel it is my role to help the parent establish credibility with teachers and principals. I don't want to sound pessimistic but most of them have given up, because they have had some terrible experiences with the system. When parents who have credibility in the community go to the principal, the principal is more likely to help the parent get involved and answer their concerns, but if I had to give a percentage, I would say 15 percent get satisfaction.

There appeared to be a lack of knowledge among parents, active community members and students about school councils and their access to them. In MENTORS, an informal survey of approximately four hundred parents at a community-based function found that, of those surveyed, only eight reported being actively involved in a school council. Also, students knew little or nothing about school councils. Most secondary school students did not know the difference between the old and new council formations, or that they were to be guaranteed a student representative on the new councils.

Saeed, a community organizer and parent, is one of the few parents in the Muslim community who had been able to negotiate the system. He felt that school councils could be very effective if parents with different perspectives had access and could be assured of a greater role within the councils and the school system:

> It depends what happens with school boards, but these advisory councils could play a very significant role, depending what direction they take. If they use the New Brunswick model where they have totally abolished school boards, and have councils for individual schools, where the parents play a very important role ... but at the moment it is sort of in between ... the parents do not have much of a say. They can only advise within the policies of the school and it is up to the principal or the board to decide whether to accept it.
> Q — Would you favour a direct role for parents in the councils?
> It should be, we are working for that. These boards of education are so big, and such a Eurocentric system, the problem is that most of the new groups who are not familiar with the system have difficulty gaining access. But at the moment it is very difficult, you have to wonder if these groups will ever have access, you have to be grounded and informed to understand the system and to know what powers you have, and that takes a generation.

Parents were also very aware of the relatively short tenure they have in their children's school, even when they seek re-election, as most said they would. In the end they were worried that the strides that they had made would be lost when the next group of parents had to re-learn strategies and establish relationships of respect with school officials. From these discussions it was clear that school councils, and their success, face several challenges:

1. *Communication*: not being made aware of the council and being able to speak effectively to school officials.
2. *Superficial involvement*: only having an advisory role and feeling as though important decisions are being made without their input.
3. *Structural and social disincentives to join*: evening meetings, use of educational jargon, and intimidation by principals and other staff members.
4. *Power sharing*: the need for genuine and not token parental involvement in school-based decision-making.
5. *Cohesion and consistency*: student and community participation, training new parents, performing outreach and getting distinct goals accomplished.

Still, despite these challenges, parents, community organizers and community liaison officers all agreed that school councils could be a wonderful school/ community strategy for transformative educational outcomes. However, for the councils to be truly inclusive, greater effort must be made to include all parents and community members.

CONCLUSION AND DISCUSSION

The many diverse and important strategies of homes, communities and stakeholders involved in education bring to mind once again the proverb stated earlier: "It takes a whole village to raise (educate) a child." Heading into the next century, that village is often a global village as we began discussing at the outset of this chapter. As cities and countries become increasingly technologically interconnected, they also become economically and socio-politically interdependent. While many argue that education must become workplace focused and technologically driven, an equally compelling line of thought takes into account the reality of everyday schools and classrooms. There is simply not enough time, resources or personnel available in the traditional classroom, with the traditional teacher using the traditional curriculum.

NEW DIRECTIONS:
LEARNING TO INCORPORATE SOCIAL CHANGE

Four broad categories of practices could be a useful paradigm for schools, families and communities that want to achieve the full benefits of inclusive schooling practices:

1. Increasing Access;
2. Participation and Power Sharing;
3. Effective Participation — Parents;
4. Effective Participation —Students.

Increasing Access

Schools and educators need to work around the diverse time constraints that are faced by parents. Varied meeting times for school councils and parent-teacher meetings would allow for all parties to work around difficult job schedules. Community liaison counsellors could have a more visible presence in the schools to co-ordinate programs and act as a resource. The more parents, students and teachers get to know and trust their counsellors, the more likely their services will be successfully accessed. Informal or semi-formal membership and mentoring for other parents and community members will also tackle some of the many barriers to inclusivity that parents face. With larger numbers, sub-committees for literacy, fundraising, sports activities, technology, et cetera, could be created, easing the burden placed on a few active parents. Some parents and community members could benefit from professional development workshops, and in turn teachers may be invited to attend meetings or events in specific communities. *Examples:* Meetings could be set in advance, but could change time and venue to accommodate working parents. New parents could be partnered with experienced council members. Teachers could meet parents at home or in a neutral setting.

Participation and Power Sharing

The powers and responsibilities of the principal and other school administrators in the school council should be clearly defined and well known to other members. The same should hold true for student councils and other student initiatives or clubs. The principal, administrators or teachers should not run the councils/initiative; they should use their influence to ensure that marginalized and/or new voices are heard. Parents and students involved in home learning practices should be sought out especially encouraged to participate in school governance bodies, such as student and school councils. *Examples:* Administrators and teachers could take non-voting advisory roles. Teachers could be available on an ad hoc basis when school rules dictate supervision is needed. Older students could be responsible for the club's/council's/initiative's administration (typing permission slips, taking attendance, calling members, et cetera), thus freeing teacher prep time and giving students a skill building opportunity.

Effective Participation — Parents

Persons with real knowledge of and connections to the larger community should be mandated to be recruited into school councils and school-community partnerships. Diligent care must be taken to be inclusive of other peoples, groups and interests. Special care should also be taken to include members of the schools' racial, religious and ethno-cultural groups. *Examples:* If it is noticed that the same few parents are always involved, these parents could be asked to think of other candidates. If one community is only represented by men, then steps should be taken to understand how to make participation possible for more women. If a religious group has certain sects/denominations in the student body and community, then parent representatives should reflect such religious diversity. Translation services should be provided for parents who do not speak English so that language does not become a barrier to participation.

Effective Participation — Students

Student participation should be encouraged, even at the elementary level. Students need to know that their voices can make a difference. Greater care should be taken by school officials and parents alike that students have specific goals and roles on the new school councils, and actively communicate with student councils/initiatives and larger community initiatives. *Example*: Designated student council members participate in school council meetings, board of education meetings, and community education organization meetings (such as Saturday Schools). In this way, the students will know and be able to have input in decisions made at many different areas that effect their education.

Resource Co-ordination

New or reallocated funds should be used to facilitate outreach. Businesses should be encouraged to donate goods or services where possible. In poorer communities, more effort needs to be made to involve parents and community members personally who are already wary of the school system. *Example:* If a school is to form a business partnership with a large high-tech firm, then special care should be taken to ensure that marginalized students qualify for co-op placements, and that those with weaker skills are trained. Also, alternative partnerships such as a health care facility, small community business or social service agency could also be sought. Resources could be shared and students would have greater opportunities for job experience.

The Benefits of Transformative Home-School Practices

What these strategies and stakeholders demonstrate is that they are willing and able to complement, supplement and challenge public schools and educators. These stakeholders have recognized that "those who control the curriculum also control most of the society's institutions and utilize the curriculum to reflect their social and cultural reality" (Collins, 1993, p. 201). While the consequences of that statement are problematic, it does give some insight into why parents, community educators and community liaison counsellors engage in alternative inclusive educational practices. Teachers and especially administrators are still overwhelmingly members of the dominant group while their students are becoming increasingly diverse (Carson, 1996, p. 12) Many parents and community educators believe that children are being harmed when the best intentioned teacher "reduces *all* non-Western societies to the exotic, the primitive or the quaint" (Klein, 1985, pp. 17-18). They also strongly believe that such harm results in inequitable job and educational opportunities, when dominant employers and educators subscribe to the Eurocentric ideologies and assumptions they learned in school. Furthermore, in their view, *all* students are missing valuable opportunities to learn not only about other cultures, ethnic groups and races, but to learn to *respect, understand, value and advocate for* oppressed groups, whether or not they are themselves members of such groups.

In times past "the school was the focal point of the community," but now in many communities it is simply the educational institution where children are sent (Berlin and Alladin 1996, p. 151). Our study demonstrates just how much that model fails to offer students the cultural pride, global knowledges, self-discipline and "belongingness" that they need to form meaningful connections with the larger society. Therein lie the truly transformative possibilities of inclusive schooling. A Portuguese child who learns to value her/his culture is more likely to retain fluency and value the acquisition of other languages, than one whose language is ignored and culture disparaged. Our study shows how Portuguese community liaison counsellors have been facilitating such learning opportunities. A Jamaican child who learns about his own culture and history is more likely to find history relevant, and therefore engage in learning about other world cultures. Our study illustrates how Jamaican parents are instilling historically and culturally positive curricula in their children. Finally, a principal or teacher who facilitates the diverse participation of activist parents and students is more likely to achieve school success than school officials who are not inclusive. Our parent and liaison counsellor narratives amply demonstrate that inclusive school governance directly and indirectly translates into better learning outcomes for students and skills development for parents.

NOTES

1   Dei et al., 1997. *Home, Family and Community-Based Learning: Lessons for Curriculum and Pedagogy.*

CHAPTER 9

MAKING CONNECTIONS
TO PUBLIC SCHOOLING:
MULTICENTRIC EDUCATION

RECASTING THE MODEL

The writing of this book arose out of a mutual desire to re-think the delivery of education in racialized and plural contexts. In this exploration of how critical theory might inform educational pedagogy and practice, we felt that an integrative anti-racist framework would best interrogate the realities of promoting equity in education. While this entails a radical re-examination and revision of the status quo, it is also a project that is realistically attuned to the political and institutional formations that make educational change so onerous in the present social climate.

As an entry point to our project, we felt that it was important to examine how certain schools were attempting to deal with issues of inclusion within some of their policies, practices and curricula. Our intent was not to present these initiatives as idealized representations of "the good school," but rather to map them out as innovative alternatives to existing models of mainstream schooling. We intended that the schools and community-based initiatives examined in this work be seen as "possibilities" that could contribute, in part, to the overall process of educational change, and improvement. Specifically, we felt that these schools and communities had developed viable and compelling models with which to address issues of exclusion, bias and Eurocentrism in educational sites. That being said, these programs may not be the answer to inclusivity and equity in schooling, but they are at the very least, a strong beginning; a foundation that should pave the way for future transformations.

The educational sites and programs outlined herein were chosen in part because they provided for an especially rich interpretation of the insurgent work being undertaken at the institutional and grassroots levels. The initiatives explored in this work, and other established practices of inclusive schooling speak to us, and encourage us to move ahead to a more comprehensive and equitable pedagogical model. Our work in this project suggests that any such forward thinking pedagogy must take difference and equity into account when attempting to address the needs of all students. To these ends, we assert that the factors of visual and knowledge representation, staff equity, language integration, spirituality and community are all fundamental to the future of education in this society. Further, these factors take on even greater importance when placed relative to the growth of cultural diversity in our schools and the globalization of our society.

The theoretical orientation employed in this text highlights the salient role that race must play in any moves that would shift "the talk" away from tolerance and diversity, and towards the pointed notions of difference and power. Race and racism are central to how we claim, occupy, and defend spaces in schools. The task of an integrative, inclusive education is to identify, challenge and change the values, structures, and behaviours that perpetuate systemic racism and other forms of oppression such as sexism, classism, and homophobia. An inclusive education discourse should highlight persistent inequities among communities focusing on relations of domination and subordination. This critical discourse sees the issue of exclusion/inclusion starkly as entrenched in inequities and power imbalances. The approach perceives prejudice as an integral part of the social order. Like anti-racism, the approach views the mechanism of redress though fundamental structural/societal change. The assumption underlying empathy, commonality and goodwill promoted by multiculturalism is that we start from a relatively level playing field, that we have access to similar resources and that we have comparable values, aspirations and concerns to those who align themselves with the dominant discourse. Nothing can be further from the reality of those racially minoritized members of our communities (see also Price, 1993).

According to Bennett (1999) there are two primary factors guiding multicultural education today: *a movement toward equity* and *curriculum reform*. A movement toward equity she argues, attempts to transform the total school environment, especially the hidden curriculum that is expressed in teacher expectations for student learning, grouping of students and instructional strategies, school disciplinary policies and practices, school and community relations, and classroom climates (p. 12). This perspective acknowledges the multiplicity of factors involved in creating an inclusive context for educational delivery. Bennett goes on to say that: "the process of becoming multicultural is one whereby a person develops competencies in multiple ways of perceiving, evaluating, believing and doing" (p. 12). She articulates this as a goal or outcome of multicultural education for all learners. We would add to this understanding, that in addition to developing these "cultural competencies," in an inclusive environment, learners must develop an understanding of the cultural achievements of colonized peoples and historically disadvantaged groups in society through the process of de-centring Eurocentric knowledge and providing space for these alternative ways of knowing. This approach is more significant than simply a museum-like appreciation for "exotic ways," as it extends to the dimensions of how we come to think and read the world and the many constituents of its historical and cultural development.

Bennett also outlines curriculum reform as a guiding force in current multicultural education. She refers to the inclusion of multi-ethnic and global perspectives, which entail: "… active inquiry and the development of new knowledge and understanding about cultural differences and the history and contributions of contemporary ethnic groups and nations, as well as of various civilizations in the past" (p. 12). We captured this approach in our model of "knowledge representation" in schools that takes a critical role in interrogating how knowledges are produced with respect to issues of power. In our model, community-based and marginalized knowledges are seen as part of a multi-centred focus and enter into the sphere of public education as alternative discourses which decentre dominant Eurocentred traditions. This represents an integrative approach to addressing issues of race and social difference and the politics of social justice and educational reform. However, attempting to integrate marginalized knowledges through the approach of what their "contributions" were, still maintains Eurocentric knowledge as a dominant centre, to which one can add on "other" kinds of knowledge. The history of dominant societies is never told solely thorough "contributions." It is only those realities and histories that are marginalized through omission, that are relegated to examination through what cultural goods and products they may have "contributed" to the undisputed centrality of the European tradition.

According to Banks (1988), who outlines several ways that non-European knowledges are conventionally integrated into the curriculum since the 1960s:

The Contributions Approach often results in trivialization of ethnic cultures, the study of their strange and exotic characteristics, and the reinforcement of stereotypes and misconceptions. When the focus is on the contributions and unique aspects of ethnic cultures, students are not helped to understand them as complete and dynamic wholes (p. 1).

The partiality of what Banks refers to as the "Heroes and Holidays Approach" leads to the "Brown Heroes and Holidays Approach" that limits and confines non-European knowledges to the realm of special days and pageants. This, as Banks points out, has a trivializing effect on the representation of these peoples and cultures.

A second approach within the multicultural framework outlined by Banks is called the "Additive Approach," which is another example of token representation. Here multi-cultural content is "added" into the curriculum, usually in the form of a book or novel or unit, which does not substantially alter the hegemony of the dominant Eurocentric focus. According to Banks, this form of limited inclusion:

... allows the teacher to put ethnic content into the curriculum without re-structuring it, which takes substantial time, effort, training and rethinking of the curriculum and its purpose, nature, goals (p. 2).

However, Banks goes on to point out that such an approach can provide a starting point for further change and meaningful transformation:

The Additive Approach can be the first phase in a more radical curriculum reform effort designed to restructure the total curriculum and to integrate it with ethnic content, perspective and frames of reference (p. 2).

Nevertheless, if this approach does not move beyond token representation it fails to be truly integrative and inclusive and, as with the Contributions Approach, it does a disservice to the knowledges of historically marginalized communities by representing them as partial and incomplete appendages to the grand narrative of Eurocentric discourse. Banks goes on to critique the use of resources which "view ethnic content from the perspectives of mainstream historians, writers, artists, and scientists because it does not involve a re-structuring of the curriculum" (p. 2). He also notes that when minority cultures and experiences are included, all too often they mirror dominant norms rather than resist or challenge their saliency:

> When these approaches are used to integrate cultural content into the curriculum, people, events and interpretations related to ethnic groups and women often reflect the norms and values of the dominant culture rather than those of cultural communities. Consequently, most of the ethnic groups and women added to the curriculum have values and roles consistent with those of the dominant culture. Men and women who challenged the status quo and dominant institutions are less likely to be selected for inclusion into the curriculum (Banks, 1999, p. 30).

To counter the selective tokenism of the "Contributions" and "Additive" Approaches, Banks poses another alternative called the "Transformative Approach," which enables students to view concepts, issues, themes and problems, from several ethnic perspectives and points of view (1988, p. 2). Likewise, we see the essence of our multicentric model, which allows for a polyvocal, or multi-voiced discussion to take place within the production and dissemination of knowledge, as the central organizing principle for the delivery of education.

We have started from the partiality of the various multicultural approaches outlined by Banks, and moved towards an anti-racist framework which examines the issues of power and privilege that underscore how minority cultures, histories and experiences are taken up in our schools. We have extended the dimensions of the discussion to include representation of community and Indigenous knowledges, spirituality and language as sites where knowledge and identity are molded and transformed. As history, culture and "the everyday" are experienced in intertwined and connected ways, multiple knowledges should be synthesized through collaborative and collective efforts. Similarly, we have viewed education as a space from which to enact a transgression from the existing values, norms and ways of knowing that have come to be accorded privilege in our schools at the expense of "other" de-privileged knowledges. It is through a truly multi-centred framework that the validity and completeness of non-European cultures, histories and societies can be understood and valued as being equally as significant as those of the Anglo-European tradition.

We are also cognizant (as Dei, 1999 considers in another context) that in pushing for the synthesis of knowledges, there are some dangers posed to local/Indigenous knowledges as they co-exist in North American schools and the Western academy. For example, there is the problem of using Indigenous peoples as "data" while discounting the theoretical knowledges of local peoples. Holmes (1999) also notes that we can be reformatting and reformulating Indigenous knowledges problematically using Eurocentric scholarly theoretical formulations and assumptions that become the "defining grid" to evaluate local knowledges. Furthermore, we must always guard against the appeal to stratifying, codifying, and systematizing Indigenous knowledges that further a project of knowledge commodification and appropriation. We need to be aware of the limits posed by the processes through which oral knowledges are "surviving" the transition to literate, corporeal and consumptive forms.

The host of existing studies on "inclusive schooling" offer useful and at times penetrating insights into the challenges of inclusion in plural communities. The literature has relevance for understanding the challenges of inclusive schooling and ways in which genuine inclusive practices can be implemented in schools. Critical educators argue that inclusive schooling cannot be effectively addressed without challenging inequitable relations of power, based on race, ethnicity, religion, gender, sexuality, class, and language.

There are some questions in the pursuit of the educational agenda as set out in this book. For example, relative to current educational trends in Ontario, it would be pragmatic to interrogatre how we might achieve the inclusion of local knowledges into schooling when a curricula that is both highly centralized and ultra-standardized has been put in place. In the resource guide produced for this book (Dei, James-Wilson and Zine, 2000), we deal with this question. But it should be reiterated that what we are calling for is a radical disruption of the current school system. The ideas of inclusive education as promised here are antithetical to the view of education as promoted in conservative regimes such as that of the Harris government in Ontario (see also Dei and Karumanchery, 1999).

A multicentric education infused into the conventional curriculum seeks to create a "balance and holistic nature to education." It is believed that students will be able to adjust to this new way of looking and thinking about others. The greatest effect of exclusion may be seen to occur when different oppressions are interconnected so that, for instance, race is gendered and gender is racialized. The fluidity of an anti-racist, inclusionary approach provides the greatest potential to transform the current school system. It displaces the centre-margin dichotomy of racism with the possibility of multiple centres for all groups of people (Dei, 1996).

In developing a multi-centred focus for the delivery of education, Nieto (1995) warns of some of the conceptual pitfalls with regard to how knowledges must come to be understood. She argues that there is:

> ... the danger of a simplistic reliance on a *multiplicity of perspectives*. This concept, a central tenet of multicultural education, is based on the assumption that knowledge is not neutral or fixed, but always contested negotiated and changing. A multiplicity of perspectives needs to be presented to students so that they can understand and appreciate why different groups, feel, perceive and behave as they do. Understanding the motives and conditions under which different groups operate, students can then "step into someone else's shoes," an often powerful and eye opening experience [original emphasis] (p. 197).

Nieto's reference to a "simplistic reliance on a multiplicity of perspectives" refers to the uncritical cultural relativism that can occur as the result of "accepting all perspectives as valid, no matter how outrageous" (p. 197). By this she refers to the possibilities for some asking for "equal time" to be given to legitimating the Nazi point of view in World War II or other such examples of how the process can be co-opted by racist forces, if unqualified. Her concern raises an important point requiring clarification. Undoubtedly when we deal with education as a culturally situated and politicized endeavour, there will be challenges to any transformative imperatives that threaten to shift the base of power to accommodate marginalized communities. Rather than advocating a cultural relativist standpoint, a critical and integrative inclusive paradigm is one that seeks to de-construct the issues of racialized, gendered and class-based power that impact on our reading of social and cultural events and history. Thus an active anti-racism methodology for teaching and learning about difference is provided, rather than a passive culturally relativist model where "anything goes."

The use of simplistic inclusive formulas can also refer to the ways that minority cultures are integrated, yet still marginalized with many current multicultural education practices, as we have noted. Keeping this in mind, the question for us has been: How do educators "move aside" some knowledge in order to open up new spaces within schooling for other knowledges? The answer lies in positing different, diverse and multiple knowledge forms as equally legitimate and valid ways of knowing. However, such new and alternative knowledge forms need not necessarily be oppositional. Oppositionality emerges in the failure and refusal of hegemonic knowledge forms to recognize the existence and validity of other knowledges. The present school system is monocultural and changing this requires expanding the school and off-school curriculum to include the valid knowledge, achievements and contributions of all societies to world scholarship. Understanding the ways different cultures/knowledges have been silenced allows us to examine alternative knowledge forms and their relevance for schooling and education [without the presupposition of the hierarchy of knowledge forms].

Dei (1998) argues that part of the difficulty of achieving multicentric or inclusive education in the mainstream is the continued reliance on, and evolution of, liberal "democratic racism." The paradigms of the democratic ontology contribute to, if not generate, the unbroken chain of racism in the academies specifically, and in society as a whole. Bearing these issues in mind, acknowledging racism, oppression, and the experiences of minoritized groups, is a starting point to interrogating Eurocentrism as a hegemonic way of knowing. Schools have traditionally served, and continue to sustain certain ideological and political interests of capital. Such powerful interests are defended in myriad ways, including opposition to any attempts to challenge what is presented as "valid" and legitimate forms of knowledge. It is the "sense" of neutrality that accompanies oppression that works to silence other marginalized voices.

INTERROGATING THE POLITICS OF KNOWLEDGE PRODUCTION

Building an Inclusive Paradigm for Teaching and Learning

It can be said that mainstream education deals with the historical challenges of social inequity in ways that minimize dissonance to the status quo. That is to say, many of the current reforms being implemented in mainstream schooling, while acceptable as a step in the right direction, still effectively fail to rupture or dismantle the invasive standards of Eurocentrism. Minority cultures are allowed to add "spice" to the bland nature of pluralism in schools and society, but are never considered on equal footing when it comes to the centrality of the Western cannon in knowledge production.

Related to this are the issues of invisibility experienced by minority students. These issues have been addressed in this book along with issues of knowledge representation, language integration and the spiritual expression of students, as an integral part of how they construct their identities and read meaning into the world. It is necessary to re-think schooling in ways that will centre diverse and multiple knowledge forms in schools, to address the issues of marginality and exclusion experienced by minority students.

To address this issue, it is significant to acknowledge the histories and contexts for emerging critiques of conventional ways of knowledge production in the Euro-American schools. Two notions that we have discussed previously are key to the dialogue: *inclusivity* and *centring*. As already alluded to, "inclusivity" denotes an educational practice that is premised on the idea that the process of teaching, learning and sharing of knowledge is fundamentally a power relation. Thus, to deal with inclusiveness is to address the issues and inequities related to the distribution of power in society. Inclusionary educational practices that fail to empower the learner cannot represent genuine inclusion. Similarly, the notion of "centre" should be seen as a point of entry within the discursive practices of schooling and therefore a location for the subject in the act of knowledge production and use. The location of centre/margin is a power relation. To be included in the processes of schooling, all learners will have to be centred. This means, the experiences, histories, cultures and identities of all learners are considered as central to all levels of educational practices (e.g., teaching, instruction, curriculum and texts). Disrupting the power of Eurocentrism is a central focus of an integrative inclusive practice. But Eurocentrism is also intertwined with racism, sexism, classism, religious dominance and homophobia. We also share the view that disrupting oppression based on race must simultaneously address sexism, classism, religious discrimination, homophobia, and other forms of oppression that work to bolster and reinforce racism.

As we pursue educational practices that will transform and improve the existing system, we must remember to make the distinction between academic discourse and policy practice. For example, local community knowledge and cultural resource bases have not been fully integrated into school teaching and learning practices. Yet, the knowledge students acquire outside of school through their families and communities, can make a vital contribution to enhance youth education. In order for schools to promote genuine inclusion of the knowledge systems of local communities, the stability of conventional knowledge must be questioned, ruptured and/or interrupted. The process of interruption may well lie in how we come to understand "knowledge."

Knowledge is experienced and acquired through daily practice. Also, because of how systems of knowledge exist within disparate relations of power in society, knowledge is contested. Educators today have the arduous task of helping to equip learners with critical thinking skills necessary for interrogating all knowledge forms. They must be able to recognize the absences and monocultural epistemologies through which schools help us to understand the world in order to address change. Critical thinking ensures that there is no closure with regard to the systems of knowledge schools can legitimately use. Creating and developing a critical consciousness also means that learners are prepared to question even the "common sense knowledge" that is taken for granted and becomes part of the hegemonic apparatuses of state and capital interests. Such critical interrogation is central to the formulation of new ways of schooling and education. It is useful for educators, students, parents and community workers to search for ways to work collectively and collaboratively in order to provide critical knowledge that would be capable of meeting and addressing contemporary challenges. Such new knowledge forms will not necessarily be the search for a given/ established truth, but rather, a commitment to strive for a complete account of the social events that shaped and continue to shape human history.

Identity: Linking the Self to Schooling

In re-thinking schooling along the lines of an inclusive framework, the issue of identity or rather the multiple identities that students bring with them into their learning experiences has been central. According to Corrigan (1989), schools do not (only) teach subjects, they inform subjectivities (p. 65). Recognizing this important link between schooling and identification has been an important strand of this research. The role of teachers is a significant one in shaping the ways students come to understand themselves and others. In this regard, Montecinos (1995) makes the following assertion:

> As significant forces in shaping a child's social environment, teachers are in a unique position to help students develop identities of empowerment as opposed to identities of subordination (p. 300).

Our position has also recognized the profound impact teachers have in helping students to develop socially and feel a sense of belonging in their environment — starting with their school. Our inclusive pedagogical strategies also attempt to help students develop "identities of empowerment" based on policies of inclusion, voice and representation through the development of emancipatory knowledge as part of a critical approach to teaching and learning. We must not simply "celebrate diversity" and the diverse identities students bring and negotiate within the context of their schooling experiences, Instead, we require a social re-constructivist approach to reformulating educational thought and praxis.

It is not enough to add a few cultural artifacts or posters to the classroom and expect them to be the framework upon which marginalized students can build a sense of identity and inclusion. An inclusive pedagogy, which seeks to engender "identities of empowerment," must be responsive to how knowledge production impacts upon the development of identities as agencies of change and transformation. Critical knowledge production engenders emancipatory knowledge by examining how individuals and groups in society are differentially located according to the social indices of race, class, gender, religion or sexual orientation, including how these identities come to bear on their schooling experiences. This framework becomes transformative through the Freirean process of "conscientization," or being aware of the structural dynamics of one's "identity of subordination" as a means of engendering resistance through self-knowledge.

Such self-knowledge also becomes actualized through the relational aspect of knowledge of the other. Linking this to the relationship between teachers and students, Montecinos (1995) points out that "... when depicting the Cultural Other, teachers need to recognize that they are also depicting themselves" (p. 301). This refers to the positioning of identities that take place through the situated practices of knowledge production and engagement. If minority cultures and identities are presented through fragmented practices, then this reflects upon the way students from these backgrounds come to see themselves constituted within the knowledge practices of school. It also serves to position those from the dominant culture in an inherently privileged and salient way through the same set of discursive practices. These issues of positionality are crucial to developing awareness of what Montecinos (1995) refers to as "reciprocity," which allows teachers to examine "... how the varied ways of interpreting students' behaviours can serve the purpose of social transformation versus maintenance of the status quo" (p. 310). It is this transformative shift that allows for identities grounded in self-knowledge and actualization to recognize transcendent possibilities stemming from their social positions vis-à-vis those they categorize as others. An education based on understanding how knowledge and power relate to inequitable social outcomes, lays the groundwork for broader social change.

However, often when we discuss the role of dominant teachers educating across differences toward emancipatory outcomes, we inadvertently trigger notions of "rescuing the other." For example, teachers who regard themselves as on a mission to "save" the underclass or disadvantaged only serve to reproduce the perception of inherent privilege accorded to those from the dominant culture who must "tend to the less fortunate." What may be seen as "good intentions" serve to reproduce colonial or paternalistic relations between these teachers and students who are already positioned differentially within society. An emancipatory pedagogy is one where teachers are aware of the authoritative and social power they wield over students and must be willing to divest this power by restoring agency to their students. Transformation through conscientization requires students being the architects of social change in their own lives and within their communities. In this way, teachers are the facilitators of transformative possibilities, not the gatekeepers.

We have suggested several ways of looking at the question of identity through the perspective of different epistemologies. The various ways that knowledge and language structure identity development have been explored to examine the positive and negative implications within schooling. However, where language practices are congruent for students, they provide a vehicle for their culture and can help create a sense of cohesion and belonging for students as a form of collective identification. Where language practices are not congruent, that is, where students have a different language or dialect from that which is dominant and privileged in schools, the result is one of alienation and dissonance. Language provides a source of identification which can strengthen communal ties and provide a collective aspect of one's identity that is tied to a shared knowledge base and history. But if language is neglected within schooling, aspects of identification — as a process of becoming connected and centred within one's culture — will not be complete for these students. Language integration then, relates to identity development through the recognition of the saliency of language and the need to be responsive toward the ways it can benefit student learning.

We have also discussed the fact that a holistic education must include the spiritual dimension of learners. Not only is spirituality an integral part of the identity and self-concept, but it also provides a medium through which people come to make sense of the world. The spiritual aspect of identity development is an often neglected focus for educators, yet spirituality also connects individuals to their community and to a non-temporal existence that can be a profound aspect of their lives. Whether spirituality is connected to a religious base or to other conceptions, schools must begin to acknowledge its relationship to the holistic formation of identity, self concept and learning.

Identities are often referred to as "multiple and shifting," meaning that we occupy multiple identities based on our race, ethnicity, class, religion, gender, and sexual orientation, and that these are not static or immutable categories, but rather they represent fluid boundaries. This postmodernist notion of the shifting or fluidity of identity however is often conflated to a position where no one can claim to be grounded in any particular ontological category. For the sake of avoiding essentializing generalizations, structured sense of identity based on shared beliefs, histories or cultural practices is often sacrificed, which limits the possibilities for collective political action or self-determination based on these identities. While it important not to pigeon-hole people according to stereotypical notions of what it means to be Black or Chinese, Muslim or Jewish, or having come from the inner city or another country, there is still something common, shared, and specific that comes from these realities that is not necessarily transient or elusive. Identities can often be sites of resistance (see Giroux, 1983) that come from being situated within a particular and identifiable social framework. Attempting to disrupt these frames of reference through poetic notions of a transient identity, can also disrupt the basis for resistance. As such, there must be a balance in recognizing identities as ontologically grounded categories, while still maintaining that these categories are not necessarily monolithic or static.

In the discussion, we have highlighted questions of race, ethnicity and culture. At one level, these are distinct and yet interrelated categories and analysis. The theoretical commitment to the saliency of race is as much political as pragmatic. Our discursive approach has also highlighted the intersections of race with other forms of difference: class, gender, ethnicity, religion and sexuality. We maintain the focus on race so as not to lose its sharp and critical edge, and also to acknowledge that at the level of policy, approaches to inclusive education will have to target specific identities, yet at the same time acknowledge where these identities intersect. Similarly, the categories of race, ethnicity, and culture cannot simply be transposed on one another. These categories are not equivalent. They are distinct in the sense that race speaks of the use of socially determined physical characteristics (e.g., skin colour) as a marker of differentiation. We evoke race not strictly in terms of its biological meaning or lack of meaning, but to the symbolic meaning as a cultural and political marker of exclusion. However, through the process of racialization, groups become marked for differential treatment by culture, language, religion and other factors. Thus, at some levels, culture and ethnicity achieve similar [not necessarily equal] effects and consequences as race, but it is through ethnicity, culture, language and religion that race achieves its differential effects on groups socially constructed as different. We have shown throughout the discussion how race, ethnicity, and culture interrelate in the various components identified as essential to achieving inclusive education. The lesson is that we cannot conflate culture, ethnicity, and identity with race. We must also not deny the saliency of race and racism in affecting more profoundly the life chances, aspirations, and opportunities of students in a racialized society (see also Alexander, 1996, p. 113).

These and other significant aspects of identity construction that have been addressed throughout this work and are constructed as a historically implicated, dynamic and relational process. We outline below the perspectives or holistic approaches to deconstructing the multiple layers of identity:

Perspectives on Identity Construction:
The Historical Importance of Self-Esteem
1. Self-other as relational;
2. Collective and social identity;
3. Understanding yourself; understanding others;
4. Self-identity in relation to the issues of marginality and power;
5. "Multiplicity" — multiple locations of identity based on factors such as race, class, gender, ethnicity, religion and sexual orientation;
6. Identity and shared cultural knowledge — connective aspect of history and shared cultural heritage. How we articulate the collective experiences of oppression?

Second Perspective:
Saliency of Certain Forms of Identity —
Some Forms of Identity more Salient to a Notion of Self
7. One's self-definition as opposed to an imposed definition;
8. Language as a powerful mark of culture — you enter culture through language — speaking one's language in a school setting ruptures the dominant; destabilizes the centre; language as a form of cohesiveness;
9. Spiritual knowledge and identity — the association of one's spiritual awareness and their sense of personal and collective identity;
10. Political identities — how negative identities become a form of resistance; politics of resistance (all knowledge embodies power).

The above aspects of identity construction relate to multiple factors, social/relational, spiritual and political that are all implicated within the process of schooling and how students' sense of self comes to be structured through their schooling experiences. An inclusive pedagogy is one that is attentive to these various dimensions and formations of identity and the extent to which schooling practices can, by taking these into account, effect the development of "identities of empowerment," rather than "identities of subordination."

INDIGENOUS KNOWLEDGES AND INCLUSIVE PEDAGOGY

In this book, we have argued that Indigenous knowledges are fundamental to critical education. In their situational, contextual and localized natures, they speak to multiple experiences and ontologies. This versatility is generated through a philosophical belief in collaborative learning and a dedication to the notion that knowledges, whether Indigenous or otherwise, are publicly owned and accessible. Therefore, as an educational resource, this openness makes them generally applicable in spite of their obvious specificities.

All knowledges develop in and through multiple contexts, some are social while others originate within the self and the body. For instance, intuition offers the individual a reading of larger socio-political contexts and may move her/him toward broader social actions. Let us reiterate this point because the need for social action and equitable reform are the most important messages that we would have readers take from this work. The promotion of Indigenous knowledges in schools is about power and the empowerment of subordinate groups. In the articulation of these alternative knowledges, local peoples and communities become empowered to develop their own accounts of marginalization and oppression. In so doing, they engage in the development of new theoretical frameworks that will be invaluable to the future of social change. However, as aforementioned, the developing frameworks and strategies must be articulated relative to questions of credibility, accountability, practice, relevance, sustainability, appropriation, validation and legitimization.

These concerns highlight the obvious problematics involved in any efforts that would seek to include Indigenous/alternative knowledges as part of the mainstream curricula. It is an important educational challenge. Dealing with the specifics of how the educators use such knowledges to teach, it is also crucial to note two pedagogic aspects of Indigenous knowledges: first, the recognition of Indigenous as a body of knowledge in itself (e.g., validation of Indigenous knowledges as one of the multiple ways of knowing; and second, using the lessons that these knowledges offer to further the cause of enhancing learning/education (e.g., using the lessons of harmony, with community and nature, human relations with environment) to teach about collaborative education, social justice and peace. In other words, using such knowledges to teach critically, to teach interpersonal relations.

Implications for Teaching

All stakeholders in the educational process have investments in Indigenous knowledges. The imperative lies in communicating the value of these knowledges to those learners, educators and stakeholders who might benefit from their use. We believe the value lies in the importance of complete/holistic education. The idea of multicentric means one is not the centre of the world, and that there are many centres of knowledge. The educator, therefore, must initiate conversations that move across boundaries and spaces to engage other ways of being. However, the pragmatics of "power-sharing" are certainly not cut and dried. So in practice, insurgent reform must begin with initial conversations about the need for change. Educators could adapt new methods of instruction that are inter-relational and interactional, and critical dialogue could begin to question the "neutrality" of the existing system. However, students can also go into their communities to interview parents and elders about their Indigenous and cultural resource knowledges. In such an approach, students will use their Indigenous languages as a means to create new knowledge. By using their own languages and going into local communities, conversations can capture the emotional, spiritual, intuitive and analytical aspects of Indigenous knowledges. Specific approaches would include students writing letters, preparing and reading stories and engaging in other correspondence in their first languages. This process allows students, parents, elders and communities to use their own languages to access and create new knowledges. Knowledge contextualized in the homes, and with families is spiritual, intuitive and emotional. It is based on lived experiences with oneself, others and the surrounding environments. The problem has been when such knowledges are brought into schools, they become disembodied and are presented outside of their spiritual and emotional dimensions.

Approaches such as these should be considered an integral part of the education process. The educational practices that permit students to engage local communities in a structured way have other pedagogic advantages. Besides providing a source of knowledge, the practice also serves as new forms of pedagogy by allowing parents, elders and communities to teach leadership responsibility, life skills and social values grounded in a sense of spirituality and emotional well-being. The educational approach using students' Indigenous languages accords a sense of "ownership" of the process to students who can be motivated to develop different types of relationships with parents, elders, community workers and other youth, and to be motivated to broaden their perspectives, as well as develop their moral skills and character.

In understanding the place of knowledge in school systems, the distinction between "systemic exclusion" and "systematized exclusion" is relevant. The former denotes the operation and enforcement of structures that consciously and unconsciously work to promote exclusion of other knowledges. For example, an educator's decision to use Canadian texts may end up excluding works of minoritized groups or historically subordinate groups where schools do not actively encourage critical writing that directly addresses minority issues and experiences in Canada. Official policy may not aim directly at excluding works of minoritized groups, and such a case may be unconscious exclusion. Alternatively, there may be cases where a policy is enacted that directly excludes work of minoritized groups; and would thus constitute institutionalized racism.

Indigenous knowledges have both generalized and specialized knowledge content. The generalized aspects of Indigenous knowledges speak to the ideas and values that broadly govern society, and they extend to commonsense knowledges about society, nature and culture. On the other hand, from a specialized perspective, Indigenous knowledges interpret aspects of society that are more distinct; aspects such as herbal medicine, pharmacology, and knowledge about oral histories. In their varied nature, Indigenous knowledges bring a unique vision to the project of educational reform.

As already argued, Indigenous knowledges have the potential of challenging conventional knowledges produced in Euro-American schools, and to offer critical discursive spaces within which to envision and enact genuine educational change. By enhancing the awareness to Indigenous subjectivity, political agency and resistance to domination, the connection between multicentric schooling and Indigenous knowledges can be made. In advocating multicentric approaches to schooling it is crucial to understand subjectivity and its role in the process of knowledge production and educational praxis. The knower is a positioned subject that actively constructs meaning and produces knowledge. Feelings and emotions are located in a spiritual realm that works with material conditionalities and forces to produce knowledge and ensure political practice. The Indigenous subjectivity can have discursive authority on social reality. The subject, therefore, has agency in interpreting her or his own culture and politics. The idea that knowledge emerges within the self and from forces outside of human agency certifies that different bodies come with different ways of knowing.

The push for a multicentric education must acknowledge that Indigenous knowledges in transnational contexts present many challenges to educators and learners. Multi-centred educational approaches must capture multiple, diverse and competing tensions in the struggle for educational change. Teaching Indigenous knowledges necessitates that we always take care to avoid strategies or practices that see these "ways of knowing" as romantic or mythical. Such perspectives actively work to devalue and mute the potential for these systems to encourage and initiate change. In this sense, we must be particularly careful to ensure these knowledges are not "hegemonized" to silence the insurgent voices therein. Some knowledges have discursive sanctions against their misuse for injurious as well as non-conforming purposes. Indigenous knowledges may have multiple sources and political interests that are not always consistent with each other. There are usually vested interests in producing, maintaining, and protecting narratives, oral histories and accounts that highlight the power of Indigenous knowledge systems to explain the past and the current. As Indigenous knowledge systems are used to rupture a linear, secular, materialistic and ahistorical reading of the reality so too can culture, tradition and history be presented as unquestioned truth.

The pathway to/between truth, discourse and narrative can be a slippery slope. All knowledges are subject to partisan, partial and limited renditions of cultures and historical realities. In social commentary, the privileging of a particular narrative/story of Indigenous knowledges may minimize the underside of history, culture and tradition. For example, the folklore, myth, fables and cultural traditions of the North American mainstream have traditionally disempowered women, ethnics and other cultural minorities. One of the dangers in parading Indigenous knowledges in Western academic contexts is for such knowledges to assume the mantle of acceptability and legitimacy as analytic and objective knowledge. In response to the racist and colonialist charge of Indigenous knowledge as "epistemologically primitive" knowledge, Western and Eurocentric standards of truth and objectivity could well be applied to the evaluation of Indigenous knowledges.

A more nuanced approach to Indigenous knowledges interrogates traditional dichotomies between old and new. In doing so, it may move beyond the problematics of dualistic thinking to integrate and synthesize multiple knowledge systems. This approach engages the possibility of attaining dialogic, communicative and/or discursive equality between systems. In other words, it encourages a balanced view and use of multiple "ways of knowing." The approach not only challenges imperial knowledge production, it critiques the insularity of knowledge systems. It also problematizes the power of transnational capital to script the Indigenous subject/"other" as without historical agency.

SPIRITUALITY IN EDUCATION

The reconciliation of the secular and the sacred (which includes individual and group conceptions of religion and spirituality) is a challenge that is often taken up in the home, family and community educational outlets and practices. In the promotion of spirituality in education, educators need to recognize the traditions, values and practices that students bring with them to school. However, that being said, we must be careful to ensure that such efforts do not amount to sugar-coated, well-meaning initiatives that suffer from the "sari, samosa and tin-drum syndrome." In order to safeguard against such problematics, educators must endeavor to make a real space for inclusion in their classrooms; a space that works to embrace and teach the whole child. In the desire to teach the whole child and to be responsive to the diverse backgrounds and histories that children bring to school, it is important that the spiritual dimension of their lives be taken into account.

The definitions and conceptions of spirituality, and religion are both various and contested. In this work we have tried to unpack these notions and to offer a new way of thinking about spirituality in education. In order to accomplish this task it is necessary to understand spirituality in education as both a conceptual and curricular construct.

Various, well established approaches to teaching and learning lend themselves well to the conception of spirituality in education offered in this text. Holistic, constructivist and anti-racist approaches can provide teachers with a framework within which to redefine practice in ways that consider children in all of their complexity and a way to challenge and propose ways that learning can happen in schools. Holistic approaches name spirituality explicitly as one of the dimensions' of students lives that it seeks to engage. Learner-centred approaches, including constructivism, recognize and honour the uniqueness of the individual and frame the teacher as a facilitator of learning instead of a giver of knowledge. Finally, anti-racist approaches critically examine schooling as it relates to issues of equity, race and oppressive practices.

Implications for Pedagogy

Before one can begin to devise strategies for incorporating practices that will encourage the development of student's spiritual lives, it is important to understand how students learn. Teachers need to be aware of how students individual and collective identities affect their ability to learn and feel empowered in the school setting. If we acknowledged the fact that the students must negotiate various environments including school, home and the larger community, including these worlds within the life of the schools would be a natural extension of teachers' work.

Similarly, it is important to frame teachers as learners and individuals who are required to sort out for themselves their personal understandings of what spirituality means and how it can be realized in their daily lives. In order to talk about religions or religious practice, one does not need to be a member of a particular religious community, nor does one need to agree with the doctrine presented. Spirituality, however, presents a new set of challenges because, as we have defined it within this text, it involves more of an inward exploration or "journey" and is mediated by our beliefs about who we are and what our place is in the world. One might argue that it would be difficult for anyone to acknowledge, support and encourage the development of a spiritual conscience, if they themselves have not come to terms with what that state could be in their own lives. We are not suggesting here that teachers have to "get it right," but we are recommending that they engage in an exploration of self discovery and actively work to understand and develop their spiritual selves before attempting to help students in this manner.

Equally as important is the environment in which this exploration is to take place. Because intuitive or spirituality understandings are not valued to the same extent as intellectual or scientific knowledge, the act of attempting to encourage the development of spirituality involves risk. It is important that the classroom and school become an environment where students feel safe, valued and empowered. It is also imperative to involve family and members of the community into the learning process by including them in the life and activities of the school in meaningful ways.

LANGUAGE INTEGRATION

Our discussion of language integration has focused on issues of linguistic integration in schooling because language plays a significant role in whether or not students retain and/or develop their sense of ethnicity, ethnic identity, self-esteem and connection to community. Further, as mentioned previously, language facility is also directly related to how minoritized people access and succeed in our educational systems. At present, mainstream schooling is not moving quickly enough to address the everyday battles that students, parents and communities are fighting as they struggle to create access and equity in their schooling experience. Bearing this in mind, if students are to develop a sense of belonging, and a sense of both space and place within their schools, it is imperative that language and other such identity factors are integrated into mainstream education. Such changes in policy and practice would work to shift our pedagogical paradigms from the present Eurocentric model, towards an inclusive environment in which minoritized students' culture, heritage and understandings of the world are incorporated into the centre of the educational process.

We understand linguistic integration in schooling as extending beyond the need to reflect the spoken language of minoritized communities, and to the more intangible and elusive qualities that shape school culture and the learning experience of all children. As noted by Cummins and Danesi (1990), language is a marker of inclusivity, and the present demand/imperative for the implementation of language integration in schooling, extends far beyond "interest group politics" as suggested by "the right." Language integration is an issue of educational improvement for *all* children, and while our primary approach works to validate and centre multiple languages within schooling, while developing an interchange between school and community, educators, administrators and others involved with the educational process must recognize the intrinsic benefits associated with such a shift in conventional pedagogy.

When questioned about the benefits of language integration in schooling, respondents in our study echoed many similar themes. Of those, the most commonly noted were:

• Heritage language use/development is crucial in sustaining cultural ties to family and community roots;

- The promotion of heritage languages in schooling could only benefit and support a greater communication between students and their families/communities;
- The centring of presently marginalized languages into the schooling experience would enhance students' sense of pride, self and belonging;
- That language integration is an important step towards establishing a greater communication base between home, school and community;
- That schools must work to motivate and include parents in the business of schooling because language often acts as a barrier to parental involvement in education;
- That linguistic integration would go a long way towards developing equity and access for first generation immigrants for whom English Skills Development are of paramount importance; and, that such initiatives are an important step towards addressing both the immediate and long-term consequences of linguistic exclusion for those for whom English is a second language;
- The importance of establishing classrooms in which both English and Heritage languages are employed as a method through which teachers could validate student languages and in turn help to empower ESL students.

Further, as noted by Cummins and Danesi (1990), the benefits of language integration extend beyond issues of heritage, cultural and equity. They assert that language development is not only an invaluable educational tool that enhances intellectual development, but that facility in multiple languages can only be beneficial to students in their academic careers and when they enter the workforce. The integration of multiple languages into mainstream schooling will ultimately result in a more educated, versatile and communicative society. Consequently, language integration, as a domain of inclusive schooling, would work directly against the sense of alienation and disengagement presently felt by linguistically minoritized youth, while developing a new resource base for *all* students. As with all other elements of schooling to be addressed through inclusivity, issues of language integration are really questions of power: Whose knowledge, language and culture are excluded, and in what overt and covert ways does this exclusion take place? Along with the other domains of inclusivity, language integration would specifically work to develop a curriculum that "speaks" of and to everybody.

Implications for Teaching

With the multiracial/multicultural/multilinguistic make-up of today's population in Canada, a move towards a more inclusive policy and practice in our schools would appear to make a great deal of sense if we are to work towards equity and social justice in our school systems. Unfortunately, within our present political milieu, such progressive and necessary transitions often get filed and dismissed under the banner of "special interest" projects and "unnecessary" expenditures. We cannot afford to continue closing our eyes to the dilemmas faced by students, families and communities. These are not special interest groups; these are actual members of our community who find that present models of schooling are to them, inaccessible, inequitable and ultimately problematic. It is no longer enough simply to teach English and French in the school system as the days of bilingualism and biculturalism are long behind us.

There is a great deal of rhetoric that portrays the practice of language integration as disruptive and strenuous. Also, within this discourse, programs that integrate language as a cultural resource to enrich student empowerment are seen as unnecessary and draining on both students and the system. In reality, however, educational research by Cummins (1986, 1989), Corson (1993), Corson and Lemay (1996), and many others, indicates that competency in first languages substantially assists second language competency, and that the possession of a second or more languages facilitates learning for students. Therefore, as schools promote multiple languages and seek to develop the language skills of students, they should recognize and focus on how multiple languages can enhance youth educational outcomes. One teacher spoke of a convergence of different conceptual linguistic patterns:

> So, inclusive would be to find out what pattern the child is more comfortable with and trying to make a link between that and the pattern I'm bringing to them ... I bring them to a different pattern ... (Ami).

This same teacher also highlighted the importance of identifying parallels between languages, and in a broader sense, cultural ways of knowing as a practice of inclusive education:

> [W]hat you're doing is just trying to show them the parallels as opposed to [the differences], and actually they like that too … to some extent they like it because it sort of gives them a bit of power in the class: "Wow, I can do it this way and I can do it this way." And then they get to see similarities between different groupings (Ami).

Language integration within an inclusive framework emphasizes the recognition of parallels in language and culture. As the above teacher notes, various practices of inclusion and language integration can prove empowering for students in that their knowledge is validated and employed within the classroom. Principles of accommodation as they exist in mainstream education today do not provide the same level of validation and empowerment as those strategies looked at herein. Even more extreme, however, is the contrast with assimilationist principles that actually serve to disempower and invalidate the knowledges that students bring with them to school.

Present practice in schooling is geared directly towards the interests of only a select sector of society. Language integration as a domain of inclusivity tries to break the language barrier that prevents some parents and students from comfortably and efficiently accessing school and succeeding in it. It is no longer acceptable for schooling to be set up such that academic success is geared only to those most able to take advantage of the system. We must make school accessible to those who find it the most difficult to access.

EDUCATIONAL SUCCESS

In discussing "success" for students we must remember that it is the families, teachers and communities that surround and support them that inform our use of the term "need." Thus, "to need" stems from turning the education system's mandate to serve *all* children from a theoretical ideal to an every-day practice. We fully acknowledge the danger and, indeed seduction of "compensatory education," which views marginalized students as pathologically disadvantaged.

For example, some new educational reforms in South Africa reject the pathological approach by developing a curriculum that asks all the children in the class, Black, white or coloured, or English, Afrikaans or Native language speakers to interrogate their views about their respective languages, body images and cultural/racial identities. The goal of the program was to "make it a total institution for the disadvantaged, rather than just grafting on compensatory or remedial classes to elementary schools with a conventional agenda" (Levin, 1990, p. 10). An integrated program was established that developed language skills, peer tutoring, parental and community involvement and an extended day to incorporate activities with the help of volunteers. Compensatory Education was rejected, not only for the classist and often racist segregation that resulted in many countries in Europe and North America, but because it often does not work. Placing students in remedial classes as a sole strategy does not fulfil their "needs" because they simply receive the same curriculum at a pace too slow to ever reach the same level of achievement as their peers in the regular class. Students then receive an inferior education in addition to limited post-secondary opportunities, social stigma and damage to self-esteem (Corson, 1998).

What made the program in South Africa succeed, just as the Saturday School, Alternative Schools, and Home Learning strategies we studied succeed, is the recognition that becoming "just like" the dominant group is an impossible and more importantly, an undesirable goal. Educating our children for "success" means educating them to develop a "critical consciousness" that recognizes and interrogates elitism and privilege, without seeking to emulated it (hooks, 1988). No matter their racial or cultural or socioeconomic background every student should work for a success that combines personal growth and achievement with community development and a desire for justice.

Implications for Pedagogy

Maslow's hierarchy of needs has become a classic expression of basic human survival (1954). The hierarchy placed physical/physiological needs at bottom, food, shelter, et cetera, leading up to the top of the pyramid, higher order personal growth processes. From psychology we borrow the term, but without the normative structure that values individualized actualization above developing relationships within a person's community. Determining the exact value of that a child may need, is less important than identifying that need itself, beyond basic biological functions and a secure socio-economic base. These categories are neither meant to outline a new theory nor to restate what might seem to be obvious, but to interrogate what we mean by the term "privilege" and how it applies in a North American school setting. As reported by educational stakeholders in this study, including the students themselves, these *success needs* include: 1) belonging to the class and school communities; 2) agency and empowerment to transform the system; 3) spiritual nourishment, whether secular or religious; 4) emotional support from peers and educators; 5) acceptance and understanding of racial/ethnic identities; 6) high expectations from self and from educators; and 7) preparation for future goals.

Each kind of "success need" is articulated in ways that reach beyond a measurement of comprehension through re-articulation, or through standardized and objective test. Instead, measurement of success should also include a child's multiple intelligences, spirituality, well-being and capacity for growth. A young minority or disadvantaged student entering the school system lacks the "cultural capital" of middle-class white students moving from a comfortable home situation to a new, yet familiar situation. At school, the majority of authority figures still come from the dominant group. The physical and social structure of the school, from the food, "play," materials and language are familiar. Educators need to interrogate just what is contained in this cultural capital, or as Peggy McIntosh has written, "invisible knapsack."

To ask if "white privilege" is found in the Canadian educational system, means first asking whether the concept exists at all. The very notion of the "invisible weightless knapsack" (1990) means that many of the dominant group who "wear" it, will not be conscious of its existence. We would argue that for others, people of colour or conscious members of the dominant group, the same question of the existence of white privilege would be like asking a non-sighted person whether the sky is blue. White dominance in society and the resulting power structure then is accepted experiential knowledge, and their denial becomes the subject of a utopic imagination. Therefore, manifestation of such privilege in the Canadian educational system would be no more than the logical extension of the exercise of power.

In exploring the "knapsack" analogy we noticed the different classes of its contents. "Passports" are simply presented, "provisions" are simply consumed, but "tools" are employed, and usually with skill and purpose. This focus on the actions of the powerful is at the heart of exposing the systemic nature of discrimination. Furthermore, looking at the purpose and effects of privilege reaches beyond the debate over its existence. Whiteness cannot be purely a passive invisible phenomenon. It is a constantly employed strategy that becomes visible to the wearer when its function is contested. White privilege is clearly evident for those who would contest it, and deployed by those would deny it. The visibility of the power may be masked by good intentions in the form of superficial multiculturalism, or through a "back to basics" sublimation of difference. The analogy of the "knapsack of privilege" does not adequately reflect the exercise of power that results.

In the social context of accepting "multicultural heritage" Canadian educators often fail to recognize that systemic inequality can lead to the accusation of bias. By allowing that a social context may *sometimes* be appropriate when applied to the *individual* student, and her/his possibilities for educational success, the teacher is in fact deciding what social contexts may be *excluded* from consideration. Consequently, the educator becomes the arbitrator of the "invisible knapsack of disadvantage." Herein lies the danger and limitation of Peggy McIntosh's analogy.

REPRESENTATION IN EDUCATION

The issues of representation have been discussed through our framework for re-inventing the familiar yet partial ways schools have traditionally dealt with non-European ways of knowing, being and engaging in the world. By creating a plural centre within educational discourse and praxis, new vantage points for understanding social, cultural, and religious/spiritual diversity is opened. According to Murtadha (1995), "Centring students not only in their historical knowledges, but also in the cultural struggles of diverse groups, prepares them for the global diversity to which they are intimately linked" (p. 366). This has been the focus of how we have come to frame issues of representation in schooling, through an understanding of globalization and diversity as well as through equity education. There is a difference between these two aspects of inclusive schooling although they may seem like mutually inclusive notions. For example when we speak of presenting a global vantage point in which to centre student learning, we are talking about developing a framework of learning for all students. All too often when teachers are asked to begin integrating knowledge from different communities into their classroom, this is seen as a way to placate certain minority and "special interest groups" rather than as simply being good education for all.

Also, in developing an equity pedagogy we go beyond the immediate pedagogical benefits of broad based cultural learning, and challenge the inequities that exist within the production of knowledge and hiring of staff that serve to marginalize particular disadvantaged groups in society. The outcome is one of social as well as intellectual transformation, although these processes work hand in hand.

The practices of visual and knowledge representation, therefore, serve to provide a broader canvas for students to build a global understanding of the world and their place within it. This not only allows for minority students to feel represented and *present* within the curricular practices of the school and the school culture, but also provides an enriched program of learning for all students. Montecinos (1995) however, points out some of the pitfalls of how attempts at representation are taken up in schools. She warns of the dangers of developing a "master narrative" or representations of ethnic groups through "patterned depictions" that are narrow and essentializing. The example of Asian students representing the "model minority" and being exceptional in math or science is one example of the use of a master narrative. Other examples may include the representation of women who occupy more traditional roles in certain cultures as being reticent and docile, particularly when compared to the master narrative of the "liberated" Western woman. The use of these essentialized paradigms as a means to convey an understanding of non-Western or Western cultures, gives the impression that cultures are fixed, ahistorical and hence predictable patterns of behaviour that individuals submit to, devoid of any sense of agency. According to Montecinos (1995):

> This type of representation ignores the cultural life of students who belong to multiple, over-lapping cultural groups. A monovocal account will engender not only stereotyping but also curricular choices that result in representations in which fellow members of a group represented cannot recognize themselves (pp. 293-294).

The ways in which these representations are read by students from a given group and their peers can influence the way people come to know and understand their realities. Montecinos goes on to write about the importance of teacher's conceptions and representation of their students as "Cultural Others" who are nevertheless connected to the same world they live in:

> This interdependence among groups implies that the Cultural Other teachers must learn about and represent in the curriculum does not live in a world completely separated from the one the teacher lives in. Learning about the Cultural Other is learning about oneself as one's own life is, in a sense, shaped by the life of the Cultural Other (pp. 296-97).

This sense of "interconnectedness" and "interdependence" is an important vehicle through which teachers can gain an understanding of difference that does not automatically become exoticized and pushed outside of the predetermined and socially regulated framework of dominant culture. It enables the teacher to move beyond Eurocentrism as a framework for understanding and measuring other cultures in terms of their "development" vis-à-vis this master order. The intrinsic nature of a given culture can be understood as socially constructed through the prevailing norms and ideological orientations of a particular society, as well as through the permutations and developments that occur through contact with other cultural forms. This presents a parallel and dynamic representation of cultures as fluid forms, rather than as monolithic and fixed notions of cultural difference.

Another way representation can work to provide non-essential understandings of "Cultural Others" is through staff representation or employment equity. This form of representation, begins to recognize the need for diverse bodies to be present within schools as teachers and administrators, not as token representatives, but in recognition of their skills, abilities and the broad funds of knowledge they bring with them into the classroom. Aside from providing role models that make minority students more aware of possibilities for their own advancement, teachers and administrators with varied backgrounds provide a richer context for all students through the lived experiences and knowledge they are able to share. However, these teachers should not be regarded as "speaking for" or representing their entire cultural or ethnic group, nor should they be on call to "perform" as part of the school's multicultural offerings. Rather these teachers bring alternative ways of knowing that can provide greater points of access for students in developing broader worldviews.

Implications for Teaching

Understanding the importance the various modes of representation in education that we have outlined: visual and knowledge representation and staff equity, is the first step in re-framing the practices of schooling as part of a conceptual shift in how we come to think about the delivery of education in a plural society. The second step is to enact this change in ways that are consistent with the principles of equity, polyvocality and multicentrism upon which this framework or conceptual understanding has been built. Some of the practical dilemmas with regard to essentializing cultures, stereotyping and using minority representatives as "cultural performers" have been discussed already. Other pragmatic concerns for teachers in the way they represent other cultures or knowledges deal with the shift from concept to practice.

All too often when teachers follow an "add-on" rather than integrated multi-centred approach, pieces are carved out from a cultural knowledge base that become abstracted "artifacts" that provide only a narrow window for understanding otherwise rich cultural histories. Nieto (1995) comments on how certain strategies that attempt to be inclusive but operate from a limited conception of what inclusion means, end up further marginalizing and compartmentalizing these cultures:

> The tendency to separate people from their experience may result in for example, a treatment of Navajo culture through an art project or a representation of the Independence struggle in Puerto Rico through a single poem. These may indeed be worthy projects, but decontextualized as they are from any sense of connection with the larger history of a people, they can easily become mere artifacts that have no meaning in and of themselves. In the final analysis, a culture cannot be understood through one art project or a complex era of history through a poem (Nieto, 1995, p. 196).

Rooting histories within a framework where their intrinsic nature is held intact is a prescriptive strategy that allows for truly representative inclusion, rather than a patchwork quilt made up of "different differences" that are superficial trappings. To accomplish this, teachers must begin to integrate the domains of visual and knowledge representation so that an art project or poem does not come devoid of its cultural context and hence, its culturally inscribed meaning.

Many of the practices of representation that came from schools in our case studies were the entry points for broader changes. It is important to recognize that there is no sense of closure here on the kinds of possibilities for educational transformation that still exist. Therefore while certain practices may appear to be only superficial at first glance, such as providing chopsticks in the kindergarten house centre, when integrated with consistent and holistic practices of knowledge representation within a multi-centric paradigm, become integral symbols of inclusion rather than token ornaments. The inclusive practices we observed were a starting point for this conceptual shift and re-structuring of practices, but still had some length to go toward true multicentrism. We have taken the step of imagining beyond the practices that exist, and engaging further possibilities.

In working toward the necessary shifts that lead toward greater transformation based on a more global paradigm and equity pedagogy, there are clear choices that need to be made. Educators must decide whether it is a cultural fair that they are choosing to "display" for their students, or whether they seek to develop a pedagogy that will allow students the broadest academic possibilities for understanding the world and the multiple histories and ways of being that continue to propel human social and cultural development. The latter choice is one that moves beyond the "tourist curriculum" and seeks to develop an enduring understanding of multiple worldviews. Once the choice is made, teachers must engage their own understandings, biases, and lack of understanding toward other bases of knowledge that will ultimately take them out of the safe, familiar, terrain that they have come to know, and are perhaps afraid to venture from. In this case, there needs to be a clear understanding that education is a dynamic and engaging force that requires change to maintain currency and relevance. The alternative of maintaining the centrality of Eurocentric knowledge is limiting and undesirable in this world of global integration. These days a limited focus in knowledge representation simply means a limited education. Representation in education therefore, is a means to capture change and fluidity in the cultural forms that constitute our modern, cosmopolitan context. These changes, through the various mediums of globalizing technology, become spatially transcendent and are able to permeate even into the most remote regions and enclaves of our society. Therefore, an inclusive education is one that is timely, relevant and focused toward building the necessary skills of cultural literacy required within a changing global dynamic.

COMMUNITY SCHOOLING

Moving from global implications to local concerns is not as disjointed a process as it sounds. The boundaries of local and global are increasingly obscured through economic and cultural integration. There is a sense of connectedness we experience to the world at large through transnational economic and political integration and the emergent diasporas that disrupt the boundaries of culture and space. The local is not so far from the global context. Yet, localized forms of knowledge are still far from many classrooms.

A study by Moll (1992) examined the community-based knowledge of 30 families of language minority students and found that they possess broad funds of knowledge in areas from agriculture to medicine that could be beneficial to students' learning. He remarked how the teacher drew upon the family and community as funds of knowledge and "invited them to contribute *intellectually* to the development of lessons." [original emphasis] (see Nieto, 1995, p. 203). The teacher developed a social network that allowed the school to draw upon the community as a source of knowledge and academic support for the school. This is one example of how the integration of school and communities can lead to mutually beneficial outcomes. Integrating community-based learning allows schools to capitalize on all the resources brought by children and their families to school.

According to Martin (1987), community-based education is about "breaking down barriers between learning and living." Creating communities for learning suggests a reciprocity in the relationship between schools and communities. Martin argues that the nature of this relationship:

> ... should be about promoting new and more democratic forms of educational access, accountability and control. In short, community education should be about power. In turn, this implies more flexible definitions of "what counts as knowledge" in curriculum and of educational roles and relationships (p. 15).

Re-defining the relationships of power and knowledge is integral to creating an integrative and inclusive focus on community in education. Re-negotiating the roles and responsibilities for various stakeholders in education as active participants in knowledge production is a challenge to the traditional structures of authority within today's classrooms.

As mentioned previously, education is a changing dynamic and must be responsive to both local and global concerns. According to Martin (1987):

These new versions of community education deliberately seek to reflect the changing and often grim reality of people's lived experience and to engage purposefully with it. Education must now, for example, be about the social, economic, and political implications of new patterns not only of education, work and leisure (including, for the time being, mass unemployment), but also of demography, race relations, family life and gender roles (in both the domestic and public sphere). If community education is to remain relevant to the experience and expectations of people in the community, it is essential that it is continually redefined and reconstructed to reflect the changing reality of their lives (p. 27).

However this process of educating towards "needs" within the community should not be confused with the notion of "compensatory education" that was based on the idea that marginalized and disadvantaged groups in society were culturally deprived. Here the focus is on making education a socially responsive process that can promote activism and change within local communities as part of a community-directed grassroots movement.

We saw this process being encouraged by community liaison counsellors, who although representing school board employees, had the dual role of being advocates for the communities they served. Part of their role involved making parents aware of the best way to channel their concerns so that they would be heard and to help organize the participation of their communities within schools through different types of programming.

The role of parents as educators and the importance of the "pedagogy of the home" is another area where school and community-based knowledge intersect. The way that parents promote learning at home or how learning takes place within community-based sites provide important insights for educators on how to respond to the needs of a diverse student population. These areas are resources that teachers can tap into to provide additional strategies that can help generate a greater connection between students' modes of learning both in and outside of school.

Implications for Pedagogy

One of the pedagogical possibilities that emerges from the discussion of community schooling is the idea of "Site Schools." Establishing school sites to generate knowledge and resource materials for teaching is one important strategy to promote and integrate such knowledges throughout the entire school system. There are examples of such educational sites in local communities that provide useful lessons for educational change in conventional schools. Within these community school sites, education about Indigenous knowledges is seen as a different type of education. The goal is to develop the full person and her/his personality. Community schools have a personal and communitarian approach to schooling.

For example, there are the Six First Nation schools where parents, community elders and youth learn about Aboriginal culture, history, language and traditions. These schools are run by the Aboriginal community and they can offer resources and lessons toward the promotion and integration of Indigenous knowledges in mainstream schools. Site schools could be established to produce resource materials and train student teachers in the cultural knowledge and histories of Indigenous peoples. These teachers could then go back into mainstream schools to share ideas and train other students and teachers.

Preservice teachers could conduct their teaching practices in these school sites. Community practices of egalitarianism could challenge the authoritarian and hierarchical structures of conventional schooling. Community schooling has a different philosophical approach to education that seriously takes into account what educators and students do after school, the use of physical environments of the school setting, and the invitation of outsiders into the schools. Teaching practices could allow students to go into communities to research and write about their own communities and create their own resource materials based on traditional crafts, storytelling and art.

CONCLUSION: RE-THINKING SCHOOLING

Education in the new millennium involves many challenges for educators in the North American context. The politics of race and social difference are salient features of schools and society at large. Teachers must be equipped to deal with the changing faces of our society and must respond to the challenge prepared with a methodology for teaching and learning that is inclusive of the diverse aspects of students lives, identities and experiences, as a basis for their pedagogy.

For many racial and ethnic minority students, schools are not seen as sites of opportunity, but of disenfranchisement. The alienation of minority youth in our schools means that the public education system, the hallmark of liberal pluralism, is failing to provide an equitable environment for the delivery of education for all youth. So long as there are positions of dominance within the cultural and knowledge bases in our schools and society, there will, by consequence, continue to be spaces of marginality, which have historically existed along the lines of race, ethnicity, class, gender, religion, and ability. It is time for these boundaries to be re-drawn and for educational practices to respond to the need for anti-racism and equity in education.

Schooling today is an increasingly problematic environment for our youth. Amidst social pressures, violence, drugs and discrimination, there is a demand for youth to become movable commodities in the labour market at the end of their academic careers. The ideological and practical demands of our market-driven political economy has altered the lexicon of schooling so that students are now seen as an "educational clientele." Murtadha (1995) comments on the resistance of students to fall into the predetermined patterns that they are being required to oblige:

> After examining this political hierarchy of knowledge, we can easily recognize that the current emphasis in most schools is global economic competitiveness and what becomes persistently devalued are the students' thoughts languages and lives (p. 365).

Murtadha goes on to argue that students are resisting a dominant curriculum that does not take into account their histories and experiences, even though this further compromises their life chances:

> Coupled with this is the devaluing of the students' life currency and the insistence that they are to know a pre-arranged state approved curriculum which is devoid of any relevancy. Students continue to resist the dominant curriculum along with its promise of high test scores and future rewards. What becomes most alarming

is that the student is blamed for not caring, the parent is blamed for not being involved and, teachers for incompetency and principals for lack of visionary leadership (Murtadha, 1995, p. 365).

When the system does not work, there is always plenty of blame to go around: the problem lies with disaffected youth, negligent parents, over-worked teachers, et cetera. We would equally point to the many systemic causes and barriers to the achievement of minority youth. Instead of merely adding to the cycle of blame, which can itself lead to inertia, we have attempted to proactively posit some educational possibilities that could make education in a plural society more responsive to the social and cultural milieu of our society. This is not intended as a panacea, but rather as a project to begin to re-think the delivery of education so that it becomes a broader and consequently less alienating and marginalizing experience.

Part of this process lies in understanding the conceptual difference between the process of "schooling" and "education." Schooling is a process that takes place in a formal institutional setting where children are socialized to conform to the dominant cultural paradigm. Education on the other hand can be regarded as a broader concept. We see education as a process that takes place in various sites and settings, such as within homes and communities. While schooling is a limited process, education is part of life long learning. Part of the "conceptual shift" we spoke of earlier also entails an understanding of the disjuncture between these concepts, and must provide a way to bridge the gap. According to Nieto (1995):

These criticisms help us move forward in developing stronger links between critical pedagogy and multicultural education because they suggest that all ideologies need to be evaluated on a number of dimensions. The issue becomes one of authentically and realistically incorporating the cultures, lifestyles and histories of formerly excluded groups into the curriculum while at the same time maintaining a critical eye about how they are included (p. 211).

Nieto raises an important point in her final sentence where she speaks of the need to maintain a "critical eye" on how inclusion becomes implemented. It is not enough to say that schools must provide an inclusive curricula and environment, but there must be a methodology that they can follow, which can help to avoid some of the unobvious pitfalls of conventional, multicultural approaches.

For example, in pursuing a multicentric educational approach, the postmodernist posture of "equal narratives" may be seductive in according some validity and legitimacy to multiple ways of knowing. However, as we have discussed, it can also lead to essentializing difference. Within the Western academy, in making all voices heard [and not to privilege any one voice], the discursive space of bland pluralism could end up reproducing the dominance of Eurocentric knowledge systems. This is particularly the case when knowledge and power issues are not confronted to implicate fundamental questions of discourse, physical bodies and representation. This book has attempted to bring these issues to the forefront of the discursive practices of schooling and provide some methodological concerns and strategies that teachers can use to make the conceptual and pragmatic shifts required in re-thinking education along more integrative and inclusive lines.

The overall objective of this book was to present some of the challenges and possibilities of inclusive, multicentric education. Our goal in promoting integrative inclusivity is to achieve a radical disruption of the status quo, conventional schooling and education. While we are interested in increasing educational access for all youth, we believe that inclusivity is more than just a question of access. There are other fundamental issues at stake: the production, validation and dissemination of multiple knowledge forms, the affirmation of learners' identity and social practice, and the pursuit of meaningful power-sharing that destabilizes the dominance of hegemonic power. This, to us, is a more critical reading that can be brought to the understanding of inclusivity. In the discussion, at times we appear to target certain groups. This is understandable given the severity of educational issues for certain groups in the school system. For example, there are those groups disproportionately disadvantaged as evidenced by high rates of dropout, disengagement and disaffection from the school system. There are also those groups for whom language, culture and religion present additional challenges for engaging the school system. But our "gaze" on these groups does not mean that in the approach to inclusivity, marginalized racial minorities should be presented, taught, and reinforced as discrete, valued entities operating in separate settings or enclaves. We see any attempt to draw this distinction as false. Inclusive practices must move beyond specific targets to reach all social groups. This means, therefore, that we must read the practices of inclusive schooling at two interrelated levels: first, as a recognition of practices that target specific groups because of the severity of issues facing those groups, and second, that the goal of a truly inclusive practice must have implications for all social groups.

This text is an invitation to all educators, including those working in schools across North America constituted primarily by white students, and not just educators in schools characterized by bodies marked by racial, cultural, ethnic, religious, linguistic, gender, class, age, dis/ability, sexuality, health, heterogeniety. Rather, all schools, regardless of demographics, are called upon to implement inclusive education. Instruction, curricular, textual, and pedagogical practices must correspond to the diverse histories and bodies of students who enter today's classrooms, and those who are denied voice or presence in these spaces. For those who claim that their classrooms are not "significantly diverse" to warrant an integrated inclusive emphasis, or where schools are primarily of the dominant [white] population, it is also essential that diverse knowledges, ideas, and values be represented in such a way as to challenge the racism of Eurocentric knowledges, attitudes, and ways of life among dominant groups (Thilen-Wilson, 1999). A recognition of the minoritized, whether or not they are physically present in the classroom, is a necessary beginning toward creating transformative possibility for social justice.

REFERENCES

Abella, R. (1984) *Equality Now: Report of the Special Committee on Visible Minorities in Canadian Society.* Ottawa: Queen's Printer.

Abercrombie, N., S. Hill and B. Turner. (1980) *The Dominant Ideology Thesis.* London: Allen and Unwin.

Ackermann, R. J. (1985*) Religion as Critique.* Amherst, MA: University of Massachusetts Press.

Alexander, C. (1996) "Street Credibility and Identity: Some Observations on the Art of Being Black." In T. Ranger, Y. Samad, and O. Stuart. (eds.), *Culture, Identity and Politics.* London: Avebury-Ashgate Publishing, 112-119.

Alladin, I., ed. (1995) *Racism in Canadian Schools.* Toronto: Harcourt Brace Canada.

Allen, G. et al. (1987) "Community Education and Education Reform," in Garth Allen, John Bastiani, Ian Martin and Kelvyn Richards (eds.), *Community Education.* London: Open University Press, 272-277.

Allingham, N. (1992) "Anti-racist Education and the Curiculum — A Privileged Perspective," in *Racism and Education: Different Perspectives and Experience.* Ottawa: Canadian Teachers Federation.

Almeida, D. A. (1998) "Indigenous Education: Survival for Our Children." *Equity and Excellence in Education,* 31(1): 6-10.

Althusser, L. (1971) *Lenin and Philosophy and Other Essays by Louis Althusser.* New York: Monthly Review Press.

Althusser, L. (1971) *Ideology and Ideological State Apparatus*. London: New Left Books.

Anderson, B. (1983) *Imagined Communities: Reflections on the Origin and Spread of Nationalism*. New York: Verso.

Anderson, J. D. (1994) "School Climate for Gay and Lesbian Students and Staff Members," *Phi Delta Kappan*. 76(2), October.

Anderson, M.L. and P.H. Collins. (1995) "Toward Inclusive Thinking Through the Study of Race, Class, and Gender" in M.L. Anderson and P.H. Collins (eds.) *Race, Class and Gender* (2nd Edition) Belmont, CA.: Wadsworth Publishing.

Apple, M. (1993) *Official Knowledge: Democratic Education in a Conservative Age*. New York: Routledge.

Apple, M. (1986) *Teachers and Texts: A Political Economy of Class and Gender Relations in Education*. New York: Routledge and Kegan Paul.

Apple, M. and L. Weis. (1983) "Ideology and Practice in Schooling: A Political and Conceptual Introduction." *Ideology and Practice in Schooling*. Philadelphia: Temple University Press.

Armour, D. et al. (1976) *Analysis of the School Preferred Reading Program in Selected Los Angeles Minority Schools*. Santa Monica, CA: The Rand Corporation. [ERIC doc. No. 130 243].

Armstrong, T. (1994) *Multiple Intelligences: in the Classroom*. Alexandria, VA: Association of Supervision and Curriculum Development.

Asante, M. K. (1992) "The Afrocentric Curriculum," *Educational Leadership*. 49(2): 28-31.

Asante, M. K. (1991) "The Afrocentric Idea in Education," *Journal of Negro Education*. 60(2): 170-180.

Assembly of First Nations Education. (1988) *Tradition and Education — Towards a Vision of Our Future*. Ottawa: National Indian Brotherhood — Assembly of First Nations.

August, D. and K. Hakuta. (1997) *Improving Schooling for Language-Minority Children: A Research Agenda*. Washington, D.C.: National Academy Press.

Austin, A. (1984) *African Muslims in Antebellum America, A Sourcebook*. New York: Garland Press.

Aylward, C. (1995) "Adding Colour: A Critique of: 'An Essay on Institutional Responsibility': The Indigenous Blacks and Micmac Programme at Dalhousie Law School." *Canadian Journal of Women and the Law* 8(3): 471-501.

Aziz, R. (1995) "Feminism and the Challenge of Racism: Deviance or Difference?" in M. Blair and J. Holland (eds.) *Identity and Diversity*. Clevedon: Multilingual Matters.

Bains, H. and P. Cohen. (eds.) (1988) *Multiracist Britain*. Basingstoke, London: MacMillan.

Baker, C. (1995) *Building Bridges: Multilingual Resources for Children*. Great Britain: Biddles Ltd.

Ball, S. (1993) "Education Markets, Choice and Social Class: The Market as Class Strategy in the U.K. and the U.S.A. *British Journal of Sociology of Education*, 14(1), 3-19.

Banks, J. A. (1999) *An Introduction to Multicultural Education*. Boston: Allyn and Bacon.

Banks, J. A. (1989) "Education for Survival in a Multicultural World," *Social Studies and the Young Learner*. 1(4) April.

Banks, J. A. (1988) *Approaches to Multicultural Curriculum Reform*. Multicultural Leader. 1(2): 1-3.

Banks, J. A. and C.A. Banks (eds.) (1993) *Multicultural Education: Issues and Perspectives*. Boston, Mass.: Allyn and Bacon.

Barman, J., Y. Herbert, and D. McCaskill. (1987) *Indian Education in Canada*, Volume 2: The Challenge. Vancouver: University of British Columbia.

Barnhardt, R. and A. O. Kawagley. (1998) *Culture, Chaos and Complexity: Catalysts for Change in Indigenous Education*. Fairbanks, AK: Alaska Rural Systemic Initiative, University of Alaska Fairbanks. http://www.ankn.uaf.edu/ccc.html.

Barth, F. (1969) *Ethnic Groups and Boundaries*. Boston: Little Brown.

Bauch, J. P. (1989) "The Transparent School Model: New Technology for Parent Involvement." *Educational Leadership*. 47(2): 32-35.

Becker, A. (1990) "The Role of the School in the Maintenance and Change of Ethnic Group Affiliation," *Human Organization*. 49: 48-55.

Belenky, M. F., Clinchy, B. M. , Goldberger, N. R., and Tarule, J. M. (1986) *Women's Ways of Knowing*. New York: Basic Books.

Bennett, C. I. (1999) *Multicultural Education: Theory and Practice*. Boston: Allyn and Bacon

Berger, P. (1978) *Readings on Religion: From Inside and Outside*. New Jersey: Prentice-Hall.

Bhabha, H. K. (1994) *The Location of Culture*. London: Routledge.

Bhabha, H. K. (1990) *Nation and Narration*. London: Routledge

Black Educators Working Group. (1993) *Submission to the Ontario Royal Commission on Learning*. Toronto.

Blair, M. (1994) "Black Teachers, Black Students and Education Markets." *Cambridge Journal of Education*. 24: 277-91.

Bloom, A. D. (1987) *The Closing of the American Mind: How Higher Education has Failed Democracy and Impoverished the Souls of Today's Students.* New York: Simon and Schuster.

Board of Education, Toronto. (1988) *Education of Black Students in Toronto: Final Report of the Consultative Committee.* Toronto.

Bourdieu, P., and J. Passeron. (1977) *Reproduction in Education, Society in Culture.* California: Sage Press.

Bourne, J. (1983) "Towards an Anti-racism Feminism," *Race and Class.* 25(1) Summer. United Kingdom.

Bowles, S., and H. Gintis. (1976) *Schooling in Capitalist America: Education Reform and the Contradictions of Economic Life.* New York: Basic Books.

Bracy, W. (1995) "Developing the Inclusive Curriculum: A Model for the Incorporation of Diversity in the Social Work Curriculum." Paper presented at the 41st Annual Program meeting of the Council on Social Work Education. San Diego, California, March 2-5, 1995.

Brand, D., and S. Bhaggiyadatta. (1986) *Rivers Have Sources, Trees Have Roots: Speaking of Racism.* Toronto: Toronto Cross Cultural Communications Centre.

Brandt, G. (1986) *The Realization of Anti-Racist Teaching.* Lewes: Falmer Press.

Brathwaite, K. (1989) "The Black Student and the School: A Canadian Dilemma" in S. Chilingu and S. Niang (eds.) *African Continuities/L'Heritage Africain.* Toronto: Terebi.

Brathwaite, K., and C. James. (1996) *Educating African-Canadians.* Toronto: John Lorimer and Co., Publishers.

Breton, R. (1964) "Institutional Completeness of Ethnic Communities and the Personal Relations of Immigrants." *American Journal of Sociology*, 70(2): 193-205.

Breton, R., W. W. Isajiw, W. Kalbach, and J. Reitz. (1990) *Ethnic Identity and Equality: Varieties of Experience in a Canadian City.* Toronto: University of Toronto Press.

Bright, J. A. (1995) "Reflections on Teaching and Learning About Diversity," *New Schools, New Communities.* 11(2) Winter.

Brookfield, S. D. (1987) *Developing Critical Thinkers: Challenging Adults to Explore Alternative Ways of Thinking and Acting.* San Francisco: Jossey Bass.

Brown, R. (1993) *A Follow-Up of the Grade 9 Cohort of 1987 Every Secondary Student Survey Participants.* Toronto Board of Education, Research Report, #207.

Brown, R.S., M. Cheng, M. Yau and S. Ziegler. (1992) *The 1991 Every Secondary Student Survey: Initial Findings*. Toronto: Toronto Board of Education, Research Services (No. 200).

Burke, M. T. and Miranti, J. G. (1995) *Counselling The Spiritual Dimension*. Alexandra, VA: American Counselling Association.

Byram, M. and J. Leman. (1990) *Bicultural and Trilingual Education: The Foyer Model in Brussels*. Clevedon: Multilingual Matters Ltd.

Campey, J., T. McCaskell, J. Miller, V. Russell. (1994) "Opening the Classroom Closet: Dealing with Sexual Orientation at the Toronto District School Board," in Susan Prentice (ed.), *Sex in Schools — Canadian Education and Sexual Regulation*. Toronto: Our Schools Ourselves Foundation, 82-100.

Canadian Alliance of Black Educators. (1992) *Sharing the Challenge, I, II, III: A Focus on Black High School Students*. Toronto.

Carby, H. V. (1982) "Schooling for Babylon." In Paul Gilroy/Centre for Contemporary Cultural Studies (ed.) *The Empire Strikes Back*. London: Hutchison, 183-211.

Carlson, D. (1997) *Making Progress: Education and Culture in New Times*. New York: Teachers College Press.

Castagna, M. (1997) "Community, Schooling and Education in North American Black Communities." Unpublished Major Research Paper, OISE, University of Toronto.

Castellano, M. B. (1998) "Updating Aboriginal Traditions of Knowledge." In G. J. S. Dei et al. (eds.) *Indigenous Knowledges in Global Contexts*. Toronto: University of Toronto Press.

Cheng, M. (1995) "Black Youth and Schooling in the Canadian Context: A Focus on Ontario." Unpublished paper, Department of Sociology, OISE.

Cherryholmes, C. (1993) "Reading Research." *The Journal of Curriculum Studies*. 25: 1-32.

Cheung, E. (1986) The Evaluation of Educational Provisions for Culturally Different Children. In R.L. Samuda and S.L. Kong (eds.), *Multicultural Education: Programmes and Methods*, 295-304.

Coelho, E. (1998) *Teaching and Learning in Multicultural Schools: An Integrated Approach*. Toronto: Multilingual Matters Ltd.

Cohen, D. L. (1990) "Parents as Partners: Helping Families Build a Foundation for Learning." *Education Week*. May issues, 9-20.

Cohen, P. (1989) *Tackling Common Sense Racism*. Cultural Studies Project Annual Report. London.

Cohen, P. (1988) *Multi-Racist Britain*. London: MacMillan.

Comer, J. P. (1989) "Parent Participation in Schools: The School Development Program Model." *Family Resource Coalition Report.* 8(2): 4 – 6.

Comer, J. P. (1988) "Educating Poor Minority Children." *Scientific American.* 259(5):42-48.

Comer, J. P. (1986) "Parent Participation in Schools." *Phi Delta Kappan.* 67, pp. 442-6.

Connelly, C. D. (1998) *Haciendo un Poquito de Des/Enlace / You'll Get It On Your Way Out: Opening a Space for Listening/Possibility.* Unpublished Master's Thesis. Kingston: Queen's University.

Contenta, S. (1993) *Rituals of Failure: What Schools Really Teach.* Toronto: Between the Lines.

Corbier,* (1998) Personal Communication.

Corrigan, P. (1989) "State Formation and Classroom Practice: Once Again 'On Moral Regulation.'" *Re-Interpreting Curriculum Research: Images and Arguments.* London: Falmer Press, 64-84.

Corson, D. (1993) *Language, Minority Education and Gender: Linking Social Justice and Power.* Toronto: Ontario Institution for Studies in Education/ Bristol, PA: Multilingual Matters.

Corson, D. (1998) *Changing Education for Diversity.* A. Hargreaves and I. Goodson (eds.) Changing Education Series. Bristol, PA: Open University Press.

Corson, D. and S. Lemay. (1996) *Social Justice and Language Policy in Education: The Canadian Research* Toronto: OISE Press/Ontario Institute for Studies in Education.

Cranton, P. (1994) *Understanding And Promoting Transformative Learning: A Guide For Educators Of Adults.* San Francisco: Jossey-Bass.

Cranton, P. (1996) *Professional Development As Transformative Learning. New Perspectives For Teachers Of Adults.* San Francisco: Jossey-Bass.

Cruikshank, J. (1992) "Oral Tradition and Material Culture: Multiplying Meanings of 'Words' and 'Things.'" *Anthropology Today,* 8 (3): 5-9.

Cummins, J. (1996) *Negotiating Identities: Education for Empowerment in a Diverse Society.* Ontario, CA: The California Association for Bilingual Education.

Cummins, J. (1995) *Brave New Schools: Challenging Cultural Illiteracy Through Global Learning Networks.* Toronto: OISE Press.

Cummins, J. (1991) *Language Learning and Bilingualism.* Japan: Sophia University.

Cummins, J. (1989) *Empowering Minority Students.* Sacramento: California

Association for Bilingual Education.

Cummins, J. (1986) "Empowering Minority Students: A Framework for Intervention." *Harvard Educational Review*. 56: 18-36.

Cummins, J., G. Feuerverger and J. M. Lopes. (1993) *The Challenge of Diversity: Adjusting to the Cultural and Linguistic Realities of the Mainstream Classroom*. Transfer Grant Project Report.

Cummins, J. and M. Danesi. (1990) *Heritage Languages: The Development and Denial of Canada's Linguistic Resources*. Toronto: Garamond Press.

Curtis, B., D.W. Livingstone and H. Smaller. (1992) "Stacking the Deck and the Streaming of Working-Class Kids in Ontario Schools," *Toronto: Our Schools, Our Selves*, 124-136.

D'Souza, D. (1991) *Illiberal Education: The Politics of Race and Sex on Campus*. New York: Free Press.

Daenzer, P., and G.J.S. Dei. (1994) *Issues of School Completion/Drop-Out: A Focus on Black Youth in Ontario Schools and Other Relevant Studies*. Background paper submitted to the Ontario Royal Commission on Learning, Toronto.

David, M. E. (1992) *Parents, Gender and Educational Reform*. London: Cambridge University Press.

Davies, S. (1994) "In Search of Resistance and Rebellion among High School Dropouts." *Canadian Journal of Sociology*. 19(3): 331-350.

Davis, A. Y. (1990) *Women, Culture and Politics*. New York: Vintage Books.

Davis, A.Y. (1981) *Women, Race, and Class*. New York: Random House.

Dehli, K. (1996a) *Between Market and State? Modalities of Power and Difference in the Marketization of Education*. Paper presented to AERA., New York, April. (Draft) OISE.

Dehli, K. (1996b) "Travelling Tales: Education Reform and Parental 'Choice' in Postmodern Times." *Journal of Education Policy*. 2(1): 75-88.

Dehli, K. (1994) [with I. Januario]. *Parent Activism and School Reform in Toronto*. Toronto: Research Report Prepared for the Ontario Ministry of Education and Training.

Dehli, K. (1987) "'Ethnic', 'Parent,' 'Community': The Proper Channelling of Local Educational Politics," in *Breaking the Mosaic: Ethnic Identities in Canadian Schooling*. Jon Young, ed. Toronto: Garamond.

Dei, G. J. S. (1999) *Rethinking the Role of Indigenous Knowledges in the Academy*. International Journal of Inclusive Education. [in press].

Dei, G. J. S. (1999) African Development: The Relevance and Implications of 'Indigenousness.' In G. J. S. Dei, et al. (eds.) *Indigenous Knowledges in*

Global Contexts. Toronto: University of Toronto Press.

Dei, G. J. S. (1998) LUND. "Why Write Back?: The Role of Afrocentric Discourse in Social Change. *Canadian Journal of Education.* 23(2): 200-208.

Dei, G. J. S. (1998) "The Politics of Educational Change: Taking Anti-Racism Education Seriously." In. V. Satzewich (ed.) *Racism and Social Inequality in Canada.* Toronto: Thompson Educational Publishing, Inc., 299-314.

Dei, G. J S. (1996) *Anti-racism Education: Theory and Practice.* Halifax: Fernwood Publishing.

Dei, G. J. S. (1996) "Black/African-Canadian Students' Perspectives on School Racism." In Ibrahim Alladin, ed., *Racism in Canadian Schools.* Toronto: Harcourt Brace Canada, 42-61.

Dei, G. J. S. (1994) "Afrocentricity: A Cornerstone of Pedagogy." *Anthropology and Education Quarterly.* 25(1): 3-28.

Dei, G. J. S. (1993) *The Examination of High Dropout Among Black Students in Ontario Public Schools.* Preliminary report submitted to the Ontario Ministry of Education and Training.

Dei, G. J. S., S. James-Wilson, and J. Zine, (2000) *Inclusive Education: A Guide to Teacher Development.* Toronto: Canadian Scholars' Press.

Dei, G. J. S., B. Hall and D. Goldin Rosenberg. (1999) Indigenous Knowledges: An Introduction. In G. J. S. Dei, B. Hall and D. Goldin Rosenberg (eds.) *Indigenous Knoweldges in Global Contexts: Multiple Readings of Our World.* Toronto: University of Toronto Press.

Dei, G. J. S. and L. Karumanchery. (1999) "School Reforms in Ontario: The 'Marketization' of Education and the Resulting Silence on Equity." *Alberta Journal of Educational Research*, 45(2) [forthcoming].

Dei, G. J. S., J. Mazzuca, E. McIsaac, and J. Zine. (1997) *Reconstructing 'Drop-out': A Critical Ethnography of the Dynamics of Black Students' Disengagement from School.* Toronto: University of Toronto Press.

Dei, George, J. S., et al. (1997) *Home, Family and Community-Based Learning: Lessons For Curriculum and Pedagogy.* Ontario Institute for Studies in Education/ University of Toronto.

Dei, G. J. S., P. Broomfield, M. Castagna, M. James, J. Mazzuca, and E. McIsaac. (1996) *Unpacking What Works: A Critical Examination of 'Best Practices' of Inclusive Schooling in Ontario.* Ontario Institute for Studies in Education/ University of Toronto.

Dei, G.J.S. and S. Razack. (1995) *Inclusive Schooling: An Inventory of Contemporary Practices Designed to Meet the Challenge of a Diverse Student Body.* Report submitted to the Ontario Ministry of Education and Training, Toronto.

Dei, G.J.S., L. Holmes, J. Mazzuca, E. McIsaac, and R. Campbell. (1995) *Drop Out or Push Out: The Dynamics of Black Students' Disengagement from School.* Report submitted to the Ontario Ministry of Education and Training, Toronto.

Delpit, L. (1988) *The Silenced Dialogue: Power and Pedagogy in Educating Other People's Children. Harvard Educational Review.* 58(3): 280-298.

Depledge, N. E. (1996) "Whom do we mean by We?" in Carol E. Harris and Norma E. Depledge (eds.), *Advancing the Agenda of Inclusive Education.* Conference of the American Association of University Women, Proceedings, 43-51.

Derman-Sparks, L. and The ABC Task Force (1991) *Anti-Bias Curriculum: Tools for Empowering Young Children.* National Association for Education Of Young Children: Washington.

DeVillar, C., J. Faltis and J. Cummins. (1994) *Cultural Diversity in Schools: From Rhetoric to Practice.* Albany: State University of New York Press.

Dickmann, L.W. (1980) "Spirituality: An Affective Facet For Curriculum Consideration." *Affect Tree* 5 (1): 8-9.

Dore, R. (1976) *The Diploma Disease: Education, Qualification and Development.* London: George Allen and Unwin.

Dornbusch, S. M. (1988) "Helping Your Kid Make the Grade." *The Stanford Magazine.* Palo Alto. [Summer Issue].

Dove, N. (1998a) *Afrikan Mothers: Bearers of Culture, Makers of Social Change.* New York: State University of New York Press.

Dove, N. (1998b) "African Womanism: An Afrocentric Theory." *Journal of Black Studies.* 28(5): 515-539.

Dove, N. (1995) "An African-Centred Critique of Marx's Logic." *Western Journal of Black Studies.* 19(4): 260-271.

Driedger, L. (1975) "In Search of Cultural Identity Factors: A Comparison of Ethnic Minority Students in Manitoba." *Canadian Review of Sociology and Anthropology,* 12:150-62.

Driedger, L. (1976) "Ethnic Self-Identity: A Comparison of In-group Evaluations." *Sociometry,* 39:131-41.

Driedger, L. (1989) *The Ethnic Factor: Identity in Diversity.* Toronto: McGraw-Hill Ryerson.

Driedger, L. (1996) *Multi-Ethnic Canada: Identities and Inequalities.* Toronto: Oxford University Press.

Durkheim, E. (1965) *The Elementary Forms of Religious Life.* New York: The Free Press. (First French Edition in 1912).

Edwards, J. (1985) *Language, Society and Identity.* Oxford: Basil Blackwell.

Edwards, J. and L. Doucette. (1987) "Ethnic Salience, Identity and Symbolic Ethnicity." *Canadian Ethnic Studies*, 19:52-62.

Eisenhart, M.A. and M.E. Graue. (1993) "Constructing Culture Differences and Educational Achievements in Schools" in E. Jacob and C. Jordan (eds.) *Minority Education: Anthropological Perspectives.* Norwood, NJ: Ablex.

Eisner, E. W. and A. Peshkin (eds.) (1990) *Qualitative Inquiry in Education: The Continuing Debate.* New York: Teachers College Press.

Elkind, D. (1992) "Spirituality in Education." *Holistic Education Review*, 12-16.

Epstein, D. (1995) *Changing Classroom Cultures: Anti-racism, Politics and Schools.* England: Trentham Books Ltd.

Epstein, D. (1990) "School and Family Connections: Theory, Research and Implications for Integrating Sociologies of Education and Family." *Marriage and Family Review*, 15(1/2): 99-126.

Epstein, D. (1988) "How do we Improve Programs in Parent Involvement?" *Educational Horizons*, 66(2): 58-9.

Epstein, D. (1986) "Parents' Reactions to Teacher Practices of Parent Involvement." *The Elementary School Journal.* 86: 277-94.

Erickson, Fred. (1987) "Transformation and School Success: The Politics and Culture of Educational Achievement." *Anthropology and Education.* 18(4): 336-356.

Ermine, W. (1995) "Aboriginal Epistemology." In M. Battiste and J. Barman (eds.) *First Nations Education in Canada: The Circle Unfolds.* Vancouver: UBC Press, 101-112.

Ernst, G., and Statzner, F. (1994) "Alternative Visions of Schooling: An Introduction." *Anthropological and Education Quarterly.* 25(3): 200-07.

Ernst, G., F. Statzner and H. T. Trueba. (1994) "Alternative Visions of Schooling: Success Stories in Minority Settings." *Anthropology and Education Quarterly*, 25 (3): 200-394 (Special Issue).

Fals-Borda, O. (1980) *Science and the Common People.* Yugoslavia.

Fals-Borda, O. and M. A. Rahman. (1991) "Some Basic Ingredients." In O. Fals-Borda and M. A. Rahman (eds.) *Action and Knowledge: Breaking the Monopoly with Participatory Action-Research.* New York: The Apex Press.

Fine, M. (1993) "Apparent Involvement: Reflections on Parents, Power and Urban Schools," *Teachers College Record.* 94(4): 682-710.

Firestone, D. et al. (1994) *Homophobia and Education — A Primer.* Toronto: Education Against Homophobia.

Fitznor, L. (1999) Unpublished Interview.

Fletcher, C. (1987) "The Meanings of 'Community' in Community Education," in Garth Allen, John Bastiani, Ian Martin and Kelvyn Richards (eds.), *Community Education*. London: Open University Press, 33-49.

Foucault, M. (1990) *The History of Sexuality — An Introduction: Volume One*. Toronto: Random House.

Foucault, M. (1987) "Body/Power" in Colin Gordon (ed.), *Power/Knowledge: Selected Interviews and Other Writings 1972-1977*. New York: Pantheon.

Foucault, M. (1980) *Power/Knowledge: Selected Interviews, 1972-77*. [Edited by C. Gordon]. Brighton: Harvester Press.

Found, W.C. (1991) *Who Are York's Undergraduates? Results of the University's 1991 Comprehensive Student Survey*. Toronto: York University.

Fowler, J. W. (1981) *Stages Of Faith: The Psychology Of Human Development And The Quest For Meaning*. San Francisco: Harper Collins.

Fox, M. (1979) *A Spirituality Named Compassion and the Healing of the Global Village*. Minneapolis: Winston Press.

Friend, R. (1993) "Choices, Not Closets: Heterosexism and Homophobia in Schools" in L. Weis and M. Fine (eds.) *Beyond Silenced Voices: Class, Race and Gender in United States Schools*. New York: State University of New York Press, 209-235.

Fullan, M. (1982) *Meaning of Educational Change*. Toronto: OISE.

Fullan, M. and S. Stiegelbauer. (1991) *The New Meaning of Educational Change*. 2nd Edition. New York: Teachers College Press.

Gans, H. (1979) "Symbolic Ethnicity: The Future of Ethnic Groups and Cultures in America." Ethnic and Racial Studies. 2:1-20.

Gans, H. (1992) *Second-Generation Decline: Scenarios for the Economic and Ethnic Futures of the Post-1965 American Immigrants*. Ethnic and Racial Studies, 2: 173-192.

Gans, H. (1994) "Symbolic Ethnicity and Symbolic Religiosity: Towards a Comparison of Ethnic and Religious Acculturation." *Ethnic and Racial Studies*, 4: 577-92.

Gardner, H. (1983) *Frames Of Mind: The Theory Of Multiple Intelligences*. New York: Basic Books.

Gaskell, J. and A. T. McLaren. (1991) *Women and Education*. Calgary: Detselig Enterprises.

Gaskell, J., A. T. McLaren and M. Novogrodsky. (1989) "Claiming an Education: Feminism and Canadian Schools," Toronto: *Our Schools, Our Selves*.

Gay, G. (1995) Mirror Images on Common Issues: Parallels between Multicultural

Education and Critical Pedagogy. In. C.E. Sleeter and P.L. McLaren (eds.), *Multicultural Education, Critical Pedagogy, and the Politics of Difference.* Albany, NY: The State University of New York Press, 155-190.

Gay, G. (1994) "Coming of Age Ethnically: Teaching Young Adolescents of Color," *Theory into Practice.* 33: 149-155.

Ghosh, R. (1996) *Redefining Multicultural Education.* Toronto: Harcourt Brace Canada.

Gill, O. (1997) "'Minority' Education in the Canadian Context." Draft thesis proposal, Faculty of Social Work, York University.

Gilligan, C. (1990) Preface: "Teaching Shakespeare's Sister." In C. Gilligan, N. P. Lyons and J. Hammer (eds.) *Making Connections: The Religious Worlds of Adolescents at Emma Willard School.* Cambridge: Harvard University Press.

Gilligan, C. (1982) *In a Different Voice: Psychology Theory and Women's Development.* Cambridge: Harvard University Press.

Gillborn, D. (1992) "Citizenship, Race and the Hidden Curriculum," *International Studies in Sociology of Education.*

Gilroy, P. (ed.) and the Centre for Contemporary Cultural Studies. (1982) *The Empire Strikes Back: Race and Racism in 70s Britain.* London: Hutchinson.

Giroux, H. (1983) *A Theory of Resistance in Education: A Pedagogy for the Opposition.* South Hadley, MA: Bergin and Harvey.

Gonzalez, V., and T. Yawkey. (1993) "The Assessment of Culturally and Linguistically Different Students," *Horizons.* 41-49.

Goodstein, L. (1994) "Achieving a Multicultural Curriculum: Conceptual, Pedagogical, and Structural Issues," *Journal of General Education.* 43(2): 102-16.

Gordon, C. (ed.) (1987) *Power/Knowledge: Selected Interviews and Other Writings 1972-1977.* New York: Pantheon.

Gordon, I. R. (1977) "Parent Education and Parent Involvement: Retrospect and Prospect." *Childhood Education*, 54: 71-9.

Greer, S. (1992) "Whose Voice? Culturally Diverse Students Need Culturally Diverse Curriculum," *Education Forum.* 18(3).

Groff, L. and Smoker, P. (1996) "Spirituality, Religion, Culture and Peace. Exploring the Foundations for Inner-Outer Peace in the Twenty-First Century." *International Journal*

Gupta, A. and J. Ferguson. (1992) "Beyond 'Culture': Space, Identity, and the Politics of Difference." *Cultural Anthropology*, 7(1): 6-23.

Guinier, L. (1995) Of Gentlemen and Role Models. In K. Crenshaw (ed.), *Critical Race Theory: The Key Writings that Formed the Movement*, New York: New Press, 73-80.

Habermas, J. (1994) "Struggles for Recognition in the Democratic Constitutional State." In A. Guttman (ed.) *Multiculturalism*. Princeton, NJ: Princeton University Press, 107–148.

Hague, W. L. (1995) *Evolving Spirituality.* Department of Educational Psychology: University of Alberta.

Hall, S. (1992) "What is this 'Black' in Black Popular Culture?" in David Morley and Kuan-Hsing Chen (eds.) *Stuart Hall: Critical Dialogues in Cultural Studies.* (London: Routledge, 1996)

Hall, S. (1991) "Old and New Identities, Old and New Ethnicities," in Anthony King (ed.) *Culture, Globalization and the World System*. New York: State University Press, 41-68.

Hall, S. (1986) "Gramsci's Relevance for the Study of Race and Ethnicity" in David Morley and Kuan-Hsing Chen (eds.) *Stuart Hall: Critical Dialogues in Cultural Studies.* (London: Routledge, 1996).

Hall, S. (1986) "The Problem of Ideology: Marxism Without Guarantees" in David Morley and Kuan-Hsing Chen (eds.) *Stuart Hall: Critical Dialogues in Cultural Studies.* (London: Routledge, 1996).

Hamdani, Daood, Hassan. (1990). Muslims in Canada. The Council of Muslim Communities of Canada, Islamic Monograph Series, 1401-3.

Haraway, D. (1998) "Situated Knowledges: The Science Question in Feminism and the Privilege of Partial Perspective." *Feminist Studies*. 14(3): 575-97.

Harris, A. P. (1997) "Race and Essentialism in Feminist Legal Theory." In A. K. Wing (ed.) *Critical Race Feminism: A Reader.* New York: New York University, 11-18.

Henderson, A. T. (ed.) (1981) *Parent Participation, Student Achievement: The Evidence Grows*. Washington, DC: National Committee for Citizens' Education.

Henderson, A. T., C. Marburger, and T. Ooms. (1986) *Beyond the Bake Sale*. Washington, DC: National Committee for Citizens' Education.

Henry, A. (1993) "African-Canadian Women Teachers' Activism: Recreating Communities of Caring and Resistance." *Journal of Negro Education*, 61(3): 392-404.

Henry, A. (1992) *Taking Back Control: Towards an Afrocentric Womanist Standpoint on the Education of Black Children."* Ph.D. dissertation, Department of Curriculum, Ontario Institute for Studies in Education, Toronto.

Henry, F. and C. Tator. (1994) "The Ideology of Racism — 'Democratic Racism.'"

Canadian Ethnic Studies, XXVI(2).

Henry, F., C. Tator, W. Mattis and T. Rees (1995) *The Colour of Democracy: Racism in Canadian Society*. Toronto: Harcourt Brace & Co.

Henry, F. (1994) *The Caribbean Diaspora in Toronto: Learning to Live with Racism*. Toronto: University of Toronto Press.

Hernandez, H. (1997) *Teaching in Multilingual Classrooms: A Teacher's Guide to Context, Process, and Content*. New Jersey: Prentice Hall.

Heschel, A. J. (1962) *The Prophets*, 2 vols. New York: Harper and Row.

Hester, H. (1989) "Start at Home to Improve Home-School Relations." *NASSP Bulletin*. 73: 23-7.

Hidalgo, N., M, Ceasar, L. McDowell and E. V. Siddle. (1993) *Facing Racism in Education*. USA: Harvard Educational Review.

Hill Collins, P. (1990) *Black Feminist Thought: Knowledge, Conscienceness and the Politics of Empowerment*. Boston: Unwin Hyman.

Hilliard, A. (1992) "Why We Must Pluralize the Curriculum," *Educational Leadership*. 49(4): 12-15.

Hirsch, E. D. (1987) *Cultural Literacy: What Every American Needs to Know*. Boston: Houghton Mifflin.

Holdberg, D. T. (1990) *Anatomy of Racism*. Mineapolis: University of Minnesota Press.

Holmes, L. (1999) "Heart Knowledge, Blood Memory and the Voice of the Land: Implications of Research Among Hawaiian Elders" In G. Dei, B. Hall, and D. Goldin Rosenberg. (eds.), *Indigenous Knowledges in Global Contexts: Multiple Readings of Our World*. Toronto: University of Toronto Press.

hooks, b. (1989) *Talking Back: Thinking Feminist, Thinking Black*. Boston: South End Press/Toronto: Between the Lines.

Houle, G. (1995) "Common Sense as a Specific Form of Knowledge: Elements for a Theory of Otherness." *Current Sociology*. 43(2/3): 89-99.

Howard, G. (1995) "Unravelling Racism: Reflections on the Role of Non-indigenous People Supporting Indigenous Education." *Australian Journal of Adult and Community Education*. (35)3: 229-37.

Ibrahim, A el K. M. (1997) "'Whassup homeboy?' Black/Popular Culture and the Politics of 'Curriculum Studies': an Anti-racism Perspective." Unpublished Paper.

Irvine, J. (1992) *Black Students and School Failure*. New York: Praeger.

Isajiw, W. W. (1974) "Definitions of Ethnicity." *Ethnicity*, 1: 111-24.

Isajiw, W., A. Sev'er and L. Driedger. (1993) "Ethnic Identity and Social Mobility: A Test of the Drawback Model and Resources." *Canadian Journal of*

Sociology. 18:177-96.

Jacob, E. and C. Jordan (1993) *Minority Education: Anthropological Perspectives*. New Jersey: Ablex Publishing Corporation.

James, C. (1995a) *Seeing Ourselves: Exploring Race. Ethnicity and Culture*. Toronto: Thompson Educational Publishing, Inc.

James, C. (1995b) "Multicultural and Anti-Racism Education in Canada," *Race, Gender, and Class*. 2(3): 31-48.

James, C. (1990) *Making It*. Oakville: Mosaic Press.

James, Irma Marcia (1998) Stitching the Ancestors' Quilt: Black Women Networking in the Law. Unpublished M.A. Thesis, Department of Sociology and Equity Studies in Education, Ontario Institute for Studies in Education of the University of Toronto, OISE/UT.

Januario, I. (1994) "A Happy Little Guy? Case Study of a Portuguese-Canadian Child in the Primary Grades," *Orbit*. 25: 44-45.

Jeffcoate, R. (1984) "Ideologies and Multicultural Education." In M. Craft (ed.), *Education and Cultural Pluralism*. Lewes: Falmer Press.

Jervis, K. (1996) "'How Come There Are No Brothers on That List?' Hearing the Hard Questions All Children Ask." *Harvard Educational Review*, 66(3): 546-576.

Karenga, M. (1988) "Black Studies and the Problematic of Paradigm: The Philosophical Dimension." *Journal of Black Studies*, 18(4): 395-414.

Karumanchery, L. (1996) *Ethnic Identity Retention: A Cross Generational Analysis of Malayalees in Toronto*. Winnipeg: University of Manitoba Press.

Karumanchery, N. (1992) "South East Asian Students' Perceptions and Experience of Racism and Their Relation to School Achievement." Masters Thesis. (Toronto: University of Toronto).

Kessler, R. (1999) "Nourishing Students In Secular Schools." *Educational Leadership*.

Kesson, K. (1993) "Critical Theory And Holistic Education: Carrying On The Conversation." In R. Miller (ed.) *The Renewal of Meaning in Education*. Brandon, VT: Holistic Education Press.

King, T. (ed.) (1992) *The Spiral Path*. Saint Paul, MN: Yes International.

Kirby, S. and K. McKenna. (1989) *Experience, Research, Social Change: Methods from the Margins*. Toronto: Garamond.

Kolander, C. A. Chandler, C. K. (1990) *Spiritual Health: A Balance Of All Dimensions*. Paper presented at the Annual Meeting of the American Alliance of Health, Physical Education, Recreation and Dance. New Orleans, LA,

March 28-April 1.

Ladson-Billings, G. (1994) *The Dream-Keepers. Successful Teachers of African-American Children.* San Francisco: Jossey-Bass Education.

Langehough, S. O., Walters, C., Knox, D. and Rowley, M. (1997, November) "Spirituality and Religiosity as Factors in Adolescents' Risk for Anti-Social Behaviors and Use of Resilient Behaviors." Paper presented at the Annual Conference for the NCFR Fatherhood and Motherhood in a Diverse and Changing World.

Larrain, J. (1991) "Stuart Hall and the Marxist Concept of Ideology" in David Morley and Kuan-Hsing Chen (eds.) *Stuart Hall: Critical Dialogues in Cultural Studies.* London: Routledge, 1996.

Lather, P. (1991) "Ideology and Methodological Attitude." *JCT: An Interdisciplinary Journal of Curriculum Studies,* 9(2): 7-26.

Lattas, A. (1993) "Essentialism, Memory and Resistance: Aboriginality and the Politics of Authenticity. *Oceania,* 63: 2-67.

de Lauretis, T. (1987) *Technologies of Gender: Essays on Theory, Film, and Fiction.* USA: Indiana University Press.

Lawson, E. (1998) "Text, Culture and Anti-Colonial Education: The Making of Jamacan Identity in the Period of Independence." Unpublished M.A. Thesis, Department of Sociology and Equity Studies in Education, Ontario Institute for Studies in Education of the University of Toronto, OISE/UT.

Leah, R. (1995) Anti-racist Studies: An Integrative Perspective. *Race, Gender and Class,* 2 (3):105-22.

Lee, E. (1994) Anti-Racist Education: Panacea or Palliative? *Orbit* 25(2): 22-25.

Lee, E. (1985) *Letters to Marcia.* Toronto: Cross-Cultural Communication Centre.

Lenskyj, Helen, Jefferson. (1997) "Changing Sex Education." *Orbit,* 28(1): 18-20.

Levin, H. (1990) "The Educationally Disadvantaged are Still Among Us." In J. Bain and J. Herman (eds.) *Making Schools Work for Underachieving Minority Students.* New York: Greenwood Press.

Lewis, M. (1988) "Without a Word: Sources and Themes for a Feminist Pedagogy." Unpublished Ph.D dissertation. Toronto: Ontario Institute for Studies in Education, University of Toronto.

Lipkin, A. (1994) "The Case for a Gay and Lesbian Curriculum," *The High School Journal.* 77: October.

Lomotey, K. (ed.) (1990) *Going to School: The African-American Experience.* New York: State University of New York Press.

Maclear, K. (1994) "The Myth of the 'Model Minority': Re-Thinking the Education of Asian Canadians," *Our School/Our Selves.* (July), 54-76.

Maguire, P. (1987) *Doing Participatory Research: A Feminist Approach.* Amherst, MA: Center for International Education, School of Education, University of Massachusetts.

Malloy, W. (1994) Inclusion: An Educational Reform Strategy for all Children. *Viewpoints.*

Marshall, J. L. (1998) *Spirituality of South Asian Women: Implications for Adult Learning.* Paper presented at the Annual Meeting of the American Educational Research Association. San Diego, CA, April 13-17, 1998.

Martin, I. (1987) "Community Education: Toward a Theoretical Analysis," in Garth Allen, John Bastiani, Ian Martin, and Kelvyn Richards (eds.) *Community Education.* London: Open University Press, 9-31.

Maslow, A. (1954) *Motivation and Personality.* New York: Harper.

McCarthy, C. (1990) *Race and Curriculum: Social Inequality and the Theory and Politics of Difference in Contemporary Research on Schooling.* London: Falmer Press.

McCombs, B. L. and Whisler, J. (1997) *The Learner-Centred Classroom and School: Strategies For Increasing Student Motivation and Achievement.* San Francisco: Jossey-Bass Publishers.

McIntosh, P. (1990) "White Privilege: Unpacking the Invisible Knapsack." *Independent School,* Winter: 31-36.

McLaren, P. (1993) *Schooling as a Ritual Performance: Towards a Political Economy of Educational Symbols and Gestures.* (2nd ed.) New York: Routledge.

McLeod, K. and E. Krugly-Smolska. (1997) *Multicultural Education: A Place to Start: Guidelines for Classrooms, Schools and Communities.* Toronto: Canadian Association of Second Language Teachers.

McRobbie, A. (1981) "Setting Accounts with Sub-Cultures: A Feminist Critique." In T. Bennett, G. Martin, C. Mercer, and Woolacott (eds.) *Culture, Ideology, and Social Process.* London: The Open Press.

Merton, R. K. (1956) *Social Theory and Social Structure.* Glencoe, IL: Free Press.

Mezirow, J. (1991) *Transformative Dimensions Of Adult Learning.* San Francisco: Jossey-Bass.

Mezirow, J. (1995) "Transformative Dimensions Of Adult Learning." In M. Welton (ed.) In *Defense of the Lifeworld.* Albany: State University of New York Press.

Mezirow, J. (1996) "Contemporary Paradigms Of Learning." *Adult Education Quarterly,* 46 (3): 158-172.

Mezirow, J. (1997) "Transformative Learning: Theory to Practice." P. Cranton (ed.) *Transformative Learning In Action, Insights From Practice*. San Francisco: Jossey-Bass.

Miller, J. P. (1996) *The Holistic Curriculum*. Toronto: OISE Press.

Miller, J. P. (1993) *The Holistic Teacher*. Toronto: OISE Press.

Miller, J. P. (1992) "Toward A Spiritual Curriculum." *Holistic Educational Review*. 43-50.

Miramontes, O.B., A. Nadeau and N. L. Commins (1997) *Restructuring Schools for Linguistic Diversity: Linking Decision Making to Effective Programs*. New York: Teachers College Press.

Miranti, J. G. and Burke, M. T. (1998) "Spirituality as a Force for Social Change." C. C. Lee and G. R. Walz (eds.) *Social Action: A Mandate For Counsellors* (161-176) Alexandra: VA, American Counselling Association.

Mitchell, G. (1987) "Community Education and School: A Commentary," in Garth Allen, John Bastiani, Ian Martin and Kelvyn Richards (eds.), *Community Education*. London: Open University Press, 83-99.

Moghissi, H. (1994) "Racism and Sexism in Academic Practice: A Case Study." In H. Afshar and M. Maynard (eds.), *The Dynamics of 'Race' and Gender: Some Feminist Interventions*. London: Taylor and Francis, 222-234.

Montecinos, C. (1995) "Culture as an Ongoing Dialogue: Implications for Multiculural Teacher Education," in Christine E. Sleeter and Peter L. McLaren (eds.), *Multicultural Education, Critical Pedagogy, and the Politics of Difference*. New York: State University of New York Press, 291-308.

Morgan, R. (1970) *Sisterhood is Powerful: An Anthology of Writings from the Women's Liberation Movement*. New York: Random House.

Mullard, C. (1985) *Race, Power and Resistance*. London: Centre for Multicultural Education.

Mullard, C. (1980) *Racism in Society and Schools: History and Policy*. London: Centre for Multicultural Education.

Murtadha, K. (1995) "An African-Centerd Pedagogy in Dialogue with Libertory Multiculturalism," in Christine E. Sleeter and Peter L. McLaren (eds.), *Multicultural Education, Critical Pedagogy, and the Politics of Difference*. New York: State University of New York Press, 349-370.

Nieto, S. (1996) *Affirming Diversity: The Sociopolitical Context of Multicultural Education*. USA: Longman Publishers.

Nieto, S. (1995) "From Brown Heroes and Holidays to Assimilationist Agendas: Reconsidering the Critiques of Multicultural Education," in Christine E. Sleeter and Peter L.McLaren (eds.), *Multicultural Education, Critical Pedagogy and the Politics of Difference.* New York: State University of New York Press, 191-220.

Nixon, J. (1984) "Multicultural Education as a Curriculum Category," *New Community.* 12: 22-30.

Nord, W. (1995) *Religion And American Education: Rethinking A National Dilemma.* Chapel Hill, NC: University of North Carolina Press.

Nord, W. and Haynes, C. (1998) *Taking Religion Seriously Across The Curriculum.* Alexandra, VA: ASCD.

Nunes, F. (1994) *Portuguese-Canadian Youth and Academic Underachievement: A Participatory Research Approach.* A thesis proposal submitted in conformity with the requirements for the degree of Doctor of Education, University of Toronto.

O'Connor, T. (1995) "Education in the Community: The Role of Multicultural Education," in Sandra Jackson and Jose Solis (eds.) *Beyond Comfort Zones in Multiculturalism: Confronting the Politics of Privilege.* Connecticut: Bergin Harvey, 195-200.

Ogbu, J. (1987) "Variability in Minority School Performance: A Problem in Search of an Explanation," *Anthropology and Education Quarterly,* 18: 312-334.

Ogbu, J. (1982) "Cultural Discontinuities and Schooling," *Anthropology and Education Quarterly.* 13: 290-307.

Ontario Ministry of Education and Training. (1993b) *School Boards/First Nations Tuition Agreements Resource Manual 1993-94.* Toronto.

Ontario Secondary School Teachers' Federation. (1995) *Antiracism Education.* Toronto: OSSTF Educational Services Committee.

Ovando, C. and V. Collier. (1998) *Bilingual and ESL Classrooms: Teaching in Multicultural Contexts.* Toronto: McGraw-Hill Ryerson.

Parsonson, K. (1986) Review of the Effects of Learning Styles on Achievement. In R.L. Samuda and S.L. Kong (eds.), *Multicultural Education: Programmes and Methods,* 33-46.

Perry, W. and M. D. Tannenbaum. (1992) "Parents, Power and the Public Schools," in L. Kaplan (ed.) *Education and the Family.* Boston: Allyn and Bacon, 100-115.

Petrash, J. (1992) "Starting Over," *Holistic Education Review.* 27-29.

Pharr, S. (1993) *Homophobia: A Weapon of Sexism.* Oakland, CA: Chardon Press.

Pinar, William F. (1993) "Notes on Understanding Curriculum as a Racial Text," in Cameron McCarthy and Warren Crichlow (eds.) *Race, Identity and Representation in Education.* New York: Routeledge.

Popkewitz, T. S. (1997) "The Production of Reason and Power: Curriculum History and Intellectual Traditions," *Journal of Curriculum Studies*. 29(2): 131-164.

Prah, K. K. (1997) "Accusing the Victims – In My Father's House: A Review of Kwame Anthony Appiah's 'In My Father's House.'" *CODESRIA Bulletin*, 1: 14-22.

Price, E. (1993) *Multiculturalism: A Critique*. Unpublished paper, Department of Sociology and Equity Studies, Ontario Institute for Studies in Education of the University of Toronto (OISE/UT)

Purkey, W. W. and J.M. Novak. (1984) *Inviting School Success*. Blemont, CA: Wadsworth.

Purkey, S. and M. Smith. (1985) "School Reform: The District Policy Implications of the Effective Schools Literature," *The Elementary School Journal*. 85: 353-389.

Purpel, D. E. (1989*) The Moral and Spiritual Crisis in Education: A Curriculum for Justice and Compassion in Education*. Granby, Mass: Bergin and Garvey Publishers.

Quick, A. H. (1996) *Deeper Roots: Muslims in the Americas and the Caribbean from Before Columbus to the Present*. London: Ta-Ha Publishers.

R. & S. Consultants. (1993) *A Study of the N'Swakamok Native Alternative School Program*. Sudbury.

Radwanski, G. (1987) *Ontario Study of the Relevance of Education and the Issue of Dropouts*. Toronto: Ontario Ministry of Education.

Raison, J. (1995) "Another School's Reality." *Phi Delta Kappan*, 76 (6) February.

Ramon, G. (1985) *Counselling Hispanic College-Bound High School Students*. Published jointed by the New York ERIC Clearinghouse on Urban Education and Las Crues, New Mexico Clearinghouse on Rural Education and Small Schools.

Razack, S. (1998) *Looking White People in the Eye: Gender, Race, and Culture in Courtrooms and Classrooms*. Toronto: University of Toronto Press.

Razack, S. (1995a) "The Perils of Talking About Culture: Schooling Research on South and East Asian Students," *Race, Gender and Class*. 2(3): 67-82.

Razack, S. (1995b) "Looking for Race in Gender: A Race Critique of How Domestic Violence as Gender Persecution is Adjudicated." Paper presented at the Critical Race Theory Workshop, Miami, Florida, June.

Razack, S. (1994) "What is to be Gained by Looking White People in the Eye? Culture, Race and Gender of Sexual Violence," *Signs*. 19(41): 894-923.

Reed, C. A. (1994) "The Omission of Anti-Semitism in Anti-Racism," *Canadian Woman Studies: Racism and Gender*. 14(2): 68-71.

Rezai-Rashti, Goli. (1997) "Gender Equity Issues and Minority Students," in *Orbit*, 28(1): 24-5.

Rich, D. (1987) *Schools and Families: Issues and Actions*. Washington, DC: National Education Association.

Rogers, C. (1969) *Freedom To Learn*. Columbus, OH: Charles Merrill.

Rooney, E. (1983) *Criticism, and the Subject of Sexual Violence*. Modern Language Notes. 98, 5 (December)

Rosaldo, R. (1989) *Culture and Truth: The Remaking of Social Analysis*. Boston: Beacon Press.

Rosaldo, R. (1980) "Doing Oral History." *Social Analysis*, 4: 8999.

Royal Commission on Learning, Ontario [RCOL]. (1994) *For the Love of Learning: Report of the Royal Commission on Learning*. Toronto: Queen's Printer for Ontario.

Russell, V. and T. McCaskell. (1995/96) *Lesbian and Gay Studies Course Readings*. Toronto: Toronto Board of Education.

Ryerson Polytechnic Institute. (1991) *1991 Survey of Students in Full-Time and Part-Time Degree and Diploma Programs*. Toronto.

Said, E. (1979) *Orientalism*. New York: Vintage Books.

Samuda, R.J. and P. Crawford. (1980) *Testing, Assessment, Counselling and Placement of Ethnic Minority Students: Current Methods in Ontario*. Toronto: Ontario Ministry of Education.

Sawicki, J. (1991) *Disciplining Foucault: Feminism, Power and the Body*. Great Britain: Routledge.

Scheurich J. and M. Young. (1997) Coloring Epistemologies: Are Our Research Epistemologies Racially Biased? *Educational Researcher*. 26(4): 4-16.

Schon, D. (1983) *The Reflective Practitioner*. New York: Basic Books.

Scott, J. W. (1988) "Deconstructing Equality-Versus-Difference: Or, The Uses of Poststructuralist Theory for Feminism." *Feminist Studies*. (Spring) 14, 1.

Sears, C. (1998) *Second Language Students in Mainstream Classrooms: A Handbook for Teachers in International Schools*. Toronto: Multilingual Matters Ltd.

Shade, B. J. (1989) *Culture, Style and the Educative Process*. Illinois: Charles C. Thomas Publisher.

Shapiro, J. P., T. Sewell and J. DuCette. (1995) *Reframing Diversity in Education*. Pennsylvania: Technomic Publishing Co. Inc.

Shujaa, M. J. (ed.) (1996) *Beyond Desegregation: The Politics of Quality in African-American Schooling*. Thousand Oaks, CA: Corwin Press.

Shujaa, M.J. (ed.) (1994) *Too Much Schooling, Too Little Education: The Paradox of Black Life in White Societies*. Trenton, N.J.: African World Press.

Simon, R. (1982) *Gramsci's Political Thought: An Introduction*. London: Lawrence and Wishart.

Siu, S.F. (1994) "Taking No Chances. A Profile of Chinese-American Family's Support for School Success," *Equity and Choice*. 10: 23-32.

Sleeter, C. (1993) "White Teachers Construct Race" in C. McCarthy and W. Crichlow (eds.) *Race, Identity and Representation in Education*. New York; Routledge.

Smart, B. (1983) *Foucault, Marxism and Critique*. London: Routledge.

Smith, D., L. McCoy and P. Bourne. (1995) *Girls and Schooling: Their Own Critique*. Gender and Schooling Papers. No.1, Toronto: Centre for Women's Studies in Education, Ontario Institute for Studies in Education.

Solomon, P. (1995) "Why Teach From a Multicultural and Anti-Racist Perspective in Canada?" *Race, Gender and Class*. 2(3): 49-66.

Solomon, P. (1992) *Black Resistance in High School: Forging a Separatist Culture*. New York: SUNY.

Sonnier, I. L. (1982) *Holistic Education: Teaching of Science in the Affective Domain*. New York: Philosophical Library.

Soper, B., Milford, G., and Rosenthal, G. (1995) "Belief When Evidence Does Not Support Theory." *Pyschology and Marketing*, 12(5): 415-422.

Sparks, C. (1996) "Cultural Studies and Marxism." In Morley, D. and K-H Chen (eds.), *Stuart Hall: Critical Dialogues in Cultural Studies*. London: Routledge.

Stallings, J. A. and D. Stipek. (1986) "Research on Early Childhood and Elementary School Teaching Programs." In M. C. Wittrack (ed.) *Handbook of Research on Teaching*. New York: MacMillan Publishing Company.

Stasiulis, Daiva K. (1990) "Theorizing Connections: Gender, Race, Ethnicity and Class" in P.S. Li (ed.), *Race and Ethnic Relations in Canada*. Toronto: Oxford University Press, 269-305.

Staton, P. and J. Larkin. (1993) *Sexual Harassment, the Intimidation Factor – A Project Report: Sexual Harassment as a Barrier to Gender Equity in Education*. Toronto: Green Dragon Press.

Steele, C. (1992) "Race and Schooling of Black Americans," *Atlantic Monthly*. April: 68-78.

Steinberg, S.R. (1995) "Critical Multiculturalism and Democratic Schooling: An Interview with Peter L. McLaren and Joe Kinscheloe." In. C.E. Slleter and

P.L. McLaren (eds.), *Multicultural Education, Critical Pedagogy, and the Politics of Difference*. Albany, NY: The State University of New York Press, 129-154.

Steward, R. J. and Jo, H. (1998) "Does Spirituality Influence Academic Achievement and Psychological Adjustment of African American Urban Adolescents?" *ERIC - 417 248*.

"Summit on Spirituality." (1995) *Counseling Today*, 38 (6): 30.

Swap, S. A. (1993) *Developing Home-School Partnerships – From Concept to Practice*. New York: Teachers College Press.

Swap, S. A. (1990) *Parent Involvement and Success For All Children: What We Know Now*. Boston: Institute for Responsive Education.

Suzuki, B.H. (1977) "Education and the Socialization of Asian Americans: A Revisionist Analysis of the 'Model Minority' Thesis," *Amerasia*. 4: 23-51.

Taylor, C. (1994) "The Politics of Recognition." In A. Guttman (ed.) *Multiculturalism*. Princeton, NJ: Princeton University Press, 25-73.

Taylor, L. (1995) "The Implications of Multicultural and Anti-Racist Pedagogies for Teaching English as a Second Language: A Personal Reflection." Unpublished paper, Department of Sociology in Education, Ontario Institute for Studies in Education, Toronto.

Tedla, E. (1992) "Indigenous African Education as a Means for Understanding the Fullness of Life: Amara Traditional Education." *Journal of Black Studies*. 23(1): 7-26.

Thiele, S. (1991a) "Introduction. Reconsidering Aboriginality." Special Issue of TAJA. 2(2): 157-60.

Thielen-Wilson, L. (1999) Review of Paper, "Rethinking Schooling in Euro-American Contexts," by George J. Sefa Dei. Unpublished paper, Department of Sociology and Equity Studies, OISE/UT.

Thomas, B. (1984) "Principles of Anti-Racist Education." *Currents*. 2(3) Edited by Tim Rees, Toronto: Urban Alliance on Race Relations.

Thomas, J. (1997) "Towards Equity in Education." *Orbit*, 28(1): 54-9.

Thornhill, E. (1986) Guidelines for Implementing More Visible Partnerships in Schools. In R.L. Samuda and S.L. Kong (eds.), *Multicultural Education: Programmes and Methods*, 287-294.

Tice, K. (1990) "Gender and Social Work Education: Directions for the 1990s," *Journal of the Social Work Education*. 26(2): 134-44.

Toronto Star, 07/14/99, "Religion and Ridicule."

Toronto Star, 07/16/99, "Law Allows for All Faiths: Province."

Troyna, B. and J. Williams. (1986) *Racism, Education and the State*. London: Croom Helm.

Vann, K. and Kunjufu, J. (1993) "The Importance of an Afrocentric, Multicultural Curriculum," *Phi Delta Kappa*. 74.

Van Sertima, Ivan. (1987) "African Presence in Early America." USA: *Journal of African Civilizations Ltd.*

Vardey, L. (1996) *God In All Worlds: An Anthology Of Contemporary Spiritual Writing*. Toronto: Vintage.

Vaugan, F. (1979) *Awakening Intuition*. Garden City: New York: Anchor Books.

Walcott, R. (1995) "Postmodernism Sociology: Music Education and the Pedagogy of Rap." Paper Presented at the Sociology of Music Education Conference, University of Oklahoma. [Forthcoming in conference proceedings].

Warren, D. M., L. J. Slikkerveer and D. Brokensha. (eds.) (1995) *The Cultural Dimension of Development*. Exeter, Great Britain: Intermediate Technology Publications.

Warshaw, R. (1988) *I Never Called It Rape: The Ms. Report on Recognizing, Fighting and Surviving Date and Aquaintance Rape*. USA: Harper Perennial.

Watts, R. and J. Smolicz (eds.) (1997) *Cultural Democracy and Ethnic Pluralism: Multicultural and Multilingual Policies in Education*. Berlin: Peter Lang.

Weedon, C. (1987) *Feminist Practice and Poststructuralist Theory*. Great Britain: Basil Blackwell.

Weil, A. (1972) *The Natural Mind*. Boston: Houghton Mifflin.

Wesley, D. C. (1999) "Believing in Our Students." *Educational Leadership*.

Willis, P. (1983) "Cultural Production and Theories of Reproduction" in L. Barton and S. Walker (eds.) *Race, Class and Education*. London: Croom Helm.

Willis, P. (1977) *Learning to Labour*. Farnborough: Saxon House.

Wolf, A. D. (1996) Nurturing the Spirit in Nonsectarian Classrooms. Hollidaysburg, PA: Parent Child Press.

Wood, A. (1995) Stop Standing on the Baby!: Spirituality and Education. Multicultural Teaching, 14 (1): 11-14.

Working Group. (1992) *Towards a New Beginning: The Report and Action Plan of the Four Level Government/African-Canadian Community Working Group*. Toronto.

Yukon Native Brotherhood. (1972) *Education of Yukon Indians*. Yukon.

Ziegler, S., N. Hardwick and G. McCrerath. (1989) *Academically Successful Inner-city Children: What They Can Tell Us About Effective Education*. Toronto: Toronto Board of Education.

Ziegler, S. N. (1987) *The Effects of Parental Involvement on Children's Achievement: The Significance of Home/School Links.* Toronto: Toronto Board of Education, Research Services.

Zine, J. (1999) (Forthcoming) *Muslim Students in Public Schools: Education and the Politics of Religious Identity.* In *Race, Ethnicity and Education.*